AN AUTHENTIC INVITATION . . .

. . . to insight, growth, identity—and to life itself. Here is a completely fresh look into the most basic problems of men and women of all faiths.

THE ART OF UNDERSTANDING YOURSELF has a universal message because it deals with universal human qualities—love, anxiety, guilt, the need for improved human relationships. It teaches that there is One who listens, understands all and forgives all . . . and that when a person believes, the way is open to fulfillment through faith, and a new and rich understanding of self and of others.

The Art of UNDER-STANDING YOURSELF

Now available . . .

A Study Guide to

The Art of Understanding Yourself
by Joe Miller / Cecil Osborne

The Art of
UNDER-STANDING YOURSELF

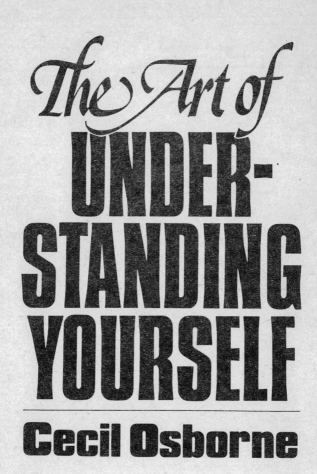

Cecil Osborne

ZONDERVAN
PUBLISHING HOUSE
OF THE ZONDERVAN CORPORATION | GRAND RAPIDS, MICHIGAN 49506

THE ART OF UNDERSTANDING YOURSELF
Copyright © 1967 by Zondervan Publishing House

Library of Congress Catalog Card Number 67-11612

Thirty-sixth printing November 1980
ISBN 0-310-30592-6

ZONDERVAN BOOKS are published by Zondervan Publishing
House, 1415 Lake Drive, S.E., Grand Rapids, Michigan 49506,
U.S.A.
Printed in the United States of America

Grateful acknowledgment is made to the following for per-
mission to use copyright material:
Atlantic-Little, Brown and Company, Publishers
    Excerpts from *The Undiscovered Self* by C. G. Jung, copy-
    right © 1958 by C. G. Jung.
Doubleday & Company, Inc.
    Excerpts from *The Listener* by Taylor Caldwell, copyright
    © 1960 by Reback and Reback.
    Excerpts from *Man's First Love* by Ralph Sockman, copy-
    right © 1958 by Ralph W. Sockman.
    Excerpts from *The Power of Sexual Surrender* by Marie N.
    Robinson, copyright © 1959 by Marie N. Robinson.
Prentice-Hall, Inc.
    Excerpts from *The Dynamics of Personal Adjustment* by
    George F. Lehner and Elle Kube, copyright © 1955.
The Westminster Press
    Excerpts from *Prayer and Personal Religion* by John B. Co-
    burn, copyright © 1957 by W. L. Jenkins, The Westminster
    Press.
    Excerpts from *The Strong and the Weak* by Paul Tournier.
The Division of Christian Education of the National Council
of the Churches of Christ
    Quotations from The Revised Standard Version of the Bible,
    copyright © 1946 and 1952.
Unless otherwise specified, all Scripture quotations are from
the Revised Standard Version of the Bible.

CONTENTS

Dr. Cecil Osborne may be contacted at the following address:

Yokefellows, Inc.
Burlingame Counseling Center
19 Park Road
Burlingame, CA 94010

FOREWORD

Dr. Cecil Osborne has conducted spiritual growth groups on the West Coast for several years. Out of his experience has come a most remarkable and insightful book, *The Art of Understanding Yourself.*

The song of the prophets is within him, but his eyes see the darkness and decay in man's soul. Only the unrealistic dreamer records nothing but the sunshine in life. No one need feel despair because of its stark realities. There is hope; there are ways out of the abyss.

This is not an armchair philosopher writing; neither is it a pious philosophy being expounded. It is a rare combination of religious insight and psychological truth born of personal experience. The blending of the two is masterfully done. One does not say or feel as he reads, "Here is religion; now here is psychology." One is only aware of the honesty, the deep meanings, the facing of reality as it is — all without moralizing. One only senses, "Here is truth that is insightful and therefore helpful."

Dr. Osborne has the rare ability to write simply — but with power. He clearly shows how man is in bondage — in bondage to things he tries to hide. The theme of alienation runs through every chapter, essentially an alienation from self. As one proceeds through the book, one is aware of the estrangement, the destiny, the division, the separation that people today are experiencing in frightening numbers. With this awareness one is challenged to examine and criticize for the essential purpose of restoring values, of re-creating self, of moving from defeat to hope.

The high-water mark in every chapter is the challenge of identity. Dr. Osborne's perspective is reassuring for he refuses to accept the doctrine that the essential nature of man is determined by condition. True identity is moral, he affirms, or it is nothing.

This book is an invitation to insight, to growth, to identity, to re-affiliation. It deserves to be read by all who are in search of a better way of life within, so they may relate meaningfully to their fellowmen. It is an invitation to move toward wholeness, by understanding how one is divided against oneself. It is therefore an invitation to life. I read this book with deep appreciation.

WILLIAM R. PARKER, Ph.D.
University of Redlands

1. YOUR LONELY SELF

> If you wish to be miserable, you must think
> about yourself; about what you want, what you
> like, what respect people ought to pay you,
> and then to you nothing will be pure. You will
> spoil everything you touch; you will make sin
> and misery out of everything God sends you
> You can be as wretched as you choose.
> —*Charles Kingsley*

PERHAPS you have never thought of yourself as lonely. You
may have friends, varied interests, and numerous activities
which occupy your time and thought. But the truth is that
no one really knows you. A friend may know certain things
about you, and may be aware of some secret longings of
your heart; but no one has ever felt precisely what you
have felt, and therefore no one can know you fully.

You feel that no one really listens to you. As you try to
share some of your deeper feelings, you may sense that the
other is waiting with ill-concealed impatience until he can
say. "Yes, and that reminds me of something that happened to me the other day." There is another reason why
we are not really known to anyone else. It is because, as
Paul Tournier has pointed out, each of us is in a state of
tension between the need to reveal, and the need to
conceal ourselves. We have an urge to share our true
feelings, but we fear that we shall become vulnerable, that
we shall be rejected or criticized. As a result we tend to
settle for commonplace discussions about the superficialities of life: "My, hasn't the weather been changeable
lately!" or some equally banal remark. "Each of us does his
best to hide behind a shield," says Paul Tournier in *The
Meaning of Persons*. "For one it is a mysterious silence
which constitutes an impenetrable retreat. For another it is
facile chit-chat, so that we never seem to get near him. Or

9

else it is erudition, quotations, abstractions, theories ... trivialities."[1]

> For who listens to us in all the world
> Whether he be friend or teacher, brother or father or
> Mother, sister or neighbor, son or ruler, or
> Servant? Does he listen, our advocate, or our
> Husbands or wives, those who are dearest to us?
> Do the stars listen, when we turn despairingly
> Away from man, or the great winds, or the seas or
> The mountains? To whom can any man say — Here I
> Am! Behold me in my nakedness, my wounds, my
> Secret grief, my despair, my betrayal, my pain,
> My tongue which cannot express my sorrow, my
> Terror, my abandonment.
> Listen to me for a day — an hour! A moment!
> Lonely silence! O God, is there no one to listen?
> Is there no one to listen? you ask. Ah, yes,
> There is one who listens, who will always listen.
> Hasten to him, my friend! He waits on the hill
> For you.
>
> —*Seneca*

Yes, there is One who listens, and many have learned to pour out their souls to God in earnest, satisfying prayer. But millions of others — perhaps the vast majority — are not so sure that He really listens and so do not seek the ear of this Listener. There is no verbal response from Him, no immediate sympathetic reply, and they doubt whether anyone is listening, after all.

Taylor Caldwell, in *The Listener*, says:

> Man does not need to go to the moon or other solar systems. He does not require bigger and better bombs and missiles. He will not die if he does not get better housing or more vitamins. ... His basic needs are few, and it takes little to acquire them, in spite of the advertisers. He can survive on a small amount of bread and in the meanest shelter. ...
>
> His real need, his most terrible need, is for someone to listen to him, not as a patient; but as a human soul. ...
>
> Our pastors would listen — if we gave them the time to listen to us. But we have burdened them with tasks which should be our own. We have demanded not only that they be our shepherds, but that they take our trivialities, our social aspirations, the "fun" of our children, on their weary backs. We have demanded that they be expert businessmen, politicians, accountants, playmates, community directors, "good fellows," judges, lawyers and settlers of local quarrels. We

have given them little time for listening, and we do not listen to them, either. . . .²

This book is, in part, the story of people, at first a small group but now numbering in the thousands, who have learned how to listen; the story of healing of mind, spirit, body and circumstance which was achieved because these people learned to share at a deeper level and discovered in the process that God's love is mediated through persons; it is the story of people who came to know God, themselves and each other in a more satisfying way than they had ever thought possible.

Joe Dandini* was a very lonely man. He dropped into my study one afternoon. I had never seen him before. He was a big, hearty, extroverted man who exuded boyish friendliness. "Look," he said, "I hardly know why I'm here. I'm a Roman Catholic, see, but I've got problems, had 'em for a long time. Well, there's this woman down the street from us. She used to be a pretty mixed up person, but all of a sudden she's gotten straightened out, and the change is so remarkable I decided to find out how it happened. I learned that she had attended some group down here at your church. That's all I know about it. I need some kind of help. Maybe I need what she's got. I've been to psychiatrists, doctors, psychologists, and I'm no better off than I was before. I keep running to the doctors with all sorts of symptoms, but they tell me it's my nerves. I guess they mean my emotions. They say there's nothing wrong with me physically, but I feel terrible most of the time.

"Besides, I have trouble holding a job. My wife's really supporting the family. I don't feel so good about that, but I no sooner get a job than I lose it. I either get into a wrangle with the boss or, if I seem to be doing pretty well, for some reason I pick a fight with a fellow employee, and bang! I'm fired again. I can't seem to hold a job over a few months, at the outside. I don't know what my trouble is. Can these groups, whatever they are, help a guy like me?"

"Such a group could help you in time," I replied, "if you work at it. The group provides the opportunity. The rest is up to you. Results depend on your honesty with yourself, and how deeply you are motivated."

"What goes on in these group meetings?" Joe asked.

---

*This name, like all the others used in case histories throughout the book, is fictitious, though the stories are true.

"It's difficult to describe. You'll have to experience it for yourself. But one thing is important — your wife should attend, too. It often helps if both husband and wife attend together."

"She wouldn't come," Joe said emphatically. "I've spent so much money on psychiatrists and doctors in an effort to get some help that she won't have anything to do with this sort of thing. Besides, I don't know how she'd feel about coming to a meeting in a Protestant church."

I suggested that he invite her, anyway, and urge her to attend for at least a month. And at the first meeting Joe did bring his wife, a charming and quietly effective person. Joe said to us during the meeting, "I went home and told her I was going to join a group down at the Baptist Church in Burlingame. I said, 'I told them you wouldn't attend.' She said, 'There you go, making up my mind for me again. Of course I'm going.'"

There was no sudden, miraculous solution for Joe's problem. He shared his deep feelings of rejection as a boy, the fear he felt toward his authoritarian father, who had been a policeman. When we learned all about his early childhood we understood why he reacted as he did. His progress was slow, but steady. There is no known method by which an immature emotional structure can be changed overnight. However, within a year Joe was back working for a man who had once fired him. He held the job this time, and began to show genuine self-assurance for the first time in his life. After two years he was promoted to assistant manager. This does not mean that his emotional and spiritual growth was complete. Spiritual growth is an open-ended process. But Joe's group experience resulted in concrete dividends, including the ability to earn a living, a new sense of self-respect, far better communication with his family, and a profession of faith which the entire family made when they asked for membership in the church. Joe and his wife and daughter now devote a great amount of time to Christian activities.

Joe's loneliness, self-rejection and sense of failure; his alienation from God, from himself and from his fellow man, were in part the result of environmental forces. It can also be said that it was sin which brought about Joe's difficulties. Sin was the sum total of the forces which caused him to be an impaired personality. Sin lay behind the factors which made his father grim and authoritarian, which made him unable to communicate with his son. Sin in Joe's case was a combination of social, psychological, and spiritual forces which left him incomplete, unable to function adequately as a person and as a father and husband. The answer for Joe was Christ's love mediated through a group of people who genuinely cared about him. In their group, Joe and his wife came to feel loved and accepted. The group was the Church in action, the family of God through which love could be channeled to bless and heal and guide.

It is extremely naive to think of sin simply as an isolated act — a lie, a theft, immorality, dishonesty — for sin is all that is less than perfection. It is rejecting God — "falling short" of the perfection which God envisioned for us. Sin is being impaired, not simply performing a wicked act. It is having impaired relationships and attitudes. It is being less than whole. It is having mixed motives. Sin is the clever rationalization by which we seek to escape from facing ourselves. It can consist in responding to a set of rigid moralistic "oughts" rather than obeying the spirit of God which dwells within us, acting solely in response to legalistic codes (and feeling virtuous in doing so) instead of learning to act spontaneously in response to divine impetus.

Many group members become able to give up their limited childhood concept of sin as something confined to "bad acts," or "evil thoughts" and discover that sin is what we *are* — faulty, impaired, lacking in spiritual maturity. They discover a new quality of love, for where sharing takes place in an appropriate setting, loving relationships normally follow. They learn to pray for one another daily with loving concern. For many, the persons within their group become their family, as some have expressed it, for they often feel closer ties with them than to their blood relations.

The small group idea is one of the most dynamic spiritual forces of the twentieth century. Since World War II we have been rediscovering its tremendous power. Under various names small groups are forming with great rapidity in churches of many denominations. Men and women are finding that the routine services and activities of the local church do not always provide sufficient motivation for significant spiritual growth.

One hour a week spent in church was never intended to

provide answers to our deepest spiritual needs. The first century Church undoubtedly consisted of small groups, in addition to the weekly meetings for worship and instruction.

Many mistakenly assume that Christianity is concerned solely with "biblical" truth (which they define narrowly), and that psychological truths are somehow not quite in keeping with spiritual matters. They forget, of course, that all truth is divine in origin, whether it be a scientific law, a philosophical principle, or a biblical truth. Theology deals in general with the nature of God and His will for man. Psychology deals with man and his inner nature. We need to know God. We need to know all we can about God, the source of our being, and everything possible about man, created in the divine image.

Therefore, throughout this book I do not distinguish between sacred and secular truth, for every aspect of life is sacred. Man, created in the image of God, is sacred; and his physical body, we are told in the Bible, is the temple of the Holy Spirit. The same God who created man designed the universe with holy intent. Every tree and blade of grass, every atom and molecule, every fragment of truth, is sacred. Every scientific law discovered by man originated with God and is sacred. There is no distinction between "sacred" and "secular," "common" and "holy."

God's command to Moses on Mt. Sinai — "Put off your shoes from your feet, for the place on which you are standing is holy ground"[2] — did not mean that only that particular ground on which Moses stood was holy. The implication is that Moses had been seeking to find God in some special "sacred" place. God was telling him that wherever he stood, *that* was a holy place, and God could meet him there.

Many tend to think of a minister's work as somehow sacred, because he is supposed to be concerned chiefly with spiritual matters, while a physician, who deals with physical bodies, is seldom thought of as being engaged in a holy task. Every person whatever his vocation, can have a sense of divine mission if he will be conscious of the loving concern of God for all of life.

Jesus made no artificial distinctions between sacred and secular. He dealt with every aspect of men's lives and thus sanctified all of life. He healed their bodies and made healing forever a sacred function. He spoke of the nature of God and of the everyday relationships between men at the same time. In the Sermon on the Mount, He taught spiritual, philosophical, psychological, and sociological principles; he discussed lawsuits, prayer, divorce, anxiety, love, forgiveness, reconciliation, anger, and a score of other things which pertained to everyday living. Jesus was interested in *everything which concerned men*, and His loving concern tells us that this is the nature of God — that He is interested in every detail of our lives. With God there are no such categories as science and religion, the sacred and the secular.

In Marc Connelly's *The Green Pastures* when "de Lawd" prepares to leave Heaven and come down to earth to see how His children are faring, He gives Gabriel some final instructions: "Gabriel, don't forget about that star that hasn't been working right. Take care of that." Gabriel assents. "And Gabriel, remember that little sparrow with the broken wing? Take care of that too, won't you?" In this delightful play, the author quite rightly portrays God as equally interested in the cosmos and the sparrows. One who has come to see the beautiful harmony which exists in all of nature, who has glimpsed the exquisite unity of the entire universe and has sensed that God is in us and we in Him and that everything in our universe is a part of God — he can never again make a distinction between sacred and secular. For "the whole earth is filled with the glory of the Lord," and everything in it is holy except where sin has touched it and marred its divine perfection.

Mystics who have pierced the veil of human consciousness and have had a glimpse of the infinite confirm that there is a unity of all things far beyond the power of the human mind to grasp in its ordinary state. Many who have explored some of the consciousness expanding drugs, such as LSD-25, although their experiences vary widely at many points, report one mystical insight: the sudden awareness, felt rather than perceived by the mind, that *the universe is one* in a way impossible to put into words. They all tell of experiencing themselves as a part of the whole, at one with God and nature, and yet still separate and autonomous.

Many people have discovered in varying degrees that for the Christian there is no boundary line between religion and life, that all life is sacred, and that Christianity was meant to apply to every aspect of life. Jesus never used the word "religion" (which appears only twice in the New Testament). He seems never to have thought of one's relationship with God as involving a "religious duty" or even a religious act in the sense that many people use such terms. He did not compartmentalize life into sacred and secular. Christians were called "followers of the way," and Christ was the One who taught the Way, who was Himself the Way, the Way to live life, and to have life abundant and eternal.

If we could once and for all see that Christianity is a way of life, not just for Sunday and emergencies, and not just a set of moral principles; if we could divest ourselves of the belief that God is concerned chiefly that we be good, we shall have taken a great step forward. God is not concerned only with the need for His children to be decent and moral and honest, desirable as these traits are. He is concerned, Jesus taught us, that our lives shall be rich and full and creative; that we shall discover our highest potential; that we shall have love, joy, peace, happiness, an abundant life, life eternal. Jesus spoke of all these at one time or another in His ministry. In the Gospel of John for example, are recorded these words:

"A new commandment I give to you, that you love one another even as I have loved you."

"Ask, and you will receive, that your joy may be full."

"My peace I give to you . . ."

"If ye know these things, happy are ye if ye do them."

"I came that they may have life, and have it abundantly."

"This is eternal life that they know thee — the only true God, and Jesus Christ whom thou hast sent."[4]

He offered this and more. Most of us would settle for any one or two of these six great blessings He offered His followers. In making Christianity another religion instead of the Way of Life, we have lost the heart of His message.

There appears to be something missing in the organized Church of today, something which was very much in evidence among the New Testament Christians. The Christian Church is the finest force for good we have on earth, and weak as it is, it is not to be disparaged. But we who love the Church can evaluate her weaknesses. They are really our own weaknesses.

In the average church ten per cent of the members do ninety per cent of the work. Thirty per cent give ninety per cent of the budget. Forty per cent attend church on Sunday morning. This is a far cry from the Church Victorious.

There is little more love among the members of the average church than there is among Rotarians or Kiwanians. In fact, there is often a more open quality of fellowship among members of service clubs than can be found in some churches. In the average church of a hundred or a thousand members, most of the members do not know each other except in the most casual way. We cannot love people until we know them, and it is impossible to know a hundred or a thousand people except at the most superficial level. Yet love was to be the hallmark of the Christian. "By this shall all men know that you are my disciples, if you love one another."

Elizabeth O'Conner recounts an experience of Gordon and Mary Cosby. Gordon is pastor of the widely known Church of The Saviour in Washington, D.C. He had preached in a church where the atmosphere was something less than vibrant. As Miss O'Conner tells it:

Gordon said, "As I looked on those granite figures, I had to repress in myself the urge to tear my robe off and to walk out of the church into the night where the air would be clean, and I could feel clean. They had supposedly come together to commemorate a high point in the church year, but the only evidence of life was the tinkling of coins falling into the collection plate."

When the service was over that night, he and Mary drove a long way. They finally stopped at a small hotel where the last vacant room was above a tavern. Noisy voices and gay jukebox melodies drifted into their room and kept them from sleeping. Reflecting on the sounds below, and the church they had left behind, Gordon recollected, "I realized that there was more warmth and fellowship in that tavern than there was in the church. If Jesus of Nazareth had His choice, He would probably have come to the tavern rather than to the church we visited."

The next morning they had breakfast at a small coffee house across from the hotel. The people who went in and out greeted one another, read their newspapers and commented on the day's news. "We thought again," said Gordon, "that Christ would have been more at home in the coffee house."[5]

Many church members, if they were to give the matter serious thought, would have to admit that they are lonely, and that they do not feel particularly loved by any appreciable number of individuals in the church. There is no one to blame; it is simply that the Church has gradually become an institution instead of a loving fellowship. But it is not impossible to change this. In the past few years it has been changed for thousands of people.

When a person visits a church for the first time, he participates in a worship service; and what is said in the sermon may or may not apply to his particular needs. He may be greeted and invited to return, but other than this, nothing of consequence may occur to lead him to believe that this is a group of people who are deeply concerned about him. If there is any love manifested it is usually limited to a friendly greeting, and one may get that almost anywhere.

At one time, if anyone had asked Margaret what her problem was, she would have said, "The whole problem is my husband. He's an alcoholic." I don't recall the first time she dropped into church, or what prompted her to come in to see me. She shared part of her need and told me that she had been seeing a psychiatrist. As the result of her counseling she had come to realize that it was not entirely her husband's fault. True, he did drink to excess, and the resultant difficulties were sufficient to cause distress to anyone. But Margaret had faced up to the fact that at heart she was what her psychiatrist called an "injustice collector." Even when things were going fairly well at home she would find some reason to prod or nag her husband, whereupon he would proceed to get drunk. She was a psychic masochist, with a deep but totally unconscious need to be punished. Entirely unaware of what she was doing, or the reason for doing it, she would manage to get her feelings hurt, or invent ways by which she could be rejected. She had come to see — at least intellectually — that she was bringing most of her suffering upon herself.

In the counseling session with her I simply listened, and at the close of our conversation I suggested that she participate in one of our group sessions. She was a faithful member for several years, and gradually shared some of her early childhood memories. Her father had been a highly moral, rigid, demanding person, and she had never been able to relate to him or feel the slightest affection for him. In fact, all she was aware of feeling was hostility and rejection, emotions which she had partially buried. She always felt vaguely guilty as a child: partly because of the unattainable standards of conduct imposed upon her, partly because she had felt rejected. The rejected child always feels guilty. Although a child does not think it out in these terms, the resultant feeling is: "I am rejected and unloved. If I were a 'good' child they would love me. Since I am not loved, I must be bad." The result is a deep feeling of guilt and unworthiness. The child simply does not feel worthy of being loved. For just such reasons Margaret "wallowed in feelings of self-pity and self-rejection," as she put it. But knowing of the rejection experienced in her childhood, one could feel only understanding and compassion, particularly since she was making a valiant effort to become a mature adult.

The change in Margaret was so marked that her brother decided to join the group. At the first session Jeff, a likeable, friendly person, told his story. Jeff had spent about $30,000 on psychiatrists, knew everything that was wrong with himself, and spouted psychiatric terms at the slightest provocation. He was suffering from "a paralysis of analysis." He told how, after he had been through nine years of Freudian psychiatric treatment and was still a very mixed up person, his wife had said thoughtfully, "Jeff, why don't you take out a lot of insurance and go shoot yourself?" He related this with no rancor, and added, "Actually she had a good point. I was no good either to myself or to my family."

Six months later Jeff had made significant progress — so much so, in fact, that he said, "I have made more spiritual and emotional progress in these six months than in my nine years of psychiatric treatment. I have learned to pray and to relate to God as a loving Heavenly Father, and I communicate with Him often through the day." His progress continues and he is finding that there is no limit to spiritual growth.

In relating Jeff's experience, I have no intention of disparaging psychiatrists. Many who have found psychiatry unavailing have also attended church for years without being able to resolve their personal problems.

Not everyone who participates in these group sessions has serious personal difficulties. Many join in order to learn how to pray, or to be a more effective Christian and while these are significant needs, they do not for most people constitute an actual crisis.

Occasionally someone says, "I have no need for such a group since I have no real problems." What they mean, of course, is that they are experiencing no great personal crisis. They are able to handle life's issues without significant difficulty. But they do have problems! Every human has inner conflicts, for the difficulty of becoming one's highest self poses a very great problem. Dr. Leon J. Saul, professor of psychiatry at the University of Pennsylvania School of Medicine, says, "No one is fully mature emotionally, or in perfect harmony with his desires, his conscience and the outer world about him. This discrepancy between the desire and the fulfillment is expressed in the degree of unhappiness, emotional tension and 'neurosis' which everyone sustains."[6]

As Fritz Kunkel has pointed out, no one makes any significant change in his personality or life situation until he is motivated by pain of some kind. Rollo May says, "People then should rejoice in suffering, strange as it sounds, for this is a sign of the availability of energy to transform their characters. Suffering is nature's method of indicating a mistaken attitude or way of behavior, and ... to the non-egocentric person every moment of suffering is the opportunity for growth."[7]

Those for whom life moves along at a more or less serene pace, who do not feel threatened by physical illness, marital distress, or mental suffering, usually are content to maintain the status quo. They are not motivated to significant spiritual commitment or growth beyond their present level.

However, apart from the sharp stab of a crisis as a motivating force in seeking relief, there is also the dull throb of frustration. In their thirties and forties many people begin to discover, for the first time, that life is considerably more frustrating than they had ever dreamed possible in their twenties. At least three-fourths of all married couples experience occasional to continuous tension and strife. They often seek out a marriage counselor only after there are so many scars and painful memories that it is difficult, if not impossible, to bring about a reconciliation.

In our groups on the West Coast we have hundreds of married couples who have no more serious difficulty than that of learning to communicate better, of sorting out their feelings, and raising the level of their tolerance for frustration, through the application of spiritual laws.

One could not imagine a more happily married couple than Chuck and Henrietta. They joined a group in the hope of achieving greater spiritual growth. After some months of discussion based on a devotional book, the group voted to take one of the spiritual growth inventories. These are basically psychological inventories to which have been added a system of evaluation slips, which the group members receive weekly or every other week. One slip received by Chuck revealed that he had a great deal of buried hostility of which he was largely unaware. He had shared with the group his terrible bouts with asthma and hay fever; and he began to wonder if his repressed hostility and dependency feelings had any bearing on his respiratory ailments, which more or less incapacitated him for part of the year.

They left the group after a year or so, and some time later I asked him about his asthma and hay fever. He said in some surprise, "Oh, didn't you know? I got over that as soon as I found out about all my buried hostility. When I learned how to handle hostility, my asthma cleared up." He had not joined the group because of his asthma, but when he resolved some of his emotional problems through a more mature form of prayer, his physical symptoms disappeared. At no time did he pray about his asthma. Rather he dealt with the underlying cause, his buried and unacknowledged hostility.

Two women, members of different groups, were seeking spiritual growth and a greater degree of inner peace. I was unaware at the time that both suffered from migraine headaches, one of them for twenty-five years, and the other for a shorter period of time. Though they did not pray for release from their physical symptoms, both were cured as a result of the new spiritual growth which they achieved. As they related themselves in love and trust to the God of peace, their physical symptoms simply vanished. Instead of praying about their physical symptoms, they focused upon God in the daily quiet time. In the group they found an opportunity to share their feelings. While they were personal, they shared no intimate detail of their lives. The healing took place as they obeyed literally the command of Jesus, "seek first his kingdom and his righteousness, and all these things shall be yours as well."

One of the gratifying discoveries made in the first eight years during which these sharing groups were in operation on the West Coast is the way in which barriers between persons are broken down easily and naturally. These invisible barriers prevent us from knowing and loving each other. The loneliness and sense of isolation experienced by reluctance to reveal ourselves to others, for fear of rejection. Within the group, barriers are lowered, and we discover ourselves loving people whom we had not even liked before. We discover that the more others learn about us, the easier it is for them to accept and love us. No one can love a mask. As we remove our masks we find ourselves being accepted at a new level.

In an initial group session, as various persons shared some of their feelings, a man said: "I have just experienced a complete reversal of my feelings toward Al. I have known him for quite a while on a fairly superficial basis. I have always thought of him as acting superior, perhaps kind of snobbish. Just now when he shared some of his feelings of inadequacy I really liked him, for I have the same feelings about myself. I no longer fear rejection from him. We're both alike. Perhaps I, too, cover up some of my feelings of inadequacy with a pretense of superiority which I do not really feel. Anyhow, Al, I've sort of endured you heretofore. Now I . . . well, I guess I can say I love you."

You may never have thought of yourself as lonely, but the feeling is there just the same, unless you have broken through the barrier of your fear of rejection. And when you can reveal your true self, however slightly, you will find yourself accepted and loved at a new level. In addition you will come to know yourself, while revealing yourself to others for our fear of being known by others is no greater than our fear of knowing ourselves.

It is "not by might, nor by power," nor by organization, crusade or campaign that the Kingdom of God will come to this earth, or to any human. It comes only by love — love for God, for others — which bridges our separateness and abolishes our loneliness.

2. THE REDEMPTIVE FELLOWSHIP

> Jesus indicates that there is absolutely no
> substitute for the tiny redemptive society. If
> this fails, he suggests all is failure; there is no
> other way.[1]
>
> — Elton Trueblood

CHRISTINE, a young married woman in her early thirties, was three years old when her father went to prison. She has borne a life-long sense of shame over the fact that her father was a convict. While he was in prison, Christine and her mother lived with her grandparents. She remembers that they were very poor and that her grandfather was a stern, authoritarian, unloving man who radiated hostility.

When her father came home on parole, she was intensely afraid of him. He had terrible outbursts of rage, and she cannot recall that he ever paid her a compliment or expressed love in any way. He told her repeatedly that she was stupid. When she became an adolescent, he warned her sternly that she must never "get into trouble with the boys." That was the sum total of her sex education from either parent, but when she was about fifteen, her father attempted to molest her sexually. She was shocked and disgusted.

Christine married at the age of twenty. Her husband wanted children, but she strongly resisted the idea of raising a family. When the first child came, she experienced a deep sense of pleasure for the first month or so, but then began to lose interest in the child. Her doctor helped her at this point. He had said, "thoughts are a habit, and you can change your thought pattern by think-

23

ing differently." She worked hard at this and eventually succeeded in accepting her first child. Ultimately she developed a wonderful relationship with him. When the second child was born, the same pattern began to manifest itself but she found it considerably easier — this time — to love the child.

Christine was a very quiet, inhibited person. At a retreat, where I first met her, I sensed that she was struggling with some deep inner conflict. After one of the sessions, I happened to walk with her toward the dining hall, and suddenly she blurted out, "I'm sick and tired of bearing my father's guilt!" I encouraged her to share her problem and slowly, painfully, she told me in considerable detail the incidents I have related. Before the retreat was over, she began for the first time to sense the extent of her violent hostility toward her father. She had never let herself feel this before. Most of it had been buried just beneath the surface. Shame, guilt, hatred, inferiority, all merged into one violent feeling of rage. I assured her that it was all right to feel whatever emotions she was experiencing at the moment, and eventually she was able to admit into consciousness all of the pent-up hostility, pain, and frustration which she had never shared with anyone nor admitted fully to herself. Christine experienced considerable relief from the telling of her story, which involved admitting that she had feelings she had never dared confront before. In the process she was able to forgive her father, which was a very healing experience. But, inexplicably, her relationship with her husband became worse. At times she could scarcely stand to be in the same room with him. She experienced the most violent and unreasoning antagonism toward him, leaving him puzzled and hurt.

In the church to which Christine belonged, a number of groups were meeting weekly, each consisting of eight to a dozen persons. Some of the groups studied a book and shared their feelings about it. Others had been taking a spiritual growth inventory and had been receiving weekly evaluation slips. The purpose of the groups was spiritual growth, which meant not only the acquiring of additional biblical knowledge but emotional maturity as well. Some sought to resolve personal problems; others wanted simply to become more mature in their Christian commitment and experience.

Christine had joined one of the groups before I met her,

and her experience was the initial step which resulted in her being willing to uncover some of her deeply buried emotions. After returning home from the retreat, profoundly disturbed by her new hostility toward her husband, she shared some of this with her group. She felt no need to tell them the whole painful story of her early life. They helped her to see that she had simply transferred her hostility from her father to her husband. She had forgiven her father to the best of her knowledge, but the pain of the past would not permit her to abandon her hatred entirely. Upon discovering what she was doing, she made a new and significant step forward in surrendering all her hostility to God.

As she described it to me later, "God became a reality to me for the first time. The God I had known before was somewhere 'up there.' Now I found that God was here within me, and a part of me. It was the greatest discovery of my life. I was on cloud nine. I can hardly remember the 'old me' of the past. I have found that I am far more tolerant of others, and I try not to make their turmoil mine. I love to help where I can, whereas I used to be afraid of people — too afraid to help them. It's wonderful to be able to love now, to be able to love both men and women and not feel guilty. Hostility and fear and guilt have been replaced by love."

Christine is active in her church and has led groups effectively. She wants her life to be as useful as possible. The will of God is her highest goal in life.

Comparatively few persons experience the events which marred the early life of Christine, but her story reveals vividly the way in which a loving fellowship can provide insight and the climate in which one is free to grow spiritually. One need not identify with Christine in order to sense the difficulty involved in learning to love and forgive. Most of us fear our hostility, whatever its origin, and feel guilty about it.

During the past few years more than twelve thousand persons have been involved with our Yokefellow groups on the West Coast. Our purpose is to help people make Christianity relevant to all of life's problems, and to help Christians toward a deeper commitment. Using several hundred groups for our experiment, we began to discover some important facts:

First, that a person can commit to God only that part of

himself which he understands and accepts; second, that a person cannot pray effectively until he deals with his emotional barriers; third, that most of these barriers are largely *unconscious;* fourth, that Christians by and large are not any better integrated as personalities than non-Christians; fifth, that it makes no difference whether a person is a Methodist, Lutheran, Pentecostalist, Baptist, Episcopalian, theological liberal or conservative — everyone has the same spiritual and emotional needs. Group members soon lost all sense of belonging to different denominations. Almost from the start they sensed that they were working at a deeper level than that provided by nice theological distinctions. Without surrendering any of their doctrinal beliefs, they simply moved into another realm where the reality of God and love transcended minor theological differences.

Another aspect of the experiment involved the use of the spiritual growth inventories, which are taken by approximately three thousand persons a year on the West Coast alone. This idea originated in Dr. William R. Parker's experiment in what he termed "prayer therapy." The inventories are basically psychological tests designed to aid spiritual and emotional growth through the use of a "feedback" system of weekly evaluation slips which are received by the group members. The slips, given out regularly over a period of fifteen to twenty-two weeks, bring into sharp focus some personality aspect and often pinpoint a buried emotion or attitude which constitutes a serious barrier to spiritual growth.

In a minister's group one of the members received a slip indicating that he experienced intense fear of his emotions, which prevented him from being able to give and receive love. He had some difficulty at first in accepting the slip, for, as he said, "I am not aware of any intense fear such as this slip describes. It's true I am rather reserved, and have my emotions well under control, but I have always considered this a virtue, not a defect." He was told to read the slip over from time to time, for occasionally it takes weeks or months, sometimes longer, for a person to accept an emotion which he has buried far below the level of consciousness.

The minister said to his group some months later, "You know that slip I got on 'fear of emotions'? It said I was largely unaware of my emotions, and frankly I was a little put out because I could not see any validity to it. I thought the psychologist who scored my test had made a mistake.

"Well, this past week, I was caught without any preparation and called upon suddenly to speak extemporaneously, something I have had to do before on occasion. For the first time in my life I was aware of the emotion of panic — just plain panic. I must have experienced it often and buried it. In fact, I almost caught myself burying the emotion in this instance. Instead, I allowed myself to feel the panic or fear or whatever it was. I admitted to myself that I was capable of feeling intense fear, and somehow I feel somewhat liberated. I don't have to hide from it any longer.

"I was taught as a child never to show fear. It was unmanly; so I suppose I have lied to myself all these years. In the process of burying fear, I imagine I dragged some other emotions down with it. Maybe that's why I am so reserved. Some people consider me inhibited. Perhaps I have been afraid all these years that people would find out how scared I really am. I don't suppose I fooled anyone but myself."

In the course of the next few months we observed that he began to lose some of his tenseness. He was much more relaxed, and more approachable. Someone said to him, "You are much more of a person." He smiled and said, "My members tell me that I preach better too. I am far more free now, and less inhibited."

Nell had an alcohol problem, and was attending Alcoholics Anonymous meetings when she first joined our group in order to speed up her cure. She had experienced an occasional lapse, and one evening she showed up at a meeting somewhat intoxicated. The group accepted her lovingly, neither feeling nor expressing the slightest criticism.

Her alcoholism, of course, was simply an outer manifestation of her feelings of self-rejection. She was unable to accept and love herself properly, nor could she give or receive love. After six months of steady spiritual and emotional growth she wrote this comment about the evaluation slips she had received:

The day I took the test I was feeling optimistic rather than depressed. However, seven of the eleven slips I received indicated more excessive emotional needs than others in the group. I have known this for a long time, I think, but was not willing to admit these "failings" — which is what I felt they were — to anyone else, to God, or to myself. I have always tried to escape my feelings by tranquillizing myself, either with alcohol or pills.

As of today, I admit and accept these emotions as part of me. I have asked God to accept them, to help me, and I feel He has. I know the group will accept them, and accept me too. And now I plan a day to day *action* program. With God's help, and the group's understanding, and my own efforts, I expect to continue my upward progress. The test pin-pointed me very accurately. Though it's taken me six months to admit openly these truths about myself, better six months than never.

The next six months constituted her period of greatest growth. She had accepted herself *as she was*. Acceptance does not imply approval. It was that she was admitting to herself, to God and to others, the kind of a person she was. After fourteen months in the group, Nell revealed a remarkable emotional maturity and spiritual poise. She had become "a new person in Christ" — through her decision.

Jung said to a group of ministers in 1932:

We cannot change anything unless we accept it. Condemnation does not liberate, it oppresses. Acceptance of oneself is the essence of the moral problem and the acid test of one's whole outlook on life. That I feed the beggar, that I forgive an insult, that I love my enemy in the name of Christ — all these are undoubtedly great virtues.... But what if I should discover that the least among them all, the poorest of all the beggars, the most impudent of all offenders, yes, the very fiend himself — that these are in me, and I myself stand in need of the alms of my own kindness, that I myself am the enemy who must be loved — what then?

To accept and love myself properly — there is the difficulty. We may challenge a Christian to a deeper commitment to Christ, but if in his innermost heart he cannot stand himself, cannot love himself, he will not be able, properly, to love anyone else. Though we may succeed in involving him in earnest service for the Kingdom of God, he will bring with him his own self-rejection, his own neurotic behavior patterns, and will poison, in some degree, everything he touches.

One of the minor miracles we see happening repeatedly in the groups is the transforming power of divine love, mediated through group members, enabling a person to accept himself. It is at this point that true spiritual growth begins.

Rollo May writes that "A human being will not change his personality pattern, when all is said and done, until he is forced to do so by his own suffering ... In fact many neurotic individuals prefer to endure the misery of their present situation than to risk the uncertainty that would come with change."[2] The pain or suffering of which he speaks may be felt either as the sharp stab of a crisis, or the dull throb of frustration; and frustration may result from a growing awareness of the meaninglessness of one's life, and a consequent sense of boredom.

Before one starts rushing about looking for ways to aid some worthy cause, he will do well to find out first who he is. After his conversion, the Apostle Paul did not hasten back to Jerusalem to engage at once in a sustained ministry of evangelism. He apparently spent three years in Arabia first, and it was years later before he accomplished anything of significance. The twelve whom Jesus chose spent three years in intensive preparation before they were considered mature enough to carry on the work which Jesus began. Even after three years of absorbing the spirit and teachings of Jesus, at the Last Supper they bickered about which ones would have the seats of honor — scarcely evidence of spiritual maturity.

Laurel joined a group solely to encourage her husband whose pressing problem was that he had lost his job as an engineer because of emotional illness. She wrote to her mother some months after she joined the group and shared the letter with me. It read, in part:

First of all let me tell you that things are happening to me in this Yokefellow group. I went along with Rob because I thought he needed my encouragement. Just now I feel that I am under the surgeon's knife and until the operation is complete I am neither my old self, nor the new self that I hope will emerge.

This daily quiet time to which we subscribe, involving thirty minutes of meditation and prayer daily, is difficult some days. Dr. Osborne says that when we resist it, it is because we are unconsciously afraid of what God is trying to reveal to us. I have often resisted my quiet time. So much has been revealed

to me so far that I can't take more of it some days. I find that
the excuses I have made for things all my life aren't excuses at
all; they are just lies I have told myself to explain away my
problems.

One perfect example, Mother, is this self-deception you and
I have practiced over the fact that we are fat. I am working on
this *acceptance* of my being fat. When I finally accept it, I may
lose weight just from refusing to fight the problem any more;
but losing weight is not the main goal.

It was six months before Laurel made any effort to
reduce. In the next three or four months she lost over
thirty pounds, with little or no struggle. This was simply
an outer manifestation of her inner spiritual growth. It
began when she "cut the umbilical cord" as she put it, and
ceased being emotionally dependent upon her mother and
her husband. Other evidences of her growth were revealed
in her remarkable new sense of self-acceptance, the loss of
her fear of people, and the surrendering of her martyr
complex which had marred the home life and her happiness. She now spends several hours daily in Christian work
on a volunteer basis.

Rob's growth was not significant for some months,
although he made a fairly consistent effort to maintain a
quiet time despite the depression which virtually immobilized him. But before the group observed its first anniversary, Rob was back at work, with only lingering traces of
his old emotional illness. Equally important was the new
sense of inner peace he manifested.

The spiritual, emotional, and physical healing that took
place in the lives of group members was the result of a
number of things:

First, a feeling of genuine love pervaded the atmosphere. Members prayed for each other daily.

Second, their love for each other was unconditional and
honest. They accepted each other just as they were. They
offered no advice but "spoke the truth in love," as commanded in the New Testament.

Third, they took two spiritual growth inventories during
their first year. Some of the evaluation slips they could
accept immediately. In other instances, it took time to
accept emotionally the things revealed to them.

Fourth, they reminded each other weekly of the daily
quiet time. They were all reading the same general recommended material during the quiet time and they often

gained great insight into their basic needs from it. Most important, they were *discovering within themselves the barriers to their own spiritual growth*. In their quiet time they then offered these newly discovered barriers to God.

The young pastor of a Methodist church wrote of his experience with small groups:

Roughly half of our adult membership has been in groups, for we now make it mandatory that all those joining the church shall go through an eight-week Spiritual Adventure Group. This policy has been in effect the last two years, and thus every member joining in this period has been in such a group. Many of these have continued in our Yokefellow program.

The Spiritual Adventure Group is basically an introduction to the small groups, and it enables the individual who is somewhat hesitant about committing himself to a long-term group to experience the meaningfulness and value of this group on a short term basis.

In every case, when an individual has participated in a group and has dropped out for one reason or another, or the group has ceased to function, these individuals have ultimately asked to unite with another group. They come to recognize that genuine needs were being met while within the group, and that the group is an essential part of their Christian experience.

We have had innumerable instances of individual lives being amazingly affected by the power of the Holy Spirit working through the group. Individuals have found meaning and purpose in their own lives, and marriages have found new hope. I am convinced that the real awakening of our church membership to what it means to be "the Church" can be traced to the initial experience which each person has had with small groups.

It is important to add that results such as these can best be achieved when the pastor himself is an active participant, and gives personal supervision to the general operation of the groups.

The dividends of finding "God as a living reality" instead of a "distant Deity" had dramatic results for many members of that church, and the experience was healing and spiritually stimulating for virtually all who participated.

One of the tragedies of the Church today is that we tend to measure our success in terms of size. In this we have fallen victim to what Jung calls "the mass mind."

The individual who is not anchored in God can offer no

resistance on his own resources to the physical and moral blandishments of the world. For this he needs the evidence of inner, transcendent experience which alone can protect him from the otherwise inevitable submersion in the mass.[3]

In speaking of the "moral blandishments of the world" Jung is not referring primarily to some blatant and scandalous form of behavior. He has in mind something far more serious than a moral lapse. It is rather the terrible danger of being engulfed by the mass mind, until we think what the mass thinks, feel what it feels, and are driven by the same materialistic goals which drive the mass of men.

The mass mind, its prevailing mood, its goals, must be resisted quite as zealously as the threat to personal morals. We may be much more aware of the temptation to obvious moral sin — theft, adultery, covetousness and the like — than of the insidious temptation to be like everyone else: to buy what others buy, seek what they seek, praise what they praise, and condone what they condone.

Jung comments on temptations which the Church experiences in this regard:

Curiously enough the churches, too, want to avail themselves of mass action ... the very churches whose care is the salvation of the *individual* soul. They, too, do not appear to have heard anything of the elementary axiom of mass psychology, that the individual becomes morally and spiritually inferior in the mass, and for this reason do not burden themselves overmuch with the real task of helping the individual achieve a metanoia, or rebirth of the spirit. ... It is unfortunately only too clear that if the individual is not truly regenerated in spirit, society cannot be either, for society is the sum total of individuals in need of redemption. I can therefore see it only as a delusion when the churches try, as they apparently do, to rope the individual into a social organization and reduce him to a condition of diminished responsibility, instead of raising him out of the torpid mindless mass, and making clear to him that he is the one important factor, and that the salvation of the world consists in the salvation of the individual soul.[4]

As a college student I once observed the mass mind in action. A man had been arrested for some sordid crime, and the city was considerably aroused over the incident. I learned that a mob was forming in the center of the city, and since I was studying psychology at the time, I was anxious to see mob action at first hand. A fellow student and I hurried to the scene, and from a safe vantage point we watched the mass mind operate. There was no single leader to direct the action, but it seemed as if gradually there emerged, not a thousand individual minds capable of rational thought, but a single mind moving the whole mob.

We could hear voices from the mob shouting, "Let's go to the jail and get him!" Others took up the cry, and, still leaderless, the crowd surged toward the county jail a few blocks away. We followed. Those in front were not so much leading as being pushed by those behind them. The angriest cries came from men safely immersed in the center of the mob. It was they who urged the crowd forward. They surged toward the jail steps, but suddenly a quiet figure emerged from the door and stood there, hand upraised.

He was a man of average size, neither commanding nor awe-inspiring; but there was something terribly authoritative about his voice: "Stop right there. Don't move, or you may get hurt."

The crowd stopped dead. A few angry mutters were heard, but they waited to see what the sheriff had to say. He began to talk in measured, quiet tones. The most significant thing about him was that he appeared unafraid. The crowd posed no threat to him, for he was right and knew it. He talked to them in simple terms about the courts, the American system of justice which each man wants for himself and must want for every other man.

He paused, then said, "Now, you will all go home, and our courts will take care of this accused man." Turning quietly he re-entered the building.

A little man far in the rear shouted, "Let's go git him anyway!" But the crowd was melting, and the little man disappeared in the mob. One person who knew he was right, backed by no visible means of enforcing the law, had stopped an angry mob of men who were temporarily insane.

Something like that has taken place in every age, wherever men have gathered. Someone shouts, "Hosanna to the Son of David!" and the crowd waves palm branches to greet the Messiah. Later a few men begin to cry, "Crucify him," and the mob takes up the cry. Or in our own day advertisers cry, "Buy this!" or "New and daring!" or they point to this or that alleged panacea for physical and mental well-being.

If one voice is heard more persuasively and more often than the others, via television, radio, or the press, an invisible mob is formed: the mass mind begins to operate. Before long, thousands, perhaps millions join in chanting the refrain, whether it be the praises of a leader, the condemnation of a cause once popular, or the demand for this or that social change. Some of the causes promoted are laudable, for the mass mind is not all evil. But as Hitler demonstrated with demonic zeal and insane genius, it is far easier to rouse the mass mind to hate than to love.

Jesus attached great importance to the conversion of the *individual*. He led no protest march to Rome or Jerusalem advocating social reform. The social injustices of the day must have caused him anguish. The poverty and misery of the oppressed masses contrasted with the revels of the wealthy. The sickness and disease, the tax-ridden tenant farmers, the blatant injustice on every hand, the heavy yoke of Rome — all this must have been a source of deepest personal sorrow to Him. Yet He resisted the temptation to make a dramatic demand for social justice. He did not command His followers to concern themselves primarily with these obvious evils. On the contrary, just before His ascension He said to the little band, "Wait here in the city until you are clothed with power from on high."⁵ They were given no other instructions than to wait prayerfully until God's Holy Spirit had united, cleansed, and empowered them. He deemed them unequal to the task of bearing the good news of the Kingdom until *something vital had happened to them personally!*

We see injustice and suffering all about us. Those with compassion feel constrained to rush about organizing, soliciting funds, launching new movements to eradicate poverty, disease, or the many different kinds of suffering which afflict humanity. This zeal is laudable. I have spent so many years as an activist, engaged in good works to alleviate human need that I find only sympathy in my heart for the zealous doer of good deeds.

It is with difficulty that I restrain myself from yielding to the impulse to share in every worthy cause. However, here as elsewhere, the good can become the enemy of the best. The obvious good of bearing food to the hungry, or solace to the bereaved, can be the enemy of the best — which might be simply to do what Jesus commanded. He said, in effect, "Don't rush off to spread the good news of the resurrection, or to change the world, until you have a special kind of power from Heaven." He did not describe the effect this power would have on them. He simply told them to wait. They would know when it came. And they waited — hours, days, in perfect obedience until the power came.

Having prayed together in quiet receptivity, they were ready to be cleansed of self-interest, pettiness, jealousy, egocentricity, and the hundred and one other spiritual sins which mar the effectiveness of zealous people. Jesus evidently spent a considerable portion of His ministry dealing with individuals, and preparing the twelve for their mission. Though He preached on a number of occasions to the multitude, His most effective results came from dealing with individuals and the little group of disciples.

And with individuals He began at the point of need: "What do you want me to do for you?" He was prone to ask. He began at the point of crisis — physical illness, sin, blindness. When the disciples argued over which of them was the greatest, he used the occasion not to settle a quarrel but to give them a long-remembered lesson in humility.

Elton Trueblood, founder of the Yokefellow movement, expressed it beautifully:

The world needed a saving faith, and the formula was that such a faith comes by a particular kind of fellowship. Jesus was deeply concerned for the continuation of his redemptive work after the close of his earthly existence, and his chosen method was *the formation of a redemptive society*. He did not form any army, establish a headquarters, or even write a book. All he did was to collect a few unpromising men, inspire them with the sense of his vocation and theirs, and build their lives into an intensive fellowship of affection, worship and work. One of the truly shocking passages of the gospel is that in which Jesus indicates that there is absolutely no substitute for the tiny redemptive society. If this fails, he suggests, all is failure; there is no other way. He told the little bedraggled fellowship that they were actually the salt of the earth and that, if this salt should fail, there would be no adequate preservation at all. He was staking all on one throw.[6]

3. ANXIETY

> A pure heart is one that is unencumbered, unworried, uncommitted, and which does not want its own way about anything, but which, rather is submerged in the loving will of God.... There can be no restlessness except it come from self-will.
>
> — *Meister Eckhart*

ONE outstanding psychiatrist affirms dogmatically that everyone is spending at least fifty percent of his psychic energy keeping repressed memories below the level of consciousness. It is at least safe to say that each of us spends a great deal of our psychic energy in trying to avoid anxiety. If this energy can be made available for creative living we can change our lives and destinies.

Behind every activity, every decision, every long-range or short-range plan, there is an unconscious effort to avoid anxiety. Since anxiety is painful to experience, we go to elaborate lengths to avoid situations which will produce it. We plan, rationalize, work, even lie to ourselves and others, in an effort to avoid it.

Psychologists agree in general that *every action is an effort to avoid anxiety*. A man who works daily at a task he dislikes, and which creates anxiety, is avoiding the greater anxiety of facing unemployment and financial distress. A woman who dislikes housecleaning, but undertakes it just the same, is doing so in an effort to avoid the still greater anxiety which would be produced by living in a dirty house. At any given moment we are doing *the thing we prefer to do*.

The manner in which we rationalize our conduct in order to avoid anxiety is illustrated by a man who disliked social events. He had been timid and withdrawn as a child, without close friends to whom to relate. He recalled a sense of being alienated from his father and older brothers. Now, in his fifties, he experienced an intense dislike for all social events. He even felt uneasy attending church.

His wife would propose attending some social event, but he would resist with any of a dozen oft-used rationalizations: he was tired, and wanted to stay home and watch television, or listen to some good music; people in general were boring; their small talk was boring; there were few intelligent people with whom one could really communicate — and so on. There was, of course, some validity to each of his contentions, but none of them was the real reason as he came to discover in the group. At first he resisted the possibility that he was simply avoiding the anxiety of close personal contact with people. He resisted even more strongly the idea that it could have originated in his early childhood. He came to see in time, however, that his real reason for avoiding personal contact with others in a social setting was because they made him feel inferior and insecure. He simply found reasons for avoiding the anxiety-producing situation.

The hoarder, whether of string, money, or odd assortments of what his family calls junk, is responding to a feeling of anxiety buried deep within the sub-conscious. He can readily rationalize his hoarding. One may need string; one will always need money; and is not saving a great virtue? Of course, there may ultimately be some possible need for all of the odds and ends he has stored, but the real reason is much deeper. He is motivated by a sense of anxiety originating in early childhood. It may have stemmed from deprivation of love when he was very young. The childhood insecurity, fear of not being loved and taken care of, now takes the form of a fear of not having enough money to take care of himself in later years. Financial insecurity in the child's home, creating a generalized anxiety, can take the form of hoarding, stinginess, fear of giving, fear of loving — all manifestations of anxiety.

It is safe to say that all anxiety-laden behavior stems not from a rationally thought out process, but from emotional factors, and that the roots usually go far back into childhood.

If we were to act other than we do, it would create

greater anxiety. To change our pattern of behavior significantly, without understanding our basic natures, tends to create additional anxiety, and thus we tend to cling to a familiar course of action.

The mountain climber is as much motivated by anxiety as is the person who cannot look over the edge of a precipice without panic. The mountain climber simply has a different kind of anxiety which drives him to conquer mountain peaks.

The course of action taken by some person may impress us as foolhardy, reckless, unwise, or just plain irrational; but to the person involved, being who and what he is, it appears to be the best possible choice. He is acting on the basis of certain emotional needs, assumptions and responses. For him to act in any other manner would create in him marked tension and anxiety.

This is not to imply, however, that all anxiety is destructive. There is a creative form of anxiety which causes a man to get out of bed in the morning and go to work. A mother answers the cry of her child in response to an inner anxiety which is also creative. Our reaction to a sudden danger marshalling all our inner resources stimulates the secretion of additional adrenalin into the bloodstream and prepares us for "fight or flight." This is a God-given instinctual response to fear. It is only when fear becomes an all-pervasive anxiety which impairs our effectiveness that it ceases to be creative and becomes destructive.

The alcoholic or problem drinker suffers from deep anxiety. His basic problem is not that he drinks too much; his excessive drinking is the outer symptom of a very strong anxiety and need. He has a low tolerance for anxiety-producing situations, and when he feels threatened by some situation, he can endure the anxiety only with the help of alcohol, which compounds the problem by causing him to feel both guilt and inferiority. Alcohol tends to paralyze the higher brain center where the judicial faculty resides. The problem drinker is no better able to cope with the situation than before he had his several drinks; in fact, his performance is usually at a lower level than before, but since his judgement is impaired he feels somewhat more effective.

Lectures by relatives, threats, condemnation, criticism and nagging serve only to make matters worse. He already feels guilty and inadequate. Criticism simply intensifies these feelings, and he feels a stronger need to drink in order to dull his guilt feelings temporarily. The Alcoholics Anonymous approach has provided a creative solution for a vast number of alcoholics. The program is psychologically and spiritually sound. Unfortunately many alcoholics cannot admit to themselves that they are problem drinkers, and they cannot be helped until they admit in all humility that they are powerless to help themselves, and are ready to turn to a Higher Power. The very admission of this fact is the absolutely essential first step.

Much anxiety is produced by repressed hostility. There are several ways of handling hostility, or any other negative emotion: One may express it, suppress it, repress it, or release it to God in complete abandonment. There are situations where hostility may be expressed to the benefit of all concerned. At other times to express deep resentment would be unwise and destructive. In such cases we learn to suppress the feeling. We know the feeling is there and we are aware of it, but we suppress it. The most dangerous procedure, one which is largely used unconsciously, is to *repress* it; that is, we pretend to ourselves that we do not feel hostility. For instance, a small child may feel hostility toward his parents, but he learns to bury or repress the feeling. After all, "we should not hate our parents." The expression of hostility is often not acceptable in the home, and the child may learn to bury it deep in the unconscious mind.

Angela is a case in point. She was that paragon of virtue dear to the parental heart: a completely obedient child. It never occurred to her to rebel openly, even in adolescence. After graduating from school she taught for several years, then became a private secretary.

Her father, toward whom she had mixed feelings of love and hate, dominated her life. He was never too successful in business, and Angela, the epitome of generosity, turned a large portion of her pay check over to the family for many years. She lived at home most of the time, often with a very limited wardrobe and a greatly circumscribed social life, because of her feeling that she should help support the family.

She had numerous offers of marriage, but could never bring herself to accept any of them until she was nearing forty. After marrying a very passive man, she continued to help support her parents for many years. Her generosity knew no bounds. But now that she had a life apart from her parents, anxiety began to take its toll. There were numerous trips to the hospital, frequent treatment by various physicians, and annual bouts with vague infections which she could not throw off.

Her parents came to live with her, intensifying the inner conflict. She worked at two jobs and kept house. Finally, with the parents safely cared for in a retirement home, Angela's life should, one would think, become somewhat more placid. On the contrary, the life-long anxiety she had experienced seemed to worsen; for it was not the actual presence of her parents, or their demands, which produced the anxiety; it was her own feeling of self-rejection and guilt which she experienced because of her mixed emotions of love and hate toward her parents.

Her physical ailments were not imaginary. They were organic illnesses, involving considerable pain. She endured them all with a mixture of cheerfulness, wit, and stoicism. She was vaguely aware that somehow her mingled love and hostility toward her parents — especially her father — were involved, but the whole area was much too painful for her to deal with it in any creative way. She resisted counseling, except in a temporary and superficial way. Angela's guilt feelings about "deserting" her parents for marriage produced anxiety, and anxiety is conflict. This inner conflict was great enough to set up an endocrine imbalance, which was the chief source of all her illnesses.

Angela had been a faithful and active churchgoer all her life. She was a firm believer in God, in Christ, and in prayer. It was not that she had no religious faith upon which to rely. It was rather that the standard format of church life had nothing to offer a person beset with deep anxieties. If she prayed, it was concerning her physical illness; but this form of prayer proved useless, for her illness was only a symptom of the basic problem: repressed hostility, creating unbearable anxiety.

She could discuss her mixed emotions toward her parents, but only in a superficial way. She refused to seek counseling or group therapy of any sort. It was obvious that the pain of her frequent illnesses was more endurable than the suffering that would be involved in facing her true feelings. She simply chose the course of action which unconsciously she felt would produce the least anxiety; but the mind tends to hand its pain — guilt and anxiety — over to the body. In Angela's case, it seemed preferable to endure physical illness for many years than to face the source of her deeply rooted anxiety. Unfortunately, hers is not an unusual case; it is highly typical.

One of the most difficult things for many persons to accept is that though consciously they want to be relieved of their physical symptoms, they have an unconscious need to have those very symptoms. We choose our symptoms — unconsciously and with inexorable finality. Specialists in the field of psychosomatic medicine believe that from fifty to eighty per cent of all physical ills originate in our emotions. In fact, *all* emotions have some effect upon the physical organism in either a creative or destructive manner. Emotionally induced symptoms can develop into actual organic illnesses in time.

Long ago the Bible recognized this. It admonishes us that "A tranquil mind is health for the body."[1] The Apostle Paul writes to the Christians at Philippi, "Have no anxiety about anything, but in everything by prayer and supplication with thanksgiving let your requests be made known to God. And the peace of God, which passes all understanding, will keep your hearts and minds in Christ Jesus."[2] God's peace can come to us only as we surrender our anxiety and fear.

The way in which mixed love and hate operate in daily life is illustrated by the young woman who wrote to her boy friend: "Dear George: I hate you! Love, Alice." These mixed emotions, ever present with us, play a large part not only in our human relations, but have much to do with our physical well-being or lack of it.

Karl Menninger describes the mechanics by which our aggressive impulses are repressed:

It is one of the recognized aims of education to deal with aggressiveness of the child's nature, i.e., in the course of the first four or five years to change the child's own attitude toward these impulses in himself. The wish to hurt people, and later the wish to destroy objects, undergoes all sorts of changes. It is usually first restricted, then suppressed by commands and prohibitions; a little later it is repressed, which means that it disappears from the child's consciousness. The child does not dare any more to have knowledge of these wishes. There is always the danger that they might return from the unconscious; therefore all sorts of protections are built up against them. the cruel child develops pity, the destructive child will become hesitant and over-careful. If education is handled intelligently, the main part of these destructive impulses will be directed away from their primitive aim of doing harm to somebody or something, and will be used to fight the difficulties of the outer world: to accomplish tasks of all kinds ... to "do good" instead of 'being bad', as the original impulse demanded.[3]

Inner peace and harmony, the absence of destructive anxiety, provide the emotional climate in which our bodies can function best, and our lives develop creatively. This is attested to by the Bible and confirmed by the findings of modern science. One may not always be able to pinpoint the cause of his anxiety. He may protest that he hasn't a worry in the world, and it may be true that he has nothing to worry about; yet he may experience a sense of diffused anxiety. It may have begun in infancy, the result of having had an authoritarian parent, or from having had unrealistic standards set for him in childhood, or from feelings of rejection. The child of four may be expected to behave like a child of six; the child of ten like one of twelve. If the report card shows a C, by parental standards it should have been at least a B. If he raises it to a B, then it should have been an A. If his grades are not all A's, the implication is that with a little more diligence on his part, they could have been.

Such a child learns that he can never win the full approval of his parents, no matter how much effort he puts forth. Nothing he ever does is good enough. He never feels quite accepted, and he can never learn to accept himself if he turns in anything less than a perfect performance. He may then go through life never able to achieve anything which meets his own inexorable demand for perfection. He did not originate this perfectionism as a philosophy of life. It was ingrained in him as a child. He may not have been taught this, but he caught it by a kind of "environmental osmosis."

The too-high standard of performance may be "caught" from a parent who never actually demands too much of the child. Children learn not only from what is told them, but by imitating parental attitudes. A child tends to develop his "emotional tone" simply by being with his parents.

There are parents who try unconsciously to get their children to achieve certain goals to compensate for their own feelings of failure or inadequacy. One college student whose parents expressed dissatisfaction with his grades attended the same university from which his parents had graduated. He asked a fellow student who worked in the office to check on his parents' grades. They were substantially lower than his!

A mother who had been denied success as a singer urged her daughter to attempt a singing career. The whole family worked toward this goal, and sacrificed to help the budding young singer secure vocal training. The daughter possessed a fair but unremarkable voice. For twenty years she struggled toward the totally unrealistic goal, and ended up emotionally and physically ill, disillusioned with life and a completely frustrated individual.

An all-pervasive anxiety operating in an adult often stems from events which happened early in the child's life and long since had been buried deep in the unconscious. At the age of four a very active and somewhat rebellious child, termed "uncooperative" by his mother, was soundly beaten into submission. Thereafter he gave her no trouble. He was a "good child," never outwardly disobedient. But the parents could never understand why he never liked to be cuddled, why he seemed to wear a look of almost constant hostility which he never expressed verbally or otherwise. Outwardly he was compliant. Inwardly he was seething with repressed hostility. To rebel would mean withdrawal of love, or abandonment, which to the child means utter annihilation. The few times he did show signs of rebellion he was whipped by his father until he gave in and again became a "good child."

The boy's repressed aggression could have taken a number of directions, depending upon many factors. In his case the first day in school he threatened a little girl on the playground, and was punished both at school and at home. He learned again the futility of showing aggression. In high school, he engaged in various types of antisocial behavior such as stealing, but was never caught.

At this point something positive happened. His family had always taken him to Sunday school and church. There he learned a moralistic kind of religion in which there was little love but a strong emphasis upon "doing right." His buried aggression and the stern demands of righteousness backed up by an avenging God battled it out in his soul, and God — the God he had learned to know — won. He entered the ministry and functioned adequately by normal standards. But his was a moralistic, unloving gospel for a number of years, until he came to understand the source of his own buried hostility. He dredged up his feelings, admitted them to consciousness, and released them to a loving Heavenly Father, who was no longer a moralistic, demanding, avenging God. He began to feel and express love to a much greater degree. His moralistic preaching changed to an emphasis upon the redeeming, forgiving love of God, revealed in Jesus Christ. He had always believed this intellectually. It had been a part of his theology. Now it became part of his life.

The change took place largely as the result of participation in a fellowship group, where honesty with one's feelings constituted one of the basic requirements. Until the change took place he had never been able to understand why he felt no particular affection for his parents. He felt a mild family tie, a sense of concern and compassion, but not the slightest affection.

He was much more aware of a nameless anxiety for which there was no apparent cause. It took its toll in nervousness, occasional bouts with colitis, arthritis, and a succession of other vague but uncomfortable symptoms. As he came to terms with his feelings — some of them long buried — most of the symptoms disappeared.

He began to see how a rigid, authoritarian, punitive family relationship had caused him to feel hostility which he had buried in his unconscious mind. There it struggled against love and obedience. Part of him wanted to love and be loved, but another part of his nature felt rejection and hostility. The resultant aggression, converted and then permeated with love and compassion, became creative.

Aggression may express itself in two ways: it can be openly hostile and possibly destructive, or it can be creative — a drive to change circumstances, to build, and to create.

Sometimes the opposing forces creating anxiety may be partially recognized. If we want to attend a concert and go bowling on the same night, a certain amount of anxiety is set up until the issue is resolved. The need to make a decision is prompted partly by the need to relieve the anxiety which persists in a mild form until a decision is made. Anxiety is inner conflict. If a husband wants to bowl and his wife wants to attend the concert, the anxiety may become a marital conflict unless resolved in a manner suitable to both.

If one gives in grudgingly and only pretends a ready acquiescence, inner anxiety ensues. The need to love and the need to have one's own way are in conflict. Only mature self-understanding and genuine Christian forgiveness and love can exorcise the demon of hostility at this point.

Anxiety may take a thousand forms. A friend of mine was seldom allowed to play as a child; he always had to be busy. His parents were harassed and debt-ridden. Their anxiety was transmitted to their three children, each of whom reacted in a different way. My friend became a compulsive worker, seldom permitting himself to relax, and feeling guilty if he took a day off. He sometimes refused to take vacations on the grounds that there was too much to do. His parents had likewise seldom taken vacations, but he failed to see any connection.

His two sisters reacted to the stress-laden atmosphere of the home in different ways. One of them determined to succeed in a highly competitive field and ruined her health, destroyed her marriage, and found neither happiness nor success. Her drive for achievement was so great that she could settle for nothing less than outstanding success. When that was denied her, she became ill and remained so for the rest of her life, although physician after physician could find little or nothing organically wrong with her. The other sister worked incredibly long hours, saved her money and spent it unselfishly on others, and worked compulsively at a succession of jobs while keeping house, until she was prostrated from sheer emotional and physical exhaustion.

There is no intention to blame the parents here. They were products of their own environment, and they used the best judgment they had. Tracing our personal ills to their source in no way fixes blame upon our parents. If we blame anything, let it be the corporate evils of society, or original sin, or a troubled and insecure collective unconscious — all of which come to about the same thing.

Many people suffering from strong anxiety would much prefer to have an operation, or be hospitalized, or undergo painful treatment, than to face the fact that the problem is emotional or spiritual in origin. Unconsciously, without any awareness of the mechanism involved, they choose to endure physical pain rather than emotional conflict. Dr. Alvarez of the Mayo Clinic has said that the vast majority of patients who complain of digestive symptoms have no organic disease which will account for their symptoms. Most prefer an operation or expensive treatment to receiving the news that their "illness" originates in their emotions. Not that these illnesses are entirely imaginary! On the contrary, there is usually genuine pain involved, or at least discomfort. But the patient insists, "The pain is here, doctor; there's nothing else wrong with me." The pain is there, but all too often it originated in anxiety, which is simply another way of saying that the problem is basically a spiritual one.

Whether we call it a mental health problem, a spiritual problem, or an impaired emotional adjustment, we are talking about the same thing. Man is body, mind, and spirit, and what affects one affects all. If there are inner conflicts and tensions, anxiety and guilt at some point in his life, the individual will tend to manifest this spiritual dis-ease by some physical symptom. If he does not, his dis-ease may take the form of psychic masochism, an unconscious need to punish himself. He may become accident-prone, trouble-prone, disaster-prone, or bad-judgment-prone. Men have been known to make a succession of incredibly bad decisions, resulting in inevitable failure, when all their friends and relatives united in warning against the results of such decisions. This is of course a totally unconscious mechanism by which the self is punished for real or imaginary guilt.

Guilt, whether real or false, can be handled in only two ways. It must be forgiven or punished. If we cannot secure forgiveness, we find a way to punish ourselves physically, mentally, or circumstantially — that seems to be an inexorable cosmic law. But then it is not God who is punishing, but the condemnatory self.

This brings us to the age-old question of why the righteous suffer. No completely satisfactory answer has ever been advanced, though volumes have been written on the subject, from the Book of Job to the latest theological work on the problem of good and evil. The righteous do suffer. Jesus said, "In the world you have tribulation."⁴ We suffer not only from the corporate evils of society (war, famine, disease, catastrophe), but we also suffer just as the "unrighteous" do from inner conflicts if we have not achieved emotional and spiritual maturity. Mere knowledge of Bible facts, plus Christian morality, will not guarantee freedom from inner conflict, much less from natural disasters.

A charming elderly woman is crippled by rheumatoid arthritis. Her hands are gnarled, and her spine twisted. She lives in constant pain. Her friends cannot understand why this dear little woman who has spent so much of her life in the service of others, who was never known to be absent from church, whose moral life has always been above reproach, should be allowed to suffer so. Here is a sweet and gentle spirit. Why? we ask — why?

Although doctors do not agree on the actual cause of rheumatoid arthritis, there is sufficient clinical evidence to warrant saying that repressed hostility often produces mild to severe arthritis. Many arthritis patients are externally placid and gentle. They are seldom aware that below the level of consciousness there has always been hostility, which they learned to repress early in life.

Loring T. Swaim, who was formerly an instructor in arthritis at Harvard Medical School and who has specialized for fifty years in the field of orthopedics, is the author of an outstanding book, *Arthritis, Medicine, and the Spiritual Laws*, in which he cites a large number of cases which were healed only after he induced the individuals to deal with their buried resentments, or with other negative emotions, in the light of Christ's teachings.

Mrs. Blandon, an excellent Sunday school teacher, had a remarkable knowledge of the Bible. She spoke on spiritual matters with quiet, authoritative emphasis, and there was always a sweet patience in her manner. She became almost totally incapacitated by arthritis in her later years, and those who visited her always went away with the feeling that it was almost a benediction to be in her presence. She never complained.

She had been reared in a rigid religious atmosphere. While very young she learned that to express resentment was sinful, and so she became a compliant, dutiful, obedient child. The normal adolescent rebelliousness never found expression in her. She grew up believing that she had no hostility. "A Christian never hates," she would say. "One never retaliates. One must always meet evil with good." Her quotations were apt, her knowledge of theology extensive, but her awareness of her emotions were almost nonexistent. She had learned to repress (deny and bury) all awareness of hostility, but the inner conflict went on in the subterranean chambers of her soul, creating anxiety, then a metabolic imbalance, and in time a crippling illness.

Mrs. Blandon would never dream of telling anyone a falsehood, but she was taught as a child to lie to herself about her true feelings. It is equally wrong to lie to God, others, or ourselves. A lie is simply the denial, repression, perversion, or distortion of the truth. God's universe depends upon spiritual laws of love and truth. It is not simple *knowledge* of the truth which sets us free, but willingness to *face* the truth about ourselves.

Not only arthritis, which we have used simply as an illustration, but scores of other physical disabilities result from anxiety born of our refusal to be honest with our emotions. Depending upon such things as tissue susceptibility, environmental factors, or one's unconscious need to choose some particular symptom, anxiety can take its toll in a hundred different ways.

For instance, many sufferers from peptic ulcers are basically dependent, hostile people. They do not usually appear dependent. On the contrary they usually give every evidence of being hard-driving, resourceful personalities. Inwardly they are divided. A part of their personalities has been rendered compliant and dependent, usually through too much maternal dominance; and another part of the personality is seeking freedom. The inner conflict creates anxiety which can be devastating. Some ulcer patients cannot accept the fact that they ever felt both love and hate towards one or both of their parents, and their buried guilt over hostile feelings toward a parent creates inner tension and anxiety.

Simple awareness of this inner conflict is not always sufficient to achieve healing. Many find that they need, first, awareness of the basic cause; second, acceptance of these emotions as valid and real at a feeling level and third, action. That is, they need to "talk out" their feelings in a proper setting.

Of course some anxiety stems from other causes. In *The*

Dynamics of Personal Adjustment, Lehner and Kube point out that anxiety may stem from:

> The discrepancies between an individual's level of achievement, and the goals and rewards a society regards as desirable. Thus an individual who is a member of a society that stresses material wealth and status may become anxious, worried, and distraught if he fails to make a lot of money and to improve his social position. This will be true especially if his close friends and associates expect him to achieve these goals.... The need to express aggressiveness or hostility may also be a source of anxiety, when such expression is stifled by cultural restrictions or threatening consequences.... Indeed, any demands with which the individual feels he cannot cope or that are in conflict with his needs can be sources of anxiety.[5]

Lehner and Kube suggest that anxiety is the common core from which all neurotic behavior arises. They mention such typical maladies as ulcers, headaches and allergies as symptoms of anxiety.

Karl Menninger quotes Ali ibn Hazm, who lived from 994 to 1064: "No one is moved to act, or resolves to speak a single word, who does not hope by means of this action or word to release anxiety from his spirit."[6] Nine hundred years ago this ancient writer anticipated the discovery of modern psychology that the avoidance of anxiety is the primary motivation in human action.

O. Hobart Mowrer stresses unresolved guilt as the major source of destructive anxiety and consequent neurosis. He says:

> Manifestly not all mistakes or "sins" lead to neurotic difficulties. Some people "get caught," and some voluntarily confess and take the consequences. And others just don't have enough conscience to be bothered. But persons of good character who are neither fortunate enough to be caught, nor wise enough to confess, develop an increasing dispositon, as time goes on, to experience the emotions and display the actions which we call "symptoms".... For ... a period the neurosis may lie dormant, latent — "the Lord is slow to wrath." But eventually the period of "grace" expires, "patience" is exhausted and the individual finds that conscience is no longer a friend and comforter, but instead a severe critic and enemy. The individual, to speak loosely, has turned *against* himself; and when this happens he is in the kind of "trouble" which we call psychopathology.[7]

Whether we call it sin, guilt, anxiety neurosis, or "an illusion of mortal mind," we are talking pretty much about the same thing. We are describing an individual who is out of harmony with divine laws and thus alienated from God, his neighbor, and himself. He can be free of his alienation and his symptoms if he will re-establish himself in a loving relationship with God and man. He can come to regard himself as forgiven and acceptable. His self-contempt, conscious or unconscious, can be replaced by a proper self-acceptance. Thousands have found that the small group, under proper conditions, can create the setting in which this spiritual transformation can take place. Here one can learn to trust his emotions, and his neighbor, and God. In the process he makes a great step forward in obeying the supreme law of love; for at its core, anxiety is an absence of love.

4. THE CURE FOR ANXIETY

> All diseases of the body proceed from the mind
> or soul.   — *Plato*

PSYCHOLOGIST Karen Horney suggests that there are four
main ways of escaping anxiety: to deny it; to avoid the
thought or feeling which arouses it; to rationalize it; to
narcotize it.[1] To these four I have added a fifth, which
seems to me the only creative way of handling anxiety on
a permanent basis.

The first method, which is to deny the existence of
anxiety, is usually an unconscious process. The individual
is conscious of certain distressing or painful symptoms,
which may be emotional or physical. He may be unaware
of the real reason for anxiety.

A woman once asked me to pray for her because she
feared a heart attack. Before praying I asked about her
symptoms. She reported a frightening palpitation of the
heart but admitted her physician had told her that the
cause was emotional rather than organic. She was certain,
however, that the violent pounding, which came on unpre-
dictably, meant that she was threatened with a heart
attack.

I asked her when the difficulty had begun. She reported
that she had first noticed the palpitations in March of the
previous year. Then she recalled that her aged mother had
died that month. She had seen no connection between the
two events. Now began the slow process of trying to
discover what it was about her mother's death which had

precipitated this tremendous anxiety. She assured me that she felt only intense sorrow over her mother's death. There was apparently no abnormal fear of death and no awareness of any other cause of undue anxiety.

As we dug just beneath the level of consciousness we found the source of her problem. It proved to be not one but two related things. She came to see that she had consciously feared her mother's death but unconsciously had desired it. She had hidden this feeling from her conscious mind. One does not wish for the death of one's mother! When this thought came perilously near the level of consciousness she pushed it down, and denied that she had ever felt this. "One shouldn't think such thoughts!" she said heatedly. "I am not that sort of person at all. I loved my mother!" Eventually, however, she came to accept the fact that she had had mixed emotions about her mother's death, both wanting it and fearing it. Since she had repressed the wish for her mother to die, she could not secure a sense of forgiveness. We can never feel forgiven for an emotion we will not admit having. It is impossible to confess to God what we will not confess to ourselves.

Another related source of her anxiety was the unrecognized fear that she, too, might die. She was haunted by certain guilt feelings. She felt just as guilty as if it had been genuine guilt before God. She knew intellectually that God had forgiven her, but she did not accept it emotionally. At an unconscious level she had begun to fear death as punishment for her sins. The unconscious mind does not operate on a logical basis. It deals in feelings — primitive and often child-like. She did not consciously think all these things, but she felt them. She "knew" better with her conscious mind, but knowing nothing of the working of the unconscious mind, she assumed that what she "knew" intellectually was precisely what she felt. She had thought that she was being truthful when she said that she had no reason for anxiety.

Now she came to see that she had a deep-seated anxiety about her mother's death, which she had partly longed for and partly feared; a deeply buried feeling that she needed to be punished for her misdeeds and "bad" thoughts, and that death might be the form of punishment. Her mother's death had brought back a flood of half-buried memories from her early childhood: dire threats of what would happen to her if she disobeyed or did wrong. For the first time she knew what to pray about. It was not an erratic heart action or a threatened heart attack, but guilt, fear and anxiety. When she was able to face her true feeling in honesty and humility, she secured release from her physical symptom. More important, she was released from much of the anxiety which had plagued her life up to this point, for she came to see that prayer is not a magical means of getting God's help in a crisis, but that it involves utter honesty with God, with others, and with ourselves.

Avoidance is the second way of dealing with anxiety. When we use this device we seek to avoid the feelings, situations or thoughts which arouse anxiety. It is no more effective than denial.

An excessively shy person finds that social contacts create anxiety, so he makes every effort to avoid people; a person who fears heights avoids tall buildings and bridges; a person who experiences undue anxiety in mountain driving, being in crowds, giving a talk in public, may simply avoid these situations. But nothing has been solved permanently. The basic anxiety still persists.

Some of our anxieties are normal. It is only when anxiety — diffused fearfulness — permeates life and destroys our peace of mind that we need to look for the underlying cause.

It is normal for a young mother to be somewhat apprehensive about her new role. One such mother, greatly distraught, shared with me her terrible fear that she might do something destructive to her child. Fear and guilt had brought her to the verge of emotional illness. She loved her baby. How could she entertain these horrible thoughts of harming him?

In the first counseling session she was led to see that it was not the child which she hated, but the added responsibilities with which she felt unable to cope. This discovery lessened her guilt feelings, and the abnormal anxiety subsided with no further help. She was able to function adequately as a mother.

She had been shocked by the thought of injuring her child and had sought first to deny the feeling and then to avoid it; but there was no way she could avoid it. It had to be dealt with and resolved.

The person who procrastinates is handling anxiety through avoidance, though he is usually unaware of it. It is not laziness which causes one to postpone unduly the writing of a letter, going to the doctor, or making a phone call. We call it procrastination, which is what it is, but procrastination arises basically because of anxiety. For some reason, usually on the unconscious level, we find it less anxiety-producing to do something else than write the letter, make the phone call, or see the doctor. Thus we "solve" the problem temporarily by avoiding it. The difficulty is that the problem is not really solved.

Some people have great difficulty with what they term "bad" thoughts. These thoughts, often having to do with sex or hostility, come to their minds unbidden. They are embarrassed and ashamed at entertaining such thoughts. They try to push them out of their minds, but the more they push the more such thoughts persist for in a struggle between will and imagination, imagination usually wins.

In the first place, there is no such thing as a "bad" thought. There are destructive thoughts, random thoughts, absurd thoughts. If, instead of putting all thoughts into two categories, "good" and "bad," one can think of them as "creative" or "destructive," he has taken the first step toward a solution. When a host of random thoughts assail the mind, one can say, "This is not a 'bad' thought. It is a destructive thought in that it destroys my peace of mind. I do not know its source, I did not invite it, I will not grapple with it, nor will I feel guilty about it. It is simply an uninvited guest, and I will gently turn my attention elsewhere, without guilt or self-condemnation." In time this gentle process of relinquishment has far more power over random, unwelcome thoughts than all the will power we can exercise.

The difficulty with using avoidance as a solution is that one tends to avoid only the symptom, which leaves the real problem undiscovered and unresolved; it then persists or breaks out in some other form.

A man once shared his paralyzing fear of going beyond a certain distance in his daily activities. He was limited to an area of roughly ten square blocks. Exceeding the boundaries of his "prison" caused the most intense fear — pounding of the heart, extreme agitation, and other symptoms so severe that he simply could not force himself to go a block beyond his self-imposed boundaries. On some occasions, without warning, his world would close in on him and he would experience difficulty in leaving the house. When he would finally force himself to go out, he would have a secondary symptom, usually a severe headache.

The origin of his problem lay in strong guilt feelings, which he had carefully denied and hidden from himself. His unresolved guilt demanded either forgiveness or self-punishment in some form. So his first step was to deny and repress his guilt feelings by pushing them down into his unconscious mind, whereupon his numerous symptoms erupted. Although he denied it he actually found his space-limitation less threatening than to face the real trouble, which was guilt.

The second effort he made to solve his problem was to avoid the anxiety-producing situation. When it caused intense fear to go beyond a given point, he simply stopped. By avoiding the symptom he relieved anxiety for the moment, but this did not solve the basic problem. On those occasions when he found it difficult even to leave the house, if he forced himself to do so, (no longer avoiding the situation) he responded unconsciously with another symptom — a headache.

All efforts to get him to look for the real cause failed, either in the group or in private counseling. He wanted the symptom removed, but he refused steadfastly to face up to the real cause — guilt — or even to admit the possibility that this could be the source of his problem. It was as if he were saying, on a deep unconscious level: "I would rather suffer the pain and embarrassment of my symptoms than the greater pain of looking within and facing up to my guilt."

It is easy to be judgmental at this point and difficult to understand the very real conflict raging in his mind. He really could not endure the pain of examining whatever brand of guilt he felt. Rather than face it and confess it he simply denied it, then tried to avoid the situations which triggered all of his symptoms. There is probably no hope of alleviating such a situation until the person finds the one real problem. The Bible calls it sin. Psychologists call it anxiety and conflict. The name matters little. Regardless of what one may call it, in order to be free, every human needs to face and confess whatever it is that alienates him from his true self, from God, and his fellow man.

A third method of dealing with anxiety is to rationalize it. All rationalizations are largely unconscious processes.

What we say by way of rationalization may be true, wholly or partially, but still not be an explanation of the action.

I overheard two men discussing the merits of their very expensive new cars. One gave an elaborate explanation for his having purchased so expensive a car. The new motor, just introduced by the manufacturer, gave surprisingly good mileage. He drove a great deal and required the added comfort provided by the car. Its power steering made driving much less fatiguing on long trips; and so on. His friend listened intently to the entire list of rationalizations, grinned, and said: "I bought mine partly because it's a status symbol!" The other heatedly denied that status had anything to do with *his* selection of the car.

A constant series of interruptions, such as a succession of phone calls, creates more tension in me than for many people I know. Tension creates anxiety and anxiety creates tension. My rationalization for years was that I had work to do and could not find time to do it if I was subject to constant interruptions. My rationalization was true as far as it went, but I always managed to avoid the basic issue.

The real problem, as I came to see, was that I had a feeling of guilt and self-criticism if I did not accomplish a given amount of work. For instance, one morning I set myself the task of dictating a given number of letters. There was an unusual number of interruptions: the buzzer sounded every few seconds, it seemed; the phone kept ringing until I asked not to be interrupted; staff members popped in, and in each instance it seemed that the interruption involved something of importance which could not wait. Irritation mounted. I had managed only a fraction of the work I had assigned myself when the secretary announced that a woman was waiting to see me. Though I had an appointment with her I had forgotten it. As I looked at the unfinished work on my desk, I asked for the woman to be brought in. Under my surface friendliness was an undercurrent of irritation because I had not been able to complete my desk work. I am certain that the visitor was aware of my frustration, for I saw it reflected in her manner.

Examining my feelings later I felt somewhat guilty over not being able to complete my desk work, which now would have to be done at night; guilty over not being able to cope with staff, visitors, telephone calls and interruptions all at the same time. Then I saw that I had been rationalizing my anxiety. I had attributed it to my zeal to finish the task, and a consequent sense of failure if I did not manage to achieve all I had outlined for myself.

The truth, as I came to see it finally, consisted of a number of things: As a child, I had felt acceptable to my parents only when I had performed my tasks well and on time. I had felt guilty in childhood if I was not constantly in motion. Parental anxiety was transmitted to me. Now as an adult I found that I could accept myself only if I had finished my self-appointed tasks on time. I felt vaguely guilty and inadequate when I did not. There was no parent to criticize, except the "parent within," who resides in each of us. My guilt feelings did not, in any sense constitute "real guilt;" they were "false guilt." I was guilty only before the accusing conscience, conditioned in childhood. By a series of clever rationalizations I had managed in adulthood to make almost a virtue out of what was a mildly neurotic reaction, based on childhood conditioning. The task I then set for myself was to insist that the "adult of the present" make decisions rather than the "inner child of the past."

A fourth method of handling anxiety is to narcotize it. This can be done by the use of drugs, alcohol, over-busyness, and in sundry other ways. Billions of dollars are spent annually on alcohol and drugs in an effort to escape from anxiety. It may be the anxiety produced by loneliness, inferiority, guilt or frustration, or by the threat of failure. Alcohol paralyzes the higher brain centers where judgment takes place and tends to lessen anxiety temporarily. The person has no more courage than before; his threshold of tolerance for anxiety has not been raised. Nothing has happened, in fact, except that he has temporarily narcotized himself. Some of the tranquilizers function in a similar way. One is no more able to cope with life, perhaps, but life appears less threatening for the moment. No one doubts the value of certain drugs as a temporary solution to the problem of anxiety, but they provide no cure for the basic "dis-ease," which is the problem of unrelieved anxiety.

A less conscious process, and a quite socially respectable one, is the narcotizing of anxiety by being excessively busy. Most compulsive workers fall into this category. Whether it is a man's compulsive devotion to his job, a mother's endless attention to innumerable details of house-keeping, or a church worker's fatiguing, never-ending, God-oriented compulsiveness, it needs to be re-examined.

A young wife and mother complained to me that she could not understand how her very relaxed but highly competent husband could "just sit and look out of the window." Exasperatedly she said, "He can sit and do nothing. I can't just sit. There are too many things to be done. A woman's work is never finished."

It developed that her problem was a mixture of rationalization and narcotizing. As a child she had never been permitted to be idle or just to read a book. Her compulsive father had insisted upon the children's being busy around the house even when there was no work to be done. Moreover, as a young wife, she was having considerable difficulty in her marriage. Communication had broken down. Constant busyness at home, together with much social activity, constituted for her an escape from the anxiety of close contact with her husband. He in turn began to devote more and more time to his office, also in an unconscious effort to avoid the anxiety generated in the home.

There are those persons, too, who seek to allay anxiety by engaging in a gay round of social activities. Such persons are not really being socially minded; they are seeking to escape from the anxiety generated by being alone, to find an answer to their own self-alienation. Their compulsive efforts may consist in constant party-going, visiting, entertaining; or they may take the form of "good works" in the community or the local church. Any or all of these can be either creative endeavors or an unconscious effort to drown out the small voice which encourages us to evaluate our inner lives and goals.

A sage has written, "Beware of the barrenness of busyness;" and another oft-repeated bit of wisdom has it, "When you're too busy to pray, you're too busy." Over-busyness is one of the marks of our society, and it is quite clear that, good as many of our frantic activities may be, much that passes for worthwhile activity is often simply an effort to relieve anxiety. The good can become the enemy of the best.

A group member at an initial session took a simple personality inventory (the Draw-A-Person Test) which was interpreted on the spot. The leader said, after examining the figure she had drawn, "You appear to be trying to escape from the universe. Why?"

She said, "Well, actually I am one of the busiest persons imaginable. Far from escaping, I am busy all day long, every day in the week, trying to minister to the needs of people all around me. There is so much that needs to be done, so many people to help. Is there anything wrong with that?"

The leader replied, "Of course there's nothing wrong with being helpful. This simple test does not reveal anything you are doing, but it does tell us that you are so dissatisfied with your life or some aspect of it that you would would like to retreat and give it all up. Why?"

Then she said, thoughtfully, "Well, really I do get terribly fatigued. I'm tired all the time from my many activities. Sometimes I have wondered how I could get out of all this and just go away someplace and..." she paused.

Someone said, "And escape from the universe, from yourself, and your inner problems?"

"Yes, maybe that's it. I just get so tired."

Further discussion revealed that she was frantically, neurotically busy in a dozen or more church and community activities. She was kind and helpful, the soul of compassion and thoughtfulness. But her fatigue, which was not so much physical as psychogenic, stemmed from her inner anxiety. She knew no way to solve the problem of anxiety except to narcotize it by being frantically busy. She helped many people and aided many good causes; but she was frustrated and inwardly discontented with life. She was solving the problems of others, but her own anxiety went unresolved.

When the time came to discuss whether the group would continue, she was the first to question whether her busy schedule would permit her to do so. She was unconsciously trying to avoid the painful necessity of examining the real source of her anxiety, which was based upon a deep sense of inadequacy.

* * *

The fifth possibility, and the only creative solution, is to seek out and remove the source of anxiety. Again it can be emphasized that there is nothing wrong with anxiety per se. It is only when our anxiety becomes so all-pervasive as to limit our effectiveness that we need to seek for the source. This is easier to suggest than to accomplish, for often the roots are buried deep within the unconscious mind. One may be totally unaware at the conscious level of the events which have created an undue amount of anxiety. Often, however, it is possible to seek out and deal with the source of this abnormal anxiety.

One young woman who was able to find the source of her anxiety in group meetings had not even been aware that anxiety was a problem in her life. By any standard she was living a normal, creative life. She was well-liked, highly competent in her work, and a faithful church member. She was to all intents and purposes a thoroughly normal young woman.

At a retreat, where those present participated in group sessions, she appeared to be confronting some inner problem, the nature of which she was unaware. After the session she came to see me to discuss certain anxieties which troubled her. I suggested the possibility that such anxieties usually originated in guilt, and asked her to bring back for our next counseling session a list of areas where she felt the pain of inferiority, shame, rejection or guilt. I explained to her that all of these tend to register on the inner nature as guilt. She brought in her list, quite a long one, the following week. She showed considerable distress as she went over her list. Her suffering was caused by the fact that she had so long kept these things hidden. She could not believe that anyone could ever respect her, much less love her, if they knew all these things about her.

Feelings of shame and fear, inferiority and rejection, were all mingled together. When she had finished I said, "I cannot see that you have so much sinned as been sinned against. To have emerged from all that to become the wonderful person you are, is to me a remarkable achievement. I have always thought highly of you. Now that I know about your early life, I feel a far greater admiration, and love besides." She asked, surprised, "How could anyone respect and love me, knowing all this about me?" I said "I do. And anyone else would, too."

The next time I saw her I sensed a radical change. There was an openness about her, a new gaiety and vivaciousness. She was a released personality and has remained so. Guilt-induced anxiety had kept a large portion of her personality under cover; or, it could be said, a large portion of her psychic energy was being spent in concealing. Now she had nothing to conceal. She no longer needed to spend a large part of spiritual resources battling anxiety. That energy now became available for creative living.

Dr. Mowrer says that humans *need* other human beings, and "when this need is frustrated — as it is bound to be by continued deception and denial of identity — there is in every socially adequate person a powerful drive to get back into satisfying and comfortable human relations." He calls attention to the conflict between our fear of being found out and this strong inner desire to discard our masks and seek creative relations with others. "As a result of a policy of duplicity, [human beings] have avoided detection and punishment; and . . . the condition which we call mental illness is the dis-ease which comes from an aggrieved conscience and . . . unresolved guilt!"[2]

Time does not diminish our feelings of guilt. The passage of time may dim one's memory of the guilt, or it may even be "forgotten" — buried in the unconscious mind. But it is still there, creating its burden of needless anxiety. While guilt is not by any means the only source of anxiety, it does play a very large part in creating destructive anxiety. By guilt, of course, we mean not only guilty acts, thoughts, and attitudes, but the general feeling of "not measuring up."

Generalizations are dangerous, as was discovered by that statistician who started to wade across a river whose *average* depth was two feet and drowned in water twelve feet deep! So, bearing in mind the risks let us make the following generalizations:

1. Anxiety is creative and necessary up to a point. Beyond that point it is destructive.
2. If one's tolerance for normal anxiety-producing situations is low, tolerance can be raised in time by a process of maturing emotionally.
3. Unbearable anxiety, exceeding our tolerance level, will always tend to produce either physical symptoms, emotional distress, or both.
4. The sources of our anxiety will usually be found in one or more of these areas:
    (a) Attempting to pursue incompatible goals.

    (b) Guilt areas, recent or of long standing; actual or false guilt (much guilt is centered on sex and hostility).

    (c) Early childhood conditioning.

    (d) Failure to achieve some goal.

The average person experiencing undue anxiety will usually find the source of his difficulty in one or more of these areas. It requires, however, a willingness to be open rather than defensive; to run the risk of exposure and consequent rejection which seldom if ever happens); and to be ruthlessly honest with oneself and with others.

The process is not an easy one, and it can seldom be undertaken alone. Our capacity for self-deception is enormous. Others in a small group can help us, gently and lovingly, to face our tendency to rationalize. We need not only psychological insight but the healing presence of One who said "For where two or three are gathered in my name, there am I in the midst of them."[3] In some mystical way the presence and power of Christ are experienced when a small group of people gather in His name, in order to be honest with Him, with themselves, and with one another. His power is then added to our human insight, and we are no longer alone in our search. We are strengthened and supported by His spirit and by others engaged in the same search.

5. WE GET WHAT WE REALLY WANT

> If you want God only, you may have all else
> besides.   — *Meister Eckhart*

I delivered a sermon one Sunday morning on the many
levels of prayer. I touched briefly on one particular aspect
of prayer, saying something like this: "Visualization plays a
vital part in effective prayer. Communion with God has
many other aspects, but it might be summed up this way:
if what you desire is in harmony with the basic will of
God; if it is in keeping with the teachings of Jesus; if it
will harm no one else and can add measurably to your
well-being or that of another; and if you want the will of
God in your life, you can receive what you want if you can
visualize it. To visualize something implies that you can
see it on the screen of your mind as an accomplished fact.
This is what Jesus meant when He said: 'If you can
believe, all things are possible to him who believes.' To
believe means that you *know* it as a fact." I elaborated on
this to some extent, and perhaps most of the congregation
gave intellectual assent to the idea.

But there was at least one person present who accepted
it at a deeper level. After the service when everyone else
had gone, the young man, a college student, said: "You're
going to the Holy Land this summer, aren't you?" I said,
"Yes, I'll be leaving sometime in July." He said casually,
"Would you mind if I went with you?" I replied, "Not at
all. I'd be delighted to have you along." I had known him

for some years, and at the time he was working with the young people of our church.

Then I did a kind of double take. I said, "Wait a minute! Where are you going to get the money for this trip?"

"I don't know," he replied, "but while you were talking this morning about the matter of visualization I suddenly saw myself in the Holy Land. I've helped you edit a lot of your film taken on previous trips to the Holy Land, and many of the scenes are very real to me. As you were speaking I suddenly found myself wishing I could go to the Holy Land, and all at once I began to visualize myself walking through the Damascus Gate into the old city of Jerusalem. I don't know how I'm going to get there, but I know I am going. I didn't plead with God for it. I just applied the tests you named, and I think I meet all of them. I do want the will of God in my life, and I believe that this is basically good. It will harm no one, and I think it will bless my own life."

A few weeks later I asked him, "Jerry, how are you coming along with your plans for going to the Holy Land?"

"Fine. I'm still going."

"Have you discovered a way to raise the money?"

"No, but it will come. I can still see myself entering the Damascus Gate."

A month later I asked about it again. He assured me that his parents were not going to help him. Just to make it clear, I told him that I was confident he could not expect any help from the church. He said, "I know. But I'm going."

About six weeks before the time of departure I began to get a little worried about Jerry. After all, he was the one who had visualized the trip; I hadn't. I told him that he would be needing to get shots and his passport and visas before long. He still had not one dollar toward the trip, but he seemed unworried. "I'm going," was all that he would say. There seemed to be no doubt, no uncertainty of any sort. He said that if he knew what to do about raising the money he would do it, but he had no guidance in this regard. He did not intend borrowing the money or asking anyone for it. "The Lord will have to work that out," he said. "I'm willing to do whatever I ought to, but I wouldn't know where to begin."

When I left by plane for the Holy Land, Jerry was there

beside me, festooned with cameras like any seasoned tourist. We visited cities in Europe, spent some time in Cairo exploring a newly discovered pyramid, then finally arrived in the old city of Jerusalem, in Jordan. As we walked through the ancient Damascus Gate into the city of Jerusalem I asked, "Jerry, is this the way you saw it?" He said, "Precisely. This is just the way I saw it."

Jerry did not borrow any money. No one embarked on a crusade to solicit funds from his friends; but he went to the Holy Land in fulfillment of a visualized dream which became a prayer. It was not the kind of prayer in which one begs God for some favor. It was rather the quiet meeting of divine conditions, and the vivid visualization of the thing as a reality, and he realized what he had visualized.

When I have related this incident people have always asked, "But you didn't tell us how he got there! Where did the money come from?" My answer has always been, "It would do little good to tell you the details, because if you were to have the same goal and pray just as Jerry did, God would probably answer it in some different way."

What actually transpired was further evidence that God often answers our prayers through persons, and that when we are fully in accord with His will, He is able to do what He has always sought to do — which is to bless us beyond our fondest dreams. The Bible declares that "He is able to do far more abundantly than all we ask or think." It was so in Jerry's case.

One day, not long before the date of departure, and with Jerry's preparations still to be made, I said, "Jerry, time is short, and you have no money yet." Half jokingly I asked, "Do you have any wealthy relatives?"

"No, not a one. I wish I did."

"No wealthy, doting uncles?"

"No, nor aunts either."

Still in a facetious vein I asked, "No wealthy friends?"

"No, not a one. Well, yes and no. I had a wealthy Sunday school teacher when I was a kid, but I wouldn't dream of asking her."

He told me about her. I knew her slightly, though she lived in another city hundreds of miles away. I asked Jerry if he would mind if I asked her. He said, "No, but I won't lift a hand to help you. I'm not asking anyone for help in this. All I know is that I am going, somehow."

Money does not drop down from heaven in a basket. Tickets have to be paid for in hard cash, and only people have cash. I knew that if God really meant for Jerry to go — and I had begun to feel some of Jerry's quiet assurance — then the answer would have to come through some individual. I wrote to his former Sunday school teacher, who, as I learned later, remembered him quite well and with great fondness. I simply told her that I wanted to see her on a matter of importance to me and to Jerry, and asked when we could get together. She replied that she would be in our area the following week to attend a dinner at one of our denominational institutions.

I was also invited to the dinner, and I told her that I would plan to see her then. As I was going into the dining hall she approached from another direction, and we met at the door. We secured our tickets and sat together during the dinner. During a brief interlude in the program I told her that I planned to make another trip to the Holy Land on a project which would take several weeks and that Jerry wanted to go with me. I did not tell her of his quiet conviction that he was going. I expressed my personal belief that it would be a significant and helpful experience for him. There was a momentary pause, and she asked, "How much would it take?" I told her, and she said, "I'll send you a check in a few days." And she did. The entire conversation had not taken two minutes.

I learned later the reason for the momentary pause. She shared with me the next time I saw her that at the time I made the request she was actually in temporary financial straits, owing to some serious mistakes made by her accountant in filing her income tax returns. "But," she added, "it was *something I felt I had to do.*"

Perhaps an isolated incident or two might be attributed to coincidence or other factors, but after discovering through personal experience the relationship between visualization and faith, I have seen this dynamic principle at work too often to ascribe it to mere coincidence.

The church of which I am pastor has sponsored a number of mission churches through the years. After the war I had watched new subdivisions being established in neighboring suburbs. In one subdivision which seemed to spring up almost overnight I approached the developer about securing a site for a church. He assured me rather ungraciously that he had no interest in churches and no intention of providing a site for one. He even refused to sell enough individual lots to provide space for a church. He explained that he needed not only the profit from the sale of lots but from the houses as well. "If people want to attend church, let them drive to the next community," he said.

I left, feeling that it was a lost cause, but a few weeks later as I drove through the subdivision I said, "Lord, if You want a church here, You can show us the way to accomplish it. Meanwhile, I'll turn it over to You." The next day, I discussed it with one of our members, a retired man familiar with real estate. I said, "I have come to feel that God wants a church in that area. If He wants it, there is some way to do it. I'm going to turn it over to you and God. Will you see what you can do?"

In a few days he came to see me. "I've found one little pie-shaped piece of land the developer will sell, but it's far too small for a church. And I looked on the city map and discovered that a private owner holds a little piece of land adjacent to the pie-shaped piece. He bought it before the developer purchased surrounding property. If we can get him to sell, I think we'd have enough for a church site. At this point I'd need some money for a cash deposit, because I can't make a bona fide offer without some cash. Are there any funds available for this project?"

I told him that our church extension funds were exhausted, but that I had discovered a basic principle long ago: when God wants something done, you go ahead and do it, and the money and other necessities are always forthcoming. I told him to ask the Finance Committee to permit the use of $1000 temporarily as a deposit on the property. They agreed, with the understanding that I would be responsible ultimately for getting the money back into the proper fund.

An offer was made and accepted on the two adjacent pieces of land, and the cash deposit put in escrow. We had ninety days to find $12,000.

A few days later I was having lunch with a member, and the conversation turned to the rapid increase in land values. I said, "Yes, and it's affecting our capacity to start new churches in this area. For instance there's a little piece of land we want for a church in a new subdivision. Five years ago we could have bought it for $5000. Today they want $12,000 and at the rate values are soaring it will be $25,000 in five years." I told him of the proposed new church, and he said thoughtfully, "I'm selling a piece of property, and the sale will be completed in less than ninety days. I give thirty per cent of my income to God, and thirty per cent of my profit on this property will be slightly over $12,000. I'll send you a check when the deal is completed." We went on with our lunch.

I had no way of knowing that my friend had $12,000 to give. I am not sure that he had intended giving it all to the church, or any part of it, since in addition to his generous gifts to our church he had numerous other interests. But for some reason — surely not coincidence — I found myself talking to the right man at the right time about a need which he had the means to meet.

When the check arrived, it was enough to pay for the church site, with sufficient left over for a down payment on a residence in which the proposed new church could meet temporarily, until it could afford to erect a building.

The young minister selected to launch the church was also given the responsibility of finding an appropriate residence-meeting place to purchase. He searched for weeks, but the houses for sale were either in the wrong location, too expensive, or too small. Finally I said, "George, let's let God in on this. He is more concerned than we are, and He is ready to guide. Let's stop looking. Do nothing until you have an overwhelming inner conviction that you ought to act. Meanwhile, visualize this as accomplished. See on an inner metal screen the accomplished fact. See the right house, at the right price, at the right location. Flash that upon your mental screen daily and hold it there. Do nothing else."

A few weeks later he phoned me in considerable excitement. "I've found the house! Last night as I was finishing dinner I suddenly thought of a house which we tried to purchase some time ago, but they wouldn't sell. It's in the right location, and the right size. I felt I ought to visit these people again and see if they'd change their minds. Well, I did, and they told me that just the night before they had decided to put the house on the market, and had planned to call a real estate broker the next morning. I got there just the night before they were going to put it on the market. We'll save the commission, but more important, it's the right house at the right time and in the right location." The house was purchased.

The small group of people he had gotten together through his calling began to meet in the new house. They arranged to start a Sunday school and sent out notices to all of the homes in the area. They had planned to have some classes meet in various rooms of the house, in the garage, and in the living rooms of members' homes nearby. On the first Sunday, nearly 150 children showed up for Sunday school! All they could do was to register them and tell them to come back next Sunday. The next week they were ready for the hundred and fifty youngsters. They requisitioned garages around the neighborhood, and one way and another they managed to conduct a Sunday school. Facilities were not the best but no one complained.

For worship services they met in the living room and adjacent dining room until they outgrew these modest quarters. Eventually George told me that they had outgrown the residence, and were still a long way from having enough money on hand to start their chapel. I looked over the facilities, and said, "George, run some lines out here behind the house. Enclose an area large enough to accommodate seventy-five persons, a small choir and a pulpit. Leave the lines there and ask God if he wants you to built a small temporary chapel there."

"What will we do for money?"

"Just what we did before. We'll put it on a mental screen, visualize it, and let God help us realize it. This is His business, you know."

A few days later I noticed that George had outlined a rectangular area on the back of the lot. It didn't look very big, but he assured me it would seat 75 persons. I suggested that he get an estimate from a contractor. "When God provides the money," I told him, "you'll want to be ready with the cost of materials. You and your people can build it. We'll pay only for materials."

They estimated that they could build a small temporary chapel as an addition to the house, with some of the congregation sitting in the house and others in the chapel. for a fairly modest amount.

A few days later one of our women phoned me. She said, "I went over to the new little church to see what they might need in their kitchen, and happened to see those strings, or whatever they are, out in the back. I asked George about it and he said they were 'faith lines' representing the new chapel. He told me what it would cost for materials, and I decided then and there that I ought to give half of the amount. Since then I have been thinking about it, and I feel the Lord wants me to give all of it."

But there were other obstacles. When they went for a building permit they were told that they could not build a chapel, even a temporary one, on a lot with a house on it. It violated all sorts of city codes. George asked me what they should do. I said, "I don't know. I suppose you could appeal it to the City Planning Commission. Try it, but keep seeing this completed chapel on your mental screen. If it is God's will no one can stop you."

I attended the Planning Commission session with him, but insisted that he do all of the talking. He made an excellent presentation, but, as they pointed out, the plan was a clear violation of city building codes. There would undoubtedly be objections from people in the community, as there had been initially when church meetings began in the residence. George just stood there before the members of the commission, and finally he said, "Well, what do you think we ought to do?"

The members were at this point united in believing that it couldn't be done. But as George stood there asking them what they thought he should do, one of the men on the Planning Commission said, "You know, we need more churches in the community. We all know that. I sure hate to turn this down. I wish we could find some way to let them do it." A second member agreed, "Yes, it's a shame, a real shame. We ought to encourage churches whenever we can." The other members of the commission nodded assent. They tried to get George to say how long they would be in the temporary chapel, but he said he had no way of knowing. It might be a year, or six months, or two years. The commission had hoped they might base their decision on the fact that it was a very, very temporary expedient. George could give no promise.

"Well," said one of the members, "I move we go ahead and let them build this chapel anyhow, whether it's legal or not. It's right even if it isn't legal, and maybe right ought to take precedence." The vote was unanimous.

"If you can believe, all things are possible. . . .'" George, discovered that, and the church did too. Ultimately, without too long a delay, a little chapel with some Sunday school rooms was built on their lot.

If we can only get the concept of a personal God who

works through impersonal laws and principles; if we can see that these principles surround us on every hand, waiting for us to reach out and receive; if we could only believe that God is infinite good, waiting for us to trust Him and love Him — then we could receive blessing upon blessing, miracle upon miracle.

There are those who protest that this is "using God." The fear of "using God" is based upon a partial truth. We must never want God's blessings without wanting Him. He is not a celestial Santa Claus who sends the desired gift in response to our childish appeals. He wants our love, as Jesus pointed out in the oft-quoted, seldom-obeyed statement, "Seek first his (God's) kingdom and his righteousness, and all these things will be yours as well" — or — "as a matter of course."[2] To seek His Kingdom must mean, among other things, to seek His will in our lives. It means that we must trust Him completely. If we cannot trust Him, if we cannot believe that His will for us is good and wonderful beyond our power to grasp, how could we ever approach Him, want Him, love Him? Why should we expect gifts from a distant deity we cannot trust fully?

To seek the Kingdom means that we give priority to the reign of God in our lives. It implies that we will want God's will above our own, knowing that what He wills is good and right and leads to more happiness and fulfillment than we can ever discover alone. Not to want His will is to refuse to trust Him. To reject His will and want our own is to be in rebellion against the God who made us and loves us.

Part of the reluctance to want His full will derives from the fear that if we surrender to Him completely He might send us to Afghanistan as missionaries, or cause us to give up some of our pleasures. Some of our difficulty springs from our stubborn, egocentric wills. We want *our* way. We fear that we shall lose our autonomy, our freedom of choice, some of our individuality as persons. It is basically an unconscious fear of losing our selfhood. Someone else would be running our lives, and we don't want that, even if that someone is God.

A small child is dependent upon his parents. In adolescence he strives to be a person in his own right, and in order to become an independent person he rebels against authority. As he matures he sees that there is something

far better than either dependence or independence, and
that is interdependence.

As Christians, many people never outgrow the phase of
spiritual adolescence, that period of willful independence
which characterizes the teenager. But as we mature spiritually, we come to discover the joy of interdependence
with God. He leaves us the free will with which He
endowed us. He will never violate our freedom of choice.

To want God's full will in our lives is simply another
way of saying that we accept the universe the way it is
created; that we accept it with joy; that we rejoice to
know that God is infinite love, and wills the best for us;
that we are willing to trust His way of running the
universe; that we want to experience the satisfaction of
having His universal laws operate on our behalf.

When I was about six years old someone died in a house
across the street. It was my first experience with death,
and I recall hearing someone say. "We must be resigned to
God's will." I came to associate God's will with death.
Perhaps many Christians have formed erroneous views of
God's will in some such fashion.

There is a phrase used by insurance men, "An act of
God," referring usually to some disaster such as a hurricane, earthquake, or an event beyond the control of men.
The original intent of the phrase was not to imply that
God wills evil things to happen to men but that such
events are not humanly caused. It may influence us to feel,
unconsciously, that God's will means something cata-
strophic, or at least unacceptable.

In prayer, as in life, we tend to place *what we really
want* at the center of our natures. The neurotic tells us
that he will do anything to be rid of his symptoms, but it
is an established fact that he will do anything rather than
give them up. To him they are preferable to facing and
dealing with the real problem. He gets what he wants
most.

In prayer we receive what we want most earnestly. It
may not be what we ask for, but it is what we want, for
"Prayer is the soul's sincere desire, uttered or unex-
pressed." If what we ask for in prayer, verbally, conflicts
with the thing we want basically at the feeling level, we
receive, not what we ask for, but what we *really* want.

One might pray. "O Lord, bless the missionaries on the
foreign field," but if he is really rather indifferent about

their welfare, then that is the nature and extent of his prayer. One might pray to have some physical symptom removed, but if at heart he is unwilling to change the basic emotional attitude which has caused the symptom, he is saying, "I want the symptom removed, but not the real cause." But since the symptom cannot be truly dealt with apart from the cause, he gets precisely what he *really* prefers under the circumstances, which is to suffer with the symptom rather than to run the risk of a change of personality or attitude.

Prayer is not mere verbalization. The words we utter have no real significance, except as they are a true reflection of what we feel or think. When what we say and what we feel are in conflict, then what we feel is the real prayer.

Prayer, then, is not merely words.

Prayer is not an effort to change God or His intent toward us.

Prayer is an effort to bring our stubborn, reluctant, egocentric wills into harmony with His loving, beneficent purpose. He wills the best for us. When we can trust His wise, creative purposes for our lives, we will have begun to pray effectively.

6. CONFESSION

> A person is not made up of acts, but of
> desires only. As is his desire, such is his
> resolve; as is his resolve, such is the action he
> performs; what action he performs, that he
> procures for himself.   — *Upanishads*

ONLY God could know how many millions of His children
have confessed their sins and mistakes without ever having
secured any real sense of pardon and cleansing. Their
number must be legion! After thirty-six years as a pastor,
during which I have counseled with hundred of persons, it
appears to me that failure to *accept* forgiveness and *feel*
forgiven constitutes the greatest single problem for most
people, though they may be partially or totally unaware of
the basic difficulty.

All Christians believe intellectually in forgiveness, and
many are able to quote the familiar passage, "If we confess
our sins, he is faithful and just, and will forgive our sins
and cleanse us from all unrighteousness." A great many of
those who quote this, however, do not experience a sense
of forgiveness at the feeling level. Often the very vigor of
their protestation that "all my sins are washed away" tells
us that there is some lingering doubt in their minds. There
are few among us who feel so fully cleansed and forgiven
that we are able to forgive ourselves fully, and to forgive
others.

There is a "false zeal" with which many good people
perform their Christian duty. This tells us that they are
seeking unconsciously to atone for some specific, or vague
and diffused, sense of guilt. We see the same thing
operating in compulsive workers.

In one of our groups a young minister was sharing his feeling of guilt over not being faithful to his daily quiet time. He had a very busy schedule, but he sensed that this was not the real cause. He said, "I have time occasionally for television, but cannot find time to visit with God. I do not know what my real barrier is."

There is often rare perception in such a group. Someone said, "Could it be that you feel guilty about something else, which you refuse to examine, and cannot face God because of this guilt with which you refuse to deal?"

The young minister smiled, but there was a tenseness in it, as though he was trying to find the answer but feared to do so. Then someone else asked the penetrating question, "Could it be that you feel uneasy about the lack of time you devote to your family, and your wife has complained about it, so that you feel genuine guilt over this but do not want to face it? Perhaps if you did face it in prayer you would have to consider some adjustments in your schedule." There was an intuitive awareness in the group that the question had struck home.

"Yes," he said, "I see now that this is my problem. If I did set aside a specific time daily for meditation and prayer I would have to deal with this matter. I know that my wife is partly right. There are the requirements of my church work — and the demands of my family. I am yielding to the demands of my work, because not to do so would create more anxiety than is aroused by the legitimate needs of my family."

With characteristic human ingenuity he had carefully hidden from himself the real reason for his refusal to meet God daily. He had not even admitted into consciousness the real basis of his problem, but it was there, just beneath the surface. A little gentle probing from others, no less guilty in this and other areas, had helped him to pinpoint his difficulty.

And with what understanding and loving concern a group probes, helping each other discover what has been avoided unconsciously! In one group session, I shared a certain guilt I felt over the resentment I experienced when "psychological sleeve tuggers" would approach me and interrupt a conversation with some obviously invented need in order to get attention. Someone has (not very graciously) referred to such a person as "bottomless pits" — persons who need love and attention in such neurotically large doses that it is as though they were bottomless, never satisfied, always returning with new excuses to get attention, no matter how flimsy the pretext.

There was a tendency on the part of some in the group to identify with me in this, having suffered as I had from such persons; but one perceptive young man asked, "Could it be that you are yourself a kind of bottomless pit, that you need love in the same degree, but do not let yourself feel it? Could you simply be projecting your own inner need upon them, hating it in yourself, and thus in them?"

My instant reaction was to reject the suggestion. The very emphasis with which I rejected it told me that he had touched something painful. I dealt with it later, and came to the embarrassing conclusion that I had indeed been projecting. I felt similar need for love at a very deep level, and had repressed it.

But it was there, nevertheless. Not having fully resolved my own unsatisfied need to receive love, I over-reacted to others who had the same problem. Now I could confess the real sin. It was not resentment which I needed to confess. I could confess this indefinitely without securing a sense of release, for I would be confessing the wrong need. What I now shared in the group was something I had been unwilling to face, my own need for love. I had been unwilling to admit that I wanted or needed it. In fact, I saw that I was partially unable to accept love. After I admitted this to myself and to the group, I no longer over-reacted when the sleeve-tuggers reached me. I had confessed the real problem.

A man once confessed to me that he had a terrible temper. He had prayed for years for some release from it without avail. I said, "Perhaps you are confessing the wrong sin. Examine your inner feelings and see if you do not discover a great deal of fear within yourself. It may be so deeply buried as to be totally unrecognized." He would not accept this possibility, even though I explained that much of our hostility stems from fear, and we then fear the hostility. Later he developed a phobia which handicapped him seriously in carrying out the simplest details of everyday living. The fear had begun to manifest itself in another manner. Now he sought my help in ridding himself of the phobia. I said, "Look within now for guilt, perhaps partly buried. When you find it you will find the root of your phobia." He was not interested, wanting only to be rid of the phobia, but without the pain of probing for buried guilt. He still has the phobia.

This is not to say that all phobias result from guilt, or that a person with a phobia is any guiltier than anyone else. It is simply one form which the guilt takes. The phobia is preferable to facing the guilt!

A man once told me of a disturbing experience. He had been making significant progress in a group, but, as he put it, "People do not warm up to me readily, and I don't think they really trust me." He had a certain reserve, a barrier which he put up unconsciously between himself and others without realizing that he did so.

He had sensed that there was repressed "material" deeply buried in his unconscious mind. In a session with a counselor he suddenly recalled a traumatic experience which had occurred when he was a small boy and which he had forgotten about until that moment. He had been sexually molested and had felt shame and guilt over it, as is usually the case, even when the child is in no sense guilty. In a later session he recalled an even more shattering experience. His own father had molested him sexually. As he recalled the experience and relived it emotionally, he experienced great distress.

His experience illustrates the fact that we feel guilt not only for what we have done but often because of shame over what has been done to us. As a child he had participated in something which he felt was shameful, and had felt guilty and "wrong." The dredging up of the memory was for him a spiritually healing experience. Confession in his case was not the usual act of admitting to some guilty act or attitude by simply admitting into awareness the memory of an event which had created false guilt.

There is a sense in which all of us are neurotic. To the degree that we "over-react" to any given situation we are neurotic. It is simply a matter of degree. Nandor Fodor says, "The neurotic has but one enemy — his conscience. It never gives him peace, and the tragedy of neurosis is that, alone, by his unaided efforts, the neurotic is unable to find out why his conscience pursues him like the Furies of the Greek tragedy. Remarkable and pathetic are the ways in which he tries to escape it, only to find that no matter what he does, it is always the wrong thing."[1]

The true neurotic is simply an individual who has not yet resolved his guilt which troubles him; but in order to live an effective life he must deal with the accusing conscience.

Occasionally there are persons who are able to handle their guilt and live normal lives until some stress-laden situation tips the scales, and then they have what is mistakenly termed a "nervous breakdown" and become unable to function normally.

A highly intelligent man in a state of deep depression, a stranger to me, came one day for counseling. He had lost all zest for living and was beset by nameless anxieties. He viewed the world through a curtain of his obsessional fears. I said, "My friend, perhaps we should go back into your earlier life and discover what it is that transpired in the past, for there appears to be some unresolved guilt area in your life. We must deal with it." He assured me that he had done things of which he was ashamed, in common with all other human beings, but that God had forgiven him. I said, "I have no doubt but that God has forgiven you, but it is apparent that you have not forgiven yourself. When I mention the word 'guilt,' what event comes to mind?" He instantly related an experience from the distant past which, he said, could not be troubling him now since it happened so long ago. I explained to him that time does not lessen our sense of guilt, but he was reluctant to believe that guilt could have anything to do with his deep depression.

Ultimately he spent considerable time in a sanitarium, where he was given shock therapy. The result of this drastic treatment provided considerable relief, so that he was able to function normally again, but experience has shown that a very large number of those receiving shock therapy ultimately regress to the old condition, unless they acquire new spiritual resources with which to meet the issues of life. He has yet to resolve his guilt over the past; and there is a strong possibility that when the pressures of daily living build up, and physical and emotional depletion occur, he will find himself suffering from the same symptoms. The accumulated stresses of life, or some traumatic event, often trigger the old sense of self-rejection which is always present until we secure a sense of divine forgiveness and are consequently able to forgive ourselves.

Jung has pointed out that when, because we cannot face the greater sin, we confess some lesser sin all the more earnestly, we fail to secure forgiveness. Not that God refuses to forgive us, it is rather that we are confessing the wrong problem.

The manner in which we confess is much less important than that we confess the right thing. To say, "Lord, forgive my many sins" may conceivably be effective, if there is in the heart a deep sense of contrition for all of one's sins. The publican's prayer, "Lord, be merciful to me, a sinner," was a highly effective prayer because there was evident in the man's mind a deep sense of contrition. He was admitting to himself and to God that he felt unworthy in a generalized sense. Another person might utter the same words and feel little or no sorrow for his sins.

As Paul Tournier has pointed out in *Guilt and Grace,*[1] one man may recount in a precise and methodical manner the nature of his wrongs, but without any real sense of remorse; while another may suddenly see for the first time the real nature of his guilt, and almost wordlessly express deepest humiliation and sorrow for his sins. It is the state of mind, the intent of the heart, which counts; not the words or the form in which the confession is framed.

Some protest emphatically, "I confess my sins only to God!" and the very vehemence with which they state this tells us that they are thoroughly defensive. Yet the Bible clearly states, "Therefore confess your sins to one another, and pray for one another, that you may be healed."[2] This does not imply that we are to blurt out our sins to the nearest human being, but rather that there is genuine spiritual healing to be found in unburdening ourselves to an appropriate person or persons — whether a minister, priest, counselor, an understanding friend, or members of a group.

One of the twelve steps of Alcoholics Anonymous has to do with sharing the precise nature of one's wrongs, for AA has discovered the tremendous value inherent in sharing our failures with some nonjudgmental person. Sometimes this can be done in a group. Obviously there are things which it might be inappropriate to share with a group, but I have observed hundreds of times the value derived by men and women who discussed in the group the defects in their lives.

We are careful to stipulate in our groups that we are not so much concerned with symptomatic sins as with sins of the spirit. One may share with the group his hostility, his fear, his sense of inferiority, and his general sense of need. It is basically sins of the spirit — greed, avarice, materialism, pride, lust, envy — which we are to confess in such a group, not necessarily the symptomatic manifestations of these spiritual failures. However, quite often someone who has come to see the nature of his spiritual need and has shared it with the group, will feel a need to share the more specific details with a counselor. In so doing he often experiences a deep sense of relief. He has gotten it off his chest, as it were; he has unburdened himself; he has gotten it out at last.

But why need one do this in a group or with a counselor? The fact that so few people *feel* genuinely forgiven gives us the answer. They have confessed to the invisible God, and if their conception of God had been vital enough they would have felt a sense of forgiveness. But to many people God is, as one college student expressed it, "a kind of oblong blur." He is invisible, "up there somewhere," rather than a living, compassionate, loving Heavenly Father.

David confessed to Nathan, when challenged by the prophet, then composed the poignant and beautiful fifty-first Psalm in which he confesses his guilt and asks for pardon. With painful honesty he has shared his confession with all mankind:

PSALM 51

Have mercy on me, O God,
   according to thy steadfast love;
     according to thy abundant mercy
     blot out my transgressions.
Wash me thoroughly from my iniquity,
   and cleanse me from my sin!
For I know my transgressions,
   and my sin is ever before me.
Against thee, thee only, have I sinned,
   and done that which is evil
     in thy sight. . . .

Create in me a clean heart, O God,
   and put a new and right spirit
     within me.

Cast me not away from thy presence,
  and take not thy holy Spirit from me.
Restore to me the joy of thy salvation,
  and uphold me with a willing
    spirit.

For thou hast no delight in sacrifice;
  were I to give a burnt offering,
    thou wouldst not be pleased.
The sacrifice acceptable to God is a broken spirit;
  a broken and contrite
    heart, O God, thou wilt not despise.

True confession is painful. If it is not painful, it is not likely to be very effective. There is no particular pain involved in saying, I find it difficult to forgive." These are generalizations and, very largely, evasions; for they could be said of almost any human being on earth. It is just another way of saying, "I am not all I ought to be, just like everyone else."

As stated before, there is within us a tension between the need to conceal and the need to reveal. The truth of our guilt demands expression. We need to tell someone, but we fear their condemnation or judgment and rejection. It is common, therefore, to feel great reluctance in facing our true guilt.

I had been a minister for quite some years before I discovered a seemingly obvious fact. Someone would make an appointment to see me, then come out with something like, "I don't understand the nature of Trinity. Will you explain it to me?" Or it might be a question concerning some moot point in Revelation. I missed many wonderful opportunities to help people by falling for this evasion. When they left it would often be, as I saw later, with a kind of reluctance, which made me feel that I had not made the theological point clear. Actually they were hoping I would say, "Now let's see what else is bothering you. If you care to tell me about it, I will not think less of you, and perhaps I can help you."

One young woman came to see me with some such unconscious evasion after I had discovered my error. Following our discussion of her supposed theological doubt I said, "But I sense that something else is bothering you. Would you care to tell me about it?" She looked genuinely surprised, and said, "Yes, I suppose there is something else, but I wasn't really aware of it until this moment. I have a serious problem, and I guess I hoped you would get it out of me." She then shared her difficulty. On subsequent visits she would say, laughingly, "Today, I don't want to talk about the Trinity but about a real problem." By this time she had discovered that I did not judge her, that I still liked her just as much, and that she was sharing guilty areas of her life with a fellow sinner.

Occasionally parents will come in to discuss a problem pertaining to their children. As they see it, it is always the child, never the parent, who is in need of help. That the relationship between the parents, and between parent and child, could have anything to do with the child's erratic behavior seldom crosses their minds. They are often irritated if I ask about their own personal relationships as parents, their spiritual lives, or the degree of inner serenity and peace they possess. "But it is the child, not us! We're getting along fine ... Well, you know how it is, there are the inevitable differences which arise between all married couples, and my husband's work does make him tense, and I suppose I do nag some, but then what parent doesn't?"

That is not a confession, but an alibi, a rationalization, an effort on the part of the parent to get the counselor to agree that it is indeed very difficult to rear a child in these unusual times, and that the parents could not be responsible in the slightest degree. Occasionally, however, it is possible to help the parents see that they have been confessing the sins of the child, not their own, and that the proper — in fact the only — place to start is with the confession of their own needs.

A mother who wanted at first to share only the terrible deeds of her fourteen-year-old boy finally was led to the shattering realization that she had never really loved her son. When he was born, the fact that she had other children to care for and that really there was not enough money even for their present family caused her to feel a surge of resentment, which she quickly repressed. "A mother shouldn't feel that way!" was her instant reaction. She could not admit to herself then, nor in subsequent years, that she had actually resented the birth of the fifth child. Now the thought came with terrifying suddenness, and she was shocked. "But I did love him, and I do! I love him dearly. I would do anything for him, anything!" Then she dealt with the question, "Could I have loved and hated him at the same time?" No, that was an intolerable suggestion. One doesn't hate one's children.

"Do you ever hate and love your husband at one and the same time?" "Oh, yes, often!" "Could you have had the same mixed feelings toward the boy?" She struggled for some time with this, and finally was able to be honest: "Yes, I see it now. I've hated him as much as I've loved him, maybe more." Then began the process of helping her to accept her feelings, not as ideal but as real. She said, "I tried to put these feelings out of my mind." *But nothing is ever put out of the mind.* Unacceptable feelings about which we feel guilty are simply rejected and pushed down deep into the unconscious mind, where they fester and breed their own deplorable litter of evil, ranging from psychosomatic ills to unaccountable rages.

The manner in which we project our guilt onto another person involves a unique, automatic, and wholly unconscious mechanism. A wife assured me that her husband was unfaithful to her. She could not actually prove it, though he had done many things which were suspicious, as she saw it, and which led her to the conclusion that he was meeting someone on the sly.

Under gentle questioning she finally looked within, and found part of the answer for herself. "Could it be that I am unduly suspicious because I started going with my husband when he was still married and before my divorce was final?" I asked her to tell me about it, and she seemed relieved to have an opportunity to share it, painful though it was to face. She had helped him to be unfaithful to his wife and had felt guilty about their relationship. Now she saw that she was feeling, "If he could be unfaithful to his first wife, he could be unfaithful to me." At a deeper level she was feeling the pain of unresolved guilt. She "deserved" to lose her husband, she felt, since she had been guilty in her relations with him before their marriage. At this point a minister or counselor or friend who is hearing the confession (for that is what it is) can ruin everything by either justifying or judging. Even if the feeling of judgment is not expressed, it can be shown in some gesture or mannerism, and the other will sense it. No one has the right to listen to a confession, a shared weakness, or even the problem of a friend, who feels judgmental or who is cursed with a need to give advice.

One must not confess only overt sins of the flesh, but

attitudes of mind, hostile feelings not yet acted out, guilty secrets, wrong motives, false goals, impaired relationships — all in fact that is less than perfect. Equally important, of course, are the sins of omission, the things we failed to do which we should have done. We might say that the rich man in Jesus' parable,[4] who ignores the beggar lying daily at his door, ends in his own private hell. He lives in torment, as he describes it. Perhaps it is the almost unbearable torment of remorse: of realizing the opportunities missed, the good intentions never acted upon, the love never expressed. It is not said that he had done anything flagrantly evil; his sin appears to be one of omission. He failed to show compassion.

Which of us is not guilty of a thousand unaccomplished deeds for which we feel guilty? This is not to burden ourselves with needless guilt: we cannot bear the burdens of all the world, nor can we die on every cross; it is a neurotic need to play God which makes us feel guilty on all counts. But we know there were times unnumbered when we neglected to do or say the things which would have expressed love. "He who does not love does not know God; for God is love,"[5] declares John.

And when we have confessed the known sins it is time to search for the unknown ones, those carefully buried guilt feelings which we dared not face at the time and so repressed them. There are the hundreds of things we have rationalized. The unconscious mind cannot accept a rationalization, because it does not deal with abstract concepts. Thus when we carefully rationalize some behavior on the ground that it was inescapable, or because everyone else does it, or with some other clever evasion, we may convince ourselves at the intellectual level but not at the emotional and spiritual level. The inner self knows better!

I was having a quiet time one morning and felt at peace with God and all mankind. I said, "Lord, I'm glad that I feel no hostility toward any living soul." I was unaware at the moment that it was not true and that I was sounding a bit like the Pharisee of old, who thanked God that he was in good shape spiritually, unlike other men. As the thought crossed my mind, I suddenly saw a face on the screen of my mind. It was the face of someone I had never particularly liked. I had not been aware of hostility until that moment. Everyone I knew felt as I did about the person, and I had unconsciously rationalized my hostility.

Suddenly I knew that I did not know God to the extent that I did not love; that I could not pray effectively until I felt unconditional love for everyone — even for this unattractive person.

I knew what I had to do, and at the first opportunity I found a way to express love. Before I was able to express it I had to pray daily for the power to do it, recognizing that I did not have the capacity within myself. I prayed, "Lord, help me to *want* to want love." Expressed sincerely, daily, this is a powerful prayer, for it is both a confession of one's failure and a prayer for help in overcoming the hostility. Soon I began to feel that I *did* want to love the unattractive person, and a delightful relationship was established as a result.

"A saint is one who sins less and less and confesses more and more," as has often been said. There is never a time when we can cease to confess. Long after the sins of the flesh are confessed, there remain all of the corrosive sins of the spirit: pride, envy, greed, avarice, lust, jealousy. And if one is almost certain that he has mastered the sins of the spirit and is quietly congratulating himself on this worthy achievement, he is horrified to discover the sin of pride operating with new vigor!

Must we always struggle, never winning, never reaching the goal line? The answer is an unqualified yes. The struggle here never ends, but with every step of the earthly pilgrimage there is a new sense of inner peace and quiet, the growing sense of a Presence working with and within us. "For God is at work in you." We are not alone in our struggle, we are not condemned by our failures. Though we fall a thousand times, if we rise again and continue to follow the Light, we are accepted and forgiven. There is no limit to His love and His forgiveness.

See how gently Jesus reproves the spiritual shortcomings of the twelve. When rejected by the inhabitants of a village, James and John asked, "Lord, do you want us to bid fire come down from heaven and consume them?" I am not certain that Jesus smiled, but I think He did, as He said, "You do not know what manner of spirit you are of." In other words, "You are not to play God, and besides, why all this hostility?" Later he referred to these two as "sons of thunder," humorously, I think, but with telling effect. He dealt with their intense hostility, but did not condemn or reject them. When the same disciples asked if they might be seated one on the right and the other on the left when He came into His kingdom, there was no condemnation of their colossal pride. He simply told them that what they asked was not His to give. The other ten disciples were indignant, but Jesus was understanding and patient with James' and John's spiritual blindness and egomania.

And there was Peter's unconsidered protestation of loyalty and fidelity: "Even if I must die with you, I will not deny you." A bit later we hear him denying vehemently that he knows Jesus at all. The cock crows, and Jesus turns and looks at him. I am sure that it was not a look of condemnation — "I told you that you wouldn't hold out. See how weak you are?" — but rather a glance of infinite love and compassion and forgiveness, for this was His nature.

Jesus regards us in the same manner, and Jesus is the manifestation of God. "If you have seen me you have seen God," he declared. So, in His compassion and forgiveness we see the nature of God, for God is like Jesus.

One basic difficulty is not that we are reluctant to confess to God but that we are unable to believe *deeply* that God could really forgive us instantly, without qualification. We find it almost incredible that God could give unconditional love, especially in view of all our previous failures. "But I've done this again and again," said one man to me. "How could God ever forgive anyone as weak and faulty as I?" I said, "You are supposing that God is no better than you. You have trouble forgiving others, especially after they have let you down numerous times, and you imagine that God is like you, able to forgive one or two failures, but not fifty. God is better than you, my friend. His love is infinite."

How, specifically, does one confess so as to receive inward assurance of forgiveness at the feeling level? What does one say? How much and how often must one confess? Far more important than that is what we have just been considering: our concept of God and His nature; for it matters little what we say or how we confess if we do not have the overwhelming conviction that God *does* forgive instantly and willingly, that He does not condemn us. If our concept of God is adequate, our prayer of contrition will be adequate. If we have a weak concept of God and His love, we will never feel fully forgiven. But assuming that one is able to believe — and feel deeply — that God is anxious to forgive, how does one go about confessing so as to have a sense of cleansing? There are many steps and many ways, but here are some of them:

First, one does not rush into the presence of God and blurt out a request for pardon, or any other kind of petition, without suitable preparation. Not that our haste and crudeness can offend God. He is beyond that. But *we* need the preparatory period. Begin first with a time of meditation. This is a part of prayer. Think about the nature of God. Affirm what you know to be true about Him. "God's love is limitless, therefore He forgives to a limitless degree. Nothing I have ever done is so bad that He loves me less. Nothing good I have ever done is sufficient to cause Him to love me more. His love is a fixed and unchanging factor. I do not increase his love for me by any good deed, nor do I decrease it by my failures. Because He loves me I can ask for and receive instant forgiveness. It is promised that 'If we confess our sins, he is faithful and just, and will forgive our sins and cleanse us from all unrighteousness.'" I believe this about God." This affirmative type of meditation is one aspect of prayer.

Second, let the confession be utterly, ruthlessly honest. A young woman told me that she and her husband had been so beset with financial troubles that they were half out of their minds with worry. Creditors telephoned and came to the door in a steady stream. There were threats of suits. She had prayed for a solution but no answer had come.

One night she went out and walked for miles, and finally she said, "God I hate you! I've asked for help and you didn't give it. I hate you!"

This was an honest confession, and a genuine prayer! God knew how she felt before she told Him, and what she did in that moment was to admit to herself and to God what she had never admitted before. Her tirade against God lasted some time, and finally, emotionally exhausted, she returned home.

She gave up praying for a miraculous deluge of money that would solve their problems. Instead she said, "God, if you want something done, you'll have to do it. I give up." This was a real prayer, a prayer of abandonment. No one would say that it was the highest form of prayer, but its very honesty had merit, and in abandoning her struggle she was, for the first time, turning it over to God. She had given up her childish prayer for a quick, easy miracle, and faced her true feelings.

Weak and human though it was, it was an honest prayer, and honesty with self and with God is the starting point. It is the absolutely essential first step. If we will not be honest with ourselves, how can we be honest with God? And if we cannot be honest with Him about our true feelings, how can He help us? Within a week she had a sudden "inspiration," which she knew was guidance. It provided temporary relief, and in a matter of months the entire problem was solved. More important, she and her husband grew spiritually in the process.

Fritz Kunkel not only sheds light on an important aspect of confession but at the same time suggests an answer to the mystery surrounding the imprecatory psalms, in which hostility and the desire for vengeance are expressed. He writes:

If we can spread out before Him all the hidden roots of our virtues and our vices, if we are honest and courageous enough to release before Him the high voltage of our unconscious hatred and love, we may discover that all our power is in the last analysis His power. . . .

Be more honest, give vent to your emotions. You hate your brother: imagine his presence; before God tell him how you feel; kick him, scratch him. You are ten years old now — get up from your chair; don't pretend to be a wise old Buddha, pace the floor, yell, scratch, punch the furniture, express yourself. Rant and rage until you are exhausted, or until you laugh at yourself. . . . God is there; tell Him the truth, be as honest as those old Hebrews: "Routed, dishonored be those who delight in doing harm to me" (Psalm 40:14, Moffatt). Pray God He should punish your brother, torture him, help you to defeat him. . . . Look, during all your rage, listening to your furious prayer, God was there. His presence encompassed you like the calm, creative smile of a father who knows that his child will spend his fury and then discover the truth, and find the right way. You will find the right way, but only when you have spent your forces. . . . It will take weeks, or months. . . . And finally you will meet the God of the inner storms.[8]

Then, Kunkel says, in time will come "God's peace that surpasses all our dreams" (Philippians 4:7, Moffatt).

John B. Coburn writes of a father

Who sat grim-faced through the funeral service of his four-year-old son who had died of polio. As he listened to the opening words, "I know that my Redeemer liveth," he kept murmuring under his breath, "God, I'll get back at you for this! I'll get back at you for this!" This was the first honest conversation he had ever had with God.

Later he commented: "That was a foolish thing to say, I suppose. How could I ever get back at God? Yet it was honest and it kept the relationship with God open. That was the way I felt, and it was right to clear up the atmosphere and get it all off my chest. For then I gradually came to myself and saw that death does have to fit into some final framework, and only God can absorb it.... I know now that my Redeemer *does* live. And I don't think I should know it, deep down inside, if I hadn't been mad at my Redeemer once—and said so."[9]

The basic sin is the emotion, the feeling, the attitude which prompts the act. Tell God how you feel. If you feel hostility, tell Him so. He knows all about human hostility in general and yours in particular. Don't justify it or rationalize it — just confess it! Tell him about your jealousy or envy, your greed, your lust for people or things, confess your fear and lack of faith and self-right-eousness, the critical attitudes which cause you to judge others and justify yourself. Confess the self-sufficiency which has caused you to depend upon yourself more than upon God. Tell him about your self-pity which you have used as a device to get sympathy. Tell him the whole sordid story of your deceit. Go back and dredge up all the past, the petty gossip, and the emotional insecurity which prompted it. Tell him about the lies you have told, or the silent deceit in which you engaged though no lie was told. Above all tell Him how unforgiving and unloving you have been.

At frequent intervals you may be beset with thoughts of how badly you have been mistreated by others. Your mind may veer off a dozen times onto side roads as you recall incidents from the past where the fault seemed to be someone else's rather than your own. But remind yourself that *you are not responsible for what people do to you; you are responsible only for the way you react to them.*

I have heard many times how people feel mistreated. My first human impulse is to feel critical of the offending husband for causing his wife such grief and pain. A bit later the husband relates his side of the story, and my initial reactions are abandoned. Both are at fault! No one can fix the blame, none can judge save God. All I can encourage them to do is to offer their own hostile, judgmental, unforgiving natures to God and seek His pardon for their own imperfections. Each has simply confessed the sins of the other.

In confession, it is worse than a waste of time to recount the sins or failures of others. We cannot solve our problems by confessing the defects of another. Though the one who has offended us may be 90 per cent in the wrong, and we only ten per cent (as we see it), our business is to examine our own guilt in the matter and confess it.

In confession we may be sure that at first — or perhaps for years — we will skim only the surface. The deeper sins will remain hidden. The poverty of spirit, the meanness and littleness, the self-will and pride — these will elude us unless we seek them out ruthlessly. There must be no rationalization, no excuses, no whining that others, too, were guilty.

But neither should we drown ourselves in a sea of remorse and self-denunciation. Our self-searching is to be as if we were looking for a faulty tube in our radio or trying to find a mislaid object. There is no reason to condemn, only to find the source of the problem.

In admitting to myself and to God that I am or have been guilty of lust, or greed, of pride and of judging, of an unforgiving nature, of hostility, I am not saying to my soul that I am worse than others and worthy to be condemned. I am simply joining the human race and confessing that I am no better than the others whom I have condemned, and that I am in need of God's forgiveness. There is no more virtue in condemning oneself than in condemning others. "Judge not that you be not judged" surely applies to myself as much as to others. I, too, am a person. I am no more qualified to judge myself than to judge others. I cannot weigh and evaluate all of the manifold factors of heredity and environment which predisposed me toward this or that fault. I need not judge. I must simply say, "This I am. I do not know precisely how I got this way. I confess it, I accept it as truth, and I now repent. I accept the loving forgiveness of God, and I now forgive myself." I may need to forgive myself a dozen or a hundred times, depending upon the degree of my refusal to accept His cleansing. There is a certain subtle pride which prevents our accepting divine forgiveness. It poses as humility, but actually it is a way of saying, "I must solve this myself. I cannot rely upon divine forgiveness. I must atone." This is nothing less than a refusal to accept the real meaning of the cross, the symbol of divine acceptance and love.

As children, when we did wrong, we learned that some form of punishment would usually follow. It might range all the way from a parental frown to total rejection for a time. Because they were human, our parents sometimes found it difficult to extend unconditional love. Often they punished in quick resentment. We learned to expect quick punishment for wrongdoing, perhaps even the withdrawal of love, the rejection which the child fears more than any form of physical punishment.

The child is not dead in the adult; it is very much alive. The emotional structure of the child is simply encased in subsequent layers of adolescence, young adulthood, adulthood, and finally an outer layer of the mature years. The pains we suffered as children are still there. They exist as scars, and because our childhood concepts are still partly alive, we tend to project onto God the feelings we had toward our parents. We may wonder if God is any more forgiving than they were.

Meister Eckhart insists that God is more ready to forgive than we are to receive forgiveness, and that the greater our sin the quicker He is to forgive us. Jesus seems never to have graded sins into various categories. The persons He chiefly condemned were the religious leaders, outwardly moral and righteous, inwardly marred by pride and other sins of the spirit. Read again His scathing denunciation of the Pharisees in the twenty-third chapter of Matthew. He says finally, "You serpents, you brood of vipers, how are you to escape being sentenced to hell?"[10]

It was the sins of the spirit then, not merely the sins of the flesh, which seemed most likely to cut one off from God, according to Jesus; and it is these basic sins which we are to confess, not only the overt deeds of the flesh. One might well examine his life for actions about which he feels guilty, then trace these back to the attitude which prompted them, then back to the emotion from which they sprang.

For instance, a man says something to me to which I reply heatedly, using stronger terms than I would ordinarily employ. Later I feel guilty about my heated reply. To confess this outer expression of irritation is relatively futile unless I go back beyond the expression to see why I reacted as I did. I relive the experience, and try to feel again what I felt during the encounter. Suddenly I realize that I was feeling threatened by what my friends had said. It was not righteous indignation at all, as I had thought originally. It was a threat to my security, and I reacted with hostility.

I could justify myself. He was wrong and I was right. I can find a dozen people who will say that I was right, but this has no bearing on the matter. We cannot summon witnesses in this encounter with God! There are just the two of us alone in this moment — God and myself; and God is asking gently:

"Did you feel threatened?" I know the answer to that. I did.
"Did it threaten your security or position?"
"Yes, no question about it."
"Then you were really afraid, weren't you?"
"No, I am never afraid! I have no fear."
"Fear is a human emotion. I do not condemn you for it. Peter was afraid and fled, remember? And Jesus did not condemn him. Peter was forgiven, and you can be. Can you admit that it was fear, not righteous indignation, and give up your pretense of virtue?"
"No, the man was wrong, he had no right ... skip it, Lord. You know and I know that whether the man was right or wrong has nothing to do with it. I was afraid. I now see that all my hostility springs from fear — fear of being dominated, fear of being wrong, fear of something. I will face this fear and look for it in all my relationships. And when I find it I will admit it and stop trying to get a popular vote on who is right and who is wrong."

This is true confession born of dialogue with God.

Confession is helped immeasurably if we can feel at a deep emotional level that sin is essentially a wrong against the self or against another human being. In His infinite love, God's stake in this matter of righteousness is not that He is outraged by our sin but that He suffers because we are injuring and destroying ourselves or others through impaired emotions and actions. Erich Fromm suggests that "sin is not primarily sin against God, but sin against ourselves."[11] Many of us have so focused our attention on the truth that "all sin is against God" and have been so fearful of playing into the hands of the relativists here that we have been unable to sense at a deep level that God's concern is that we shall not harm ourselves or others, and that sin is also "what man has done to man." Trying to resolve the apparent paradox here will not help us confront ourselves; but it may help us greatly if we can see sin as a violation of the divinely created self.

Fromm goes on to say that the proper reaction to awareness of guilt is "not self-hate, but an active stimulation to do better." Self-hate is not only not a virtue; it is a great wrong. To hate ourselves is to despise one whom God loves; it is as much a sin as hating another person.

God is not outraged because a man loses his temper, commits adultery, robs a bank, or beats his children. God's concern in all of this, or in any other set of outwardly manifested sins, is that these things are destructive of human personality and relationships. We value property so much more than human personality that we may forget that the bank robber has done himself more harm than anyone else. The money he took is covered by insurance; insurance rate hikes are passed on to the consumer, which is unfortunate but not fatal. What has happened is not simply that a man has stolen some money but that a human personality has gone wrong.

A mother who confesses that she feels guilty over yelling at her children has not "angered" God by her daily irritation; she has failed at a much deeper level. She has failed to establish the daily relationship with the Eternal which would give her the calm to deal with her children in loving patience; or she is distracted with so many "good causes" that she has little energy and time left for her primary task. Her basic sin is at a much deeper level than the shouting at her children. It goes back to her relationship with God. This may be what she needs to confess. She may even discover in confession that she is simply taking out on the children the hostility she feels toward her husband.

The adulterer has violated a divine law, but God is not outraged because His moral code has been violated. It is human personality which has been violated. Adultery is not wrong because it is forbidden in the Ten Commandments; it is forbidden in the Ten Commandments because it is destructive of human personality. Man was not made for the Sabbath; he was not designed to fit into it as into a straight jacket. Rather, the Sabbath was made for man; given to him as a day of rest which he needs.

The student who cheats on an examination has not done grave injury to God. He has simply begun a habit which is destructive of his own moral and spiritual fiber. God is "against" whatever is destructive for us. His love for us is so great that He cannot see us destroying ourselves without suffering Himself. It is the suffering of God, symbolized by the cross, which is involved in sin. We suffer _in_ our sins, Christ suffered _because_ of them. His suffering becomes redemption for us when we are able to confess the _right_ sin with true contrition.

Isaac Meir of Ger, quoted by N. N. Glatzer, says: "Whoever talks about and reflects upon an evil thing he has done is thinking of the vileness he has perpetrated; and what one thinks, therein one is caught . . . And he will surely not be able to turn, for his spirit will coarsen and his heart rot, and besides this, a sad mood may come upon him. Stir filth this way or that, and it is still filth. To have sinned or not to have sinned — what does it profit us in Heaven? In the time I am brooding on this I could be stringing pearls for the joy of Heaven. That is why it is written, 'Depart from evil, and do good'; turn wholly from evil. You have done wrong? Then balance it by doing right."[12]

Our "balancing" is not that of self-justification but an alternative to wallowing in forgiven guilt.

7. GUILT AND PUNISHMENT

> We do not hate ourselves because we are
> worthless, but because we are driven to reach
> beyond ourselves. . . . Self torture is in part an
> inevitable by-product of self-hate. Whether the
> neurotic tries to whip himself into perfection
> impossible to attain, hurls accusations against
> himself, or disparages and frustrates himself,
> he is actually torturing himself.
>
> — *Karen Horney*[1]

LARRY had served two terms in San Quentin for theft and
forgery. When he was released after serving his second
term he appeared to be driven by some inner compulsion
to continue his life of crime. He went on another check-
writing spree, but for some reason unknown to himself at
the time, he began signing his own name to the checks.
This made it ridiculously easy to trace him, and he was
apprehended, and sentenced to a third term at San Quentin.

There is within us an inner mechanism which tends to
enforce its own edict, "confess or be punished." Either we
must secure a sense of forgiveness and cleansing, or we
find a way to be punished, or to punish ourselves. In
Larry's case, when he was serving his second term, he
experienced a temporary release from guilt — — he was
being punished. But he did not feel fully forgiven, either
by God, man, or himself. Consequently, when he was
released, his inner judicial self sentenced him to further
punishment. When he signed his own name to the worthless checks, it was as though he was saying, unconsciously,
"I am still guilty. Find me and punish me."

"The soul will run eagerly to its judge," as Plato
expressed it. Man is so constituted that his guilt must be
either fully forgiven or he will find ways, by an inexorable
inner mechanism, to punish himself.

Police report that a criminal will often unwittingly leave some obvious clue at the scene of a crime, an unconscious message to the police, saying, "I am the guilty party. Come and get me!" Consciously he desires to escape. Unconsciously he feels a need to be punished. When apprehended he may feel a temporary relief but not a permanent sense of having expiated his guilt.

As long as he is in prison he may have a mixture of conscious hostility toward the authorities and some sense of relief, for he has been arrested, sentenced, and is paying the penalty for his crime. But when released, still feeling unforgiven by God, man, and his inner judicial self, he will often go to great pains to get himself locked up again. Outside prison walls again, his unresolved guilt takes over, and he feels a need to be punished in order to relieve the sense of guilt.

God has so constituted us that guilt must be resolved. We are concerned now, not simply with some overt guilty act, but with all that registers on the inner self as guilt: shame, inferiority, feelings of rejection and worthlessness, together with thoughts, desires, and impulses which we feel are "bad." God has instituted divine forgiveness, and if our concept of God's unconditional love is adequate, we can accept His pardon, and forgive ourselves. However, if we cannot believe in a God of infinite love and accept His forgiveness, then guilty feelings will persist in some form until they are resolved, one way or another.

We punish ourselves quite as inexorably for false guilt as for real guilt. A woman who had suffered from insomnia for years told me in a counseling session that she was not conscious of any unresolved guilt areas in her life; but a spiritual growth inventory clearly revealed a sense of guilt. Eventually she recalled three different things which had a bearing on her problem. One had to do with a partially buried memory of having been sexually molested as a small child. Another concerned some early childhood guilt feelings regarding sex, based upon misinformation; and a third had to do with repressed hostility which she felt toward her husband.

She had been a Christian a great part of her life, had taught a Sunday school class for the previous five or six years, and knew all about divine forgiveness at an intellectual level. A sense of shame over the childhood experience had registered as guilt; but since she had not considered herself guilty of anything it had never occurred to her to deal with that particular experience. As for the repressed hostility she felt toward her husband, she had not admitted to herself that she harbored any such unworthy feelings. It was not God who condemned her, but some portion of her inner self, the judicial system which was still pronouncing her guilty. When she was able to uncover these areas of guilt — some real and some false — and deal with them creatively, she no longer suffered from insomnia.

Freud maintained that many persons deliberately resort to wrongdoing because it is certain to bring punishment of some sort. This will alleviate their sense of guilt, which originates somewhere else in the person's life. Often the act, thought, or desire is totally repressed. Thus we have the painful spectacle of a person consciously doing wrong in an unconscious effort to be punished for unconscious guilt!

People who are accident-prone, trouble-prone, sickness-prone, or disaster-prone fall in this category. There are even instances of people who are bad-judgment-prone, who consistently make wrong decisions in an unconscious effort to fail, so that they may be punished, through failure, for their buried sense of guilt. It needs to be stressed, however, that such people may be no guiltier than anyone else. Their difficulty may be nothing more than a deep sense of inferiority, or a generalized sense of worthlessness, masquerading as guilt.

How can one secure divine forgiveness, the only alternative to self-punishment? It is not always as simple as one might think. A lovable, gentle but pathetic man looking ten years older than his actual age, came to pour out his story of grief and depression. He knew that it stemmed from guilt, from which he could secure no sense of relief. The misdeeds which he confessed were no worse than those of millions of others, yet for him they were enormous, so great that he was sure God could never forgive him. He was able to quote numerous passages from the Bible pertaining to God's willingness to forgive, but he could not apply them to himself. He was contemplating suicide as the only way out of a morass of moral, social and financial difficulties. It seemed certain that he was punishing himself for *the wrong sins*, yet so great was his need to be punished that he would not consider the solution proposed. He was determined to suffer. He could not and would not take steps which could provide relief.

Jesus made it clear, in the only comment he made about the Lord's Prayer, that we cannot be forgiven by God unless we are willing to forgive others. God cannot give to us what we are unwilling to give to another. He said, "For if you forgive men their trespasses, your Heavenly Father also will forgive you; but if you do not forgive men their trespasses, neither will your Father forgive your trespasses."² This was the basic problem of the man who could not secure a sense of forgiveness: he would not deal with his basic sin, that of refusal to forgive others.

Another aspect of God's forgiving love is revealed in the experience of Job, who, in a series of disasters, lost all of his possessions, then his children, and finally his health. Sitting among the ashes, he sought to discover the cause of his misery. Three friends came ostensibly to comfort him, but instead they argued that he must have sinned, or else God would not have permitted all the disasters to befall him. Job insisted that he had not sinned, at least not in the sense that they understood sin. Their belief, common then and still in existence today, was that in this life God always punishes the wicked and rewards the righteous. Therefore, they said, his sorrows must bear a relationship to moral failure at some point in his life. They obviously wanted the satisfaction of forcing him to reveal the precise nature of his sin.

He would have been more than human had he not resented their insinuations. Almost vehemently he protested his innocence: he had done nothing worthy of the tragedies which had befallen him. Toward the end of the drama God prevails upon the three friends to go to Job and "offer up for yourselves a burnt offering; and my servant Job shall pray for you ... And the Lord restored the fortunes of Job, *when he had prayed for his friends* ..." (italics added).³ There is, I think, a relationship between Job's willingness to pray for his friends, whom he resented, and the ultimate restoration of his health and his fortune.

We are not eligible to experience God's blessing — either His forgiveness or His guidance — so long as we are filled with resentment. Only as we accept and love others do we become able to receive what God is always seeking to bestow upon us. His desire to bless us is constant and unchanging. Our capacity to receive his love hinges upon our being willing to love. Thus Jesus explains that we fulfill the whole law when we love God with our whole nature and love our fellow man as we love ourselves. We are entitled to love ourselves properly. It is as inappropriate to hate ourselves, to blame or judge ourselves, as it is to reject and condemn others.

To say that "guilt demands punishment or forgiveness" may sound as though we are saying that God punishes us for our misdeeds and, by inference, that every disaster or sorrow we suffer must be evidence that God is punishing us for our sins. The book of Job was written chiefly to disprove this belief, for Job is portrayed as an upright man who loved God but who none the less suffered all manner of trouble. Smoking may cause cancer, but not all victims of cancer are smokers. All misdeeds, mistakes, errors of judgment, or sins carry in themselves an inevitable penalty; but not all sorrows or disasters are the result of our own misdeeds. We may suffer from the collective social evils, as a plague, for example. Our homes may be destroyed in a hurricane. Our children may be struck down by a drunken driver. Our jobs or savings may be lost through no direct fault of our own. Such disasters or sorrows could not be construed as stemming from one's own sins or mistakes, or from an unconscious need for self-punishment.

But there is another kind of trouble which does result from our own mistakes. (Whether we call it a sin or a mistake matters little for the moment. Mistakes may be the result of a mistaken way of life, and sins may be either willful or unwitting). A farmer who plants corn two feet deep, or an eighth of an inch deep, will not get a corn crop. He has made a mistake. He has violated the universal law of corn planting. God is not outraged. No one has been harmed but the farmer and his family. God has not punished him. He has simply not understood the principles of farming, or has been too lazy to learn them, or too careless in applying what he knows.

When we say that sin must be forgiven or punished, we are not saying that God does the punishing directly, but that there is an inexorable inner law which metes out a kind of impersonal justice. The farmer who planted his corn improperly was not being punished, except in the sense that the results of our actions can always be counted upon. This is a dependable universe. "Whatsoever a man soweth, that shall he also reap." This is not divine revenge, but inevitable result: cause and effect. We all sit down ultimately to a banquet of consequences.

Recognizing and confessing our mistakes does not wipe out their natural consequences. A careless driver backs his car into the side of another car in a parking lot. He is tempted for a moment to drive away, since no one appears to have noticed. He feels both guilty over his carelessness and apprehensive about the cost of the damages. His better nature triumphs, and he decides to leave his card on the windshield of the damaged car, indicating that he was at fault and will be responsible for the repairs.

He was guilty of carelessness, he has confessed his fault, and now he must be prepared to pay the penalty for his carelessness. His guilt has been both confessed and "punished" — punished in the sense that he is going to pay for the accident. He does not go free simply because he has confessed. Even if he drives away unnoticed, he will still be punished, not directly by an irate God, but by an inner voice which says, day and night, "You were dishonest." His punishment, then, lies in having to live with a dishonest person. He would have not only done a dishonest thing; he would have become a dishonest person and would have destroyed his own self-respect by that much.

The clerk who is occasionally dishonest, and who rationalizes it on the grounds that he is underpaid, may be right in his contention but at the center of his being there is an inner self which never accepts a rationalization because it knows the truth. He has not merely done a dishonest thing, he has become a dishonest person and knows it. The firm from which he has stolen may suffer no serious loss. The company can recover; the clerk cannot — until he has repented not only of the deed but the dishonest practice of rationalizing.

The government has vast reserves, and the petty amount one may deduct illegally from his income tax bears little relationship to the billions received by the Collector of Internal Revenue. The dishonest tax payer can rationalize that millions are wasted in one way or another by the government; but he suffers in that he has become a dishonest person. The government may never discover the deceit, but the taxpayer has not gone free. The inexorable inner self knows the truth. From this inner tribunal there is no escape. It demands repentance and forgiveness, or punishment; and the self does not wait for the day of judgment; it is judging constantly. "If our hearts do not condemn us, we have confidence before God." Unresolved guilt robs us of the openness with God which makes prayer effective. In some subtle way guilt condemns us to mask our true selves from the gaze of others. It is a totally unconscious mechanism. Act by act, day by day, lie by lie, we become progressively more and more opaque, less and less open. We become persons who cannot afford to be open lest we reveal the dishonesty within.

But dishonesty is not limited to overt theft or lies. A worse dishonesty consists in lying to ourselves, in denying our true feelings, in pretending that we feel one way when we really feel another, in a subtle refusal to face up to the kind of person we really are.

Among the commonest forms of self-punishment are emotional distress, physical symptoms, and mental illness. T. S. Szasz says that such a person "is in effect saying, 'admitting:' 'I have, alas, sinned, and now in expiation thereof, I am suffering,' with, of course, the implication, 'so you don't need to punish me. I'm doing it myself'."[4]

O. Hobart Mowrer writes that "a man is never whole until he is 'open to the world.' This is not to say that a person has to shout his sins 'from the housetop.' Not at all. But he is not fully 'saved' in the sense of being out of danger, until he is no longer afraid of having *anyone* know the truth about him."[5]

Elsewhere he says, "Guilt, in short, is the fear of being found out and punished. And it persists for precisely the reason that ... the mere passage of time does not reduce culpability ... The original sin is, moreover, *compounded by deception*, which becomes an ongoing 'sin,' which was not merely committed *then*, but is still being practiced and perpetuated, here and now."[6]

Sidney S. Jourard says, "Every maladjusted person is a person who has not made himself known to another human being, and in consequence does not know himself. Nor can he be himself. More than that, *he struggles actively to avoid becoming known by another human being. He works* at it ceaselessly, twenty-four hours a day; and it is work!"[7]

Some years ago a woman asked me to join her in prayer for the alleviation of a very painful physical condition for which medical men could provide no relief. Before agreeing to do so I asked about her relationships and attitudes toward those most closely related to her.

It developed that she had harbored a long-standing resentment against her husband. He had been unfaithful to her. "I can forgive him for anything else, but not for that," she said, and there was a finality about her declaration. I suspected a direct relationship between her burning hostility and her physical disability. I asked her if she would prefer the continued suffering to forgiving her husband. She said, "I will *never* forgive him!"

"Then," I said, "I think it would be fruitless for me to pray for you, since you have not met one of the basic conditions for answered prayer. Jesus makes it clear that you cannot be forgiven (healed spiritually, emotionally and physically) until you are willing to forgive anyone who has injured you." She departed, grim and unyielding. I had no definite assurance, of course, that her physical pain bore a direct relationship to her unforgiving nature; but the edict of the Bible on this matter, and the findings of modern science, point to a definite correlation. The mind simply passes its pain and dis-ease on to the body.

It is a great mistake to assume that as humans we consist of three rather loosely joined parts — body, mind and spirit. On the contrary, man is a unit, and what affects the mind or spirit will invariably affect the body to some degree. It needs to be said that not all of us have the same kind of conscience. Acts which would cause one person to experience the deepest remorse might leave another with little or no feelings of guilt. Someone contrasts Benvenuto Cellini and John Bunyan in this regard. Cellini was very devout when it came to his daily devotions, but cruel and immoral. He seems to have experienced no sense of guilt. Bunyan, on the other hand, basically moral, spiritually sensitive and highly ethical, was constantly tortured by a sense of doubt and remorse. He felt guilty over the slightest action which he deemed to be less than perfection. In one sense, Cellini would be called psychologically more healthy, although Bunyan was in every sense the finer character.

The principle here can be summarized in this way: Sin is not simply the overt act, but any attitude or emotion which is less than Christlike. Guilt must be dealt with. It may be thought of as a warning signal to indicate that there is a spiritual malfunction. When the problem of inner conflict has been resolved, the pain of guilt should cease; its function, as a warning, has been accomplished.

If we do not resolve guilt through the securing of forgiveness (God's judicial act) and self-forgiveness (our own responsibility), an inner mechanism goes into operation. We will suffer an inner dis-ease, in the form of remorse, depression or some other mental or emotional manifestation. When this becomes too great, the mind passes its pain on to the body, and actual organic disease can follow.

The victim of mental or emotional stress usually receives little sympathy; but when we transfer the difficulty to the body, great solicitude is forthcoming, ranging from expressions of sympathy to cards and flowers. God's loving concern, however, is that we as total persons shall be whole and well. "Wilt thou be made whole?" Jesus asked. To be whole is to be open with God through confession; to release the pain of guilt to Him, and to accept His divine forgiveness. For some it may mean the sharing of feelings with an individual or with a group. We have our choice: we can be open to God and man and be free of most of our ills of mind and body; or we conceal our failure and thus shut ourselves off from the healing, forgiving, redeeming power of Christ.

We began this chapter with the story of Larry, who was recommitted to San Quentin for a third term. He began a search for his basic difficulty, trying out this religious approach and that. Eventually, through the wise guidance of the chaplain, he began to search for the roots of his difficulty. In a prison fellowship group he continued his growth.

When eligible for parole, he wrote us, asking if our church could sponsor him and provide employment. This was done. Immediately upon coming to us he was invited to join a group. Within a few months he had gained sufficient confidence to share the story of his life. No one had known until then that he was an ex-convict. He shared this hesitantly, expecting rejection in some form. Instead, there were warm expressions of love and acceptance. Gradually his own self-acceptance increased. God's love and forgiveness were, in a sense, mediated through the group members.

Within a few months Larry expressed a desire to spend the rest of his life helping prisoners and ex-convicts. In order to prepare himself, he enrolled in a seminary as a special student. Though he had not completed high school, he was able to do postgraduate work with relative ease. While still in school, he was instrumental in starting a halfway house for released prisoners and upon graduation succeeded in starting a second such institution. A foundation grant then enabled him to devote himself full time to the establishing of fellowship groups in prisons and halfway houses for released prisoners. He gives every evidence of having accepted, fully and freely, the forgiveness of God, and of having forgiven himself. Those who meet him are impressed by this transparent effort to be honest with himself, with God, and with man.

Della was reared in a highly moralistic environment. Her parents were staunchly religious, and Della acquired an abnormal load of neurotic "shoulds" and "oughts." At college she associated with two widely divergent groups of friends — one highly moral and the other consisting of students determined to throw off all restraints.

A year or so out of college, with her inner conflict still unresolved, she began to drink heavily. Finally she was committed to a mental institution for acute alcoholism. When Della was released, though she had the benefit of long periods of therapy with a psychiatrist, she was still a very sick young woman emotionally. There was one other brief trip to a mental institution.

When we first encountered her she had been "dried out," as they put it, through faithful attendance at Alcoholics Anonymous, but had substituted tranquilizers, which she took at the rate of eight to twelve a day, and was unable to hold a job. Eventually a part-time job was offered her, which she was able to take, though only working an hour or two a day at first. Finally she found her way into a fellowship group. She rejected the moralistic religion of her early childhood, which had loaded her down with all manner of neurotic guilt; yet she was obviously seeking God. She feared and felt terribly guilty about her enormous hostility. In short, she was fettered by real guilt, false guilt, fear, hostility, and feelings of worthlessness.

She finally became able in a group to express some of her pent-up hostility, and when she found that the roof did not fall, gradually came to accept her emotions as a valid part of herself. Her sense of self-rejection was so great that she could neither give nor receive love at first. Eventually, as God's healing was mediated through the group, Della came to accept herself. Her sense of false guilt diminished, and she learned how to deal with real guilt. Before long she was working fulltime and doing beautifully. She is "well," "whole," in the sense that divine love has been mediated to her. Her level of self-acceptance is good, and her relationships are all creative. She is a homemaker who works full time in a highly significant Christian cause.

Larry and Della are extreme examples of the compulsion all of us have, in some measure, to punish ourselves for real or imaginary guilt. Guilt is a universal phenomenon. "All have sinned, and fall short of the glory of God."[8] Thus, all are in need of discovering and accepting God's grace — His love and unconditional acceptance.

A minister tells of the spiritual journey of Irene, an excellent illustration of the way in which the grace of God is mediated through the love of understanding Christians:

"She was one of the most unattractive young women I have ever known. I had never seen her before. She sat slumped in the chair, almost inarticulate. I asked her what I could do for her. She looked frightened, guilty, and 'lost,' in some strange way. She said, 'I don't really know why I am here. I need something, but I don't know what.'

"She had a drinking problem, but there seemed to be something much deeper. In the first counseling session all I could get out of her was a feeling of complete rejection by her parents, an intense hostility toward them, and a sense of utter self-loathing which she could not put into words. She expressed an almost venomous hostility toward her parents, especially her father. She had wanted his love and had felt completely rejected. Her appearance indicated a rejection of the feminine role. She was masculinized in appearance. In attempting to identify with her father, who rejected her, she had apparently taken on masculine 'feeling tones.'

"I could not believe all that she told me, and subsequently she confessed that much she had shared with me was untrue, but it took a year or more for her to admit this.

"In the group to which she was assigned she related to the others with difficulty. Usually a group gives a total acceptance of an individual, no matter how unappealing their personality traits may be, but they could not believe her, and had difficulty accepting her fully. She had apparently become a pathological liar, and subsequent events revealed that she was also a pathological thief, as well as a compulsive drinker. Her progress was slow. It had taken her over twenty years to become the mixed-up person she was, and we recognized that even if we could help her, it was going to take a long time. It did.

"I had a dozen or so counseling sessions with her during the four years she was in a group. I discovered that she had lied to herself so long it was virtually impossible for her to distinguish truth from falsehood. One spiritual growth test revealed that she had apparently lied on the test, but when given another test on which it is impossible to lie even to oneself, there was incontrovertible evidence of latent homosexuality. I let her score the test, in my study. When she finally looked at the results she sat stunned, struggling with the problem of trying to be honest with her real feelings.

"In that session she finally shared, under gentle probing, that much of what she had told me in the past had been a tissue of lies, told in an effort to bolster a terribly weak ego. She confessed to her dishonesty, and to all of the impaired attitudes which had marred her life. I told her that I did not condemn her, that God accepted her, forgave her, and that if she could turn her life over to Christ, she could find self-acceptance, and the meaning of life — salvation for the here and now, as well as eternal life.

"The struggle to reverse her long-held attitudes went on for some weeks. Then I noticed a change in her appearance. She began to dress in a much more feminine manner. To the surprise of everyone, she became a very attractive person. Gone were most of the traits and mannerisms which had caused her to be rejected, and as the result of which she rejected others with a kind of sullen hostility.

"Irene made an effort to re-establish a creative relationship with her parents. This in itself was redemptive. Now she could accept them, and they could relate to her, because her hostility had almost totally vanished. She began to take part in the life of the church. She became quieter, better adjusted to people, and more self-accepting.

"Her spiritual journey is not ended. No one's ever is. Her growth continues; but I can testify to the redemptive process which changed a hostile and terribly unhappy young woman into an attractive, creative person. The church provided the basic background against which her personal drama was played, but her moral and spiritual transformation took place largely because of the group.

"She is active in the church, as well as in several social groups. She has ceased to punish herself by making herself unattractive, and acting in an unacceptable manner. Her new self-acceptance, manifested in many ways, is simply the result of accepting God's love revealed in Christ, and mediated through the group."

It may not be easy for a relatively well-adjusted person to identify with Irene and Larry and some of the others whose lives are described in this chapter. They are used as illustrations chiefly because their problems are only an intensification of the difficulty experienced by every human — that of trying to pursue incompatible goals, a process which the Bible calls sin and which psychologists call inner conflict or neurosis. Whether one's inner conflict is severe enough to register as neurosis, or whether it manifests itself in impaired relationships, physical symptoms, or a general disillusionment with life, the solution for each of us is the same: *to bring our disordered lives under the control of the living Christ*. A few are able to do this alone. Most of us, however, require the fellowship and strength, the loving acceptance and inspiration provided by a group of kindred spirits pursuing the same goal, which is spiritual maturity.

8. GUILT AND FORGIVENESS

> Saints are men who permit God's forgiveness
> to come into them so fully that not only are
> their sins washed out, but also their very
> selves, their egos, and the root of their self-
> will. ... I forgive to the level that I have been
> forgiven, and if that level is moderate (be-
> cause . . . I wanted only to lose my vices and
> not myself) I can forgive only people who
> have offended moderately, and my forgiveness
> helps them only moderately. — *Anonymous*

In an effort to trap Him, the scribes and the Pharisees
brought before Jesus a woman who they said had been
caught in the act of adultery. They flung her before Him
and asked Him to judge her. The Mosaic law said that
such a woman should be stoned to death. If Jesus refused
to support the law of Moses his enemies could accuse Him
of teaching contrary to their law. Jesus bent down (perhaps to avoid towering over the crouching woman) and
wrote something in the sand. Then He said, "Let him who
is without sin among you be the first to throw a stone at
her." There must have been many a sidelong glance. Who
would be the first to declare himself sinless? There must
have been an embarrassing silence as, one by one, they
silently departed.

Left alone with the woman, Jesus asked her, "Has no
one condemned you?" "No one, Lord," she replied. Jesus
said, "Neither do I condemn you; go, and do not sin
again."[1]

There is no judgment here on the part of Jesus. He does
not seek to fix the degree of her guilt. He does not
condone the sin, but neither does He cause her to feel
rejection by giving her a lecture on the evils of an immoral
life.

Normally we feel critical of those who fall into such
temptation, but in this instance our sympathy is all with

the woman. We find ourselves condemning the ring of evil-minded men. In this we see our innate tendency to find the culprit: to discover the "good" people with whom we identify, and the "evil" people whom we reject. To do this is to judge. But we need to identify with both the woman and her accusers, for they are all sinners, perhaps no more nor less than we. If we have not committed adultery, have we not sinned as badly in our pride, jealousy, lust, materialism, and hate? None of us has ever dragged such a woman before a judge, but who among us is guiltless of judging others to be "wicked," of trying to discover the evil-doer and to fix the blame?

To understand divine forgiveness we must turn to the teachings of Jesus. His parable of the prodigal son illustrates it best.[2] The younger of two sons leaves home in reckless, youthful disregard of the father's love. In a distant country he squanders his money with dissolute companions who desert him when his money is gone. Reduced to tending swine — unspeakable depths to a Jew — he begins to compare his hunger and loneliness with the abundance and love he had experienced at home. Suddenly he resolves to return home: "I will arise and go to my father, and I will say to him, 'Father I have sinned . . .'"

The father rushes down the road to welcome the returning son. The young man begins his carefully rehearsed speech of repentance, but the father cuts it short with his glad welcome. The son's repentance is obvious; nothing matters to the father but that his son has returned. The father has not waited until now to extend forgiveness. In his mind the son was always forgiven. But he could not be aware of or accept or be healed by that forgiveness until he returned in repentance.

As we become more moral and decent, we often tend to become more judgmental. We see the obvious difference between good and evil, and we are insistent upon condemning evil. Automatically we set ourselves up as judges of what is right and wrong, good and bad, and we quote scripture to back up our judgment. Even if we do not verbalize the judgment, we feel judgmental and pronounce sentence within our hearts. We are thus quite as guilty of judging as if we had said something out loud. Painfully enough, others can feel our silent judgment. In the unconscious facial expression, the faintest lift of an

eyebrow, the change of inflection, we betray our judgmental attitude. And when we are critical or condemnatory,
we always arouse hostility in others.

A woman from another city came to see me one day.
She was suffering from deep depression and had under-
gone a year or more of psychiatric care in an effort to
discover the reason. The surface problem was evident:
there was marital distress, and divorce proceedings were
pending. But I sensed a much greater anguish of soul than
could be accounted for by the divorce.

She had been reared in an excessively moralistic home,
where the religious atmosphere was grim and unsmiling.
Love was never expressed between members of the family;
all emphasis was upon being "good." As a child she had
been thoroughly compliant, never disobeying in any respect. However, when she left home she fell in love with a
man of a different faith, whose occupation her parents
would have condemned. Her conduct upon leaving home,
while not wild or rebellious, was in many ways a violation
of all that she had been taught at home.

I called to her attention what I supposed would be
obvious to her — that her marriage to a man of a different
religious background, whose occupation would be an
affront to her parents, together with her other manifestations of rebellion, all constituted a rejection of parental
religious standards. She had never realized before that she
was in rebellion and, at some deep level of her nature, felt
conflict which was registering as guilt. She felt guilty
before her parents yet she knew that in some way they
were wrong; guilty before God, because she had violated
her old religious standards; and guilty before the tribunal
of her own soul. She had never been able to sort out false
guilt from real guilt, much less secure a sense of forgiveness.

For a year she had endeavored with a psychiatrist to
discover the source of her problem, but she still felt that
the basic difficulty was unresolved. Not until she dealt
with the matter of guilt could she have a sense of forgiveness. Whatever healing there was resulted not so much
from any insight on my part as from the fact that I could
feel with her, experience her pain, identify with her in her
guilt, and be a channel through which she could experience the divine grace of God, manifested as forgiveness.

Most of us do not realize how often we criticize and

judge and fix blame — so many are the ways this tendency of ours finds expression. To a child we may say, "For heaven's sake, must you always be doing that?" or, still worse, "If I've told you once I've told you a thousand times!" Thus sentence is pronounced. What we are saying is, "You are a very stupid person, and I don't know how I've managed to put up with you this long." No matter how we phrase it, the child gets the real message and feels condemned and rejected.

With adults, who may conceivably strike back and thus be able to defend themselves, we may be more cautious than with the defenseless child. After all, we don't particularly want to get into a verbal free-for-all with an equal who may be able to tell us off, so we are more cautious. But to the child we say, "Why did you do it that way?", implying that a mongoloid idiot would have known better. We say, "Here, let me show you!" or employ any of a hundred expressions, each of which is a judgment and a condemnation arousing hostility. Valid or otherwise, every judgment builds a barrier between ourselves and others. It is our way of saying, "I find it hard to accept you when you do that." It is very common, very human, but a far cry from unconditional love. *All* criticism is destructive, whether expressed or only felt. We may label it constructive criticism, but the victim hears it as judgment.

Speaking in a Los Angeles church one Sunday, I said that it is impossible to change others through criticism, however well intentioned; that our judgmental attitudes build barriers and destroy relationships. I said that we cannot change others directly, that we can only change ourselves; and when we change, others tend to change in reaction to us. After the service a man said he wanted to talk to me. We sat down in a pew, and he said, "I suddenly saw this morning what's wrong with my home life. For thirty years I've been trying to change my wife and children. I did it only for their good, but they resented it. My children hate me and married young just to get away from home. My wife won't speak to me, and I had thought it was just becuase they wouldn't accept my superior wisdom in a lot of things. Now I see for the first time that I have alienated them with my criticism."

We talked at some length, and he departed. That night he was back for the evening service, and at the conclusion walked up to me holding hands with a woman whom he introduced as his wife. She smiled and said, "I don't know what you said to my husband this morning, but already he's a different man." I replied, "I simply told him that we cannot change others through direct action or criticism, that it breeds hostility and destroys relationships." She turned on him with her eyes flashing, waved her finger in his face, and said with genuine hostility, "I've been trying to tell you that for thirty years!" So it had not been a one-sided affair after all; two judgmental persons had been trying to point out each other's defects.

I have often asked myself why I am able to be helpful in some counseling situations and not in others. I have come to see that when I have been genuinely helpful, when something creative has happened, it has been because I did not feel critical, because I offered no direct advice, and chiefly because I was able to feel total, unconditional acceptance and love.

Why did Jesus seem to prefer sinners to the social and religious leaders of His day? Why did He prefer to associate with the tag-ends of humanity? His enemies said that He was always eating with social outcasts, with prostitutes and the despised tax collectors, with uncultured fishermen who sometimes swore. Moreover, Jesus and those with him did not always obey the ceremonial customs as did the "decent people;" they even did things on the Sabbath which the priests said were taboo.

If we were to associate with such persons because we approve of their conduct we might well feel ashamed of our taste. But Jesus appears to have assoicated with them because, of the two kinds of sinners, He found them much to be preferred. These people were receptive. They had sinned, they knew it, and there was no secret about it. But the Pharisees, the moralists of the day, did not feel that they were sinners. They were decent, went to church, tithed, and obeyed all of the external requirements of the law. Because they could not see that they were sinners, they could not accept the grace of God, for it never occurred to them that they needed it! Only a self-acknowledged sinner can ever feel the grace of God's forgiveness, for only he is aware of his need for it.

Notice to whom Jesus revealed His divinity. It was not to the moralists of the day, the religious leaders of the nation, but to a slattern at a well in Samaria — a "foreigner" besides, with whom self-respecting Jews had no dealings.

She could not expect Jesus to speak to her, much less ask her for a drink, for a centuries-old religious feud existed between Jew and Samaritan. This woman came to the well alone, for no doubt other women despised her for her loose morals. They would also have feared her, for she had had a succession of husbands and was a threat to other women. But here was a Jew speaking to her. His voice was friendly and warm, and His smile was just as friendly as His voice.

They fell to talking about religion and, eventually, about the religious differences between the Jews and Samaritans. She said, ready to leave, "When the Messiah comes He will tell us all these things." Jesus said, "I that speak unto thee am he."[3]

It was not to religious leaders who were proud of their outward morality but to a much-married woman then living with a man not her husband that Jesus revealed His messiahship. With something akin to pain I ask myself the question, "If Jesus were to walk among us today, unknown, would He choose church people to whom to reveal Himself, or would He seek out some self-acknowledged moral derelict?" I dare not answer the question — I do not know. We read that "Christ loved the Church and gave Himself for it." But this does not mean that He could approve of the complacent moralism and the judgmental attitudes manifested by many church people.

I was once leading an interdenominational retreat held at a beautiful Boy Scout lodge in the northwest. My glance fell on the wall, where in large letters were inscribed the Scout Oath and the Scout Law. I read them aloud and said, "If all of us were to obey these principles to the letter, and if we were also to obey the Code of Hammurabi, born centuries before Moses and the Ten Commandments, we would even be better people than most of us are now." There was no dissent. I asked, "Why, then, did Jesus come? Was it simply to give us some ethical and moral precepts? Surely His coming must not have been solely to urge us toward higher standards of conduct but for another purpose as well."

The Bible is not basically a Book about morals. In The Sermon on the Mount, containing the highest ethical and moral precepts known to man, Jesus does not teach that it is solely by straining toward these ethical principles that we shall attain heaven. I do not begin to apply all of Jesus' teachings in my life, nor do I know anyone who does so in all circumstances. Yet I expect to enter heaven, and I expect to find many others there who have lived, perhaps, a less blameless life than I have. I expect to attain eternal life: not because I am good but because God is good; not because I have been able to give unconditional love under all circumstances but because He is able to do so; not because I have always been able to forgive but because God can do so and has forgiven me.

The chief characteristic of the Christian moralist is that, though he may speak fervently of the grace (the unmerited favor) of God, he bogs down in a panting, nervous, apprehensive, guilt-ridden effort to be "good" and to "avoid the things of the world." (And no two moralists have identical lists of worldly pursuits.) The moralists have a scripture quotation to hurl at anyone who engages in any activity which they themselves do not personally enjoy or approve of. Their "don't" is often a cultural taboo learned half a century or more ago at the knee of a guilt-ridden parent who spoke of grace but lived under the lash of the law.

Even after I have managed, by prayer and patience and the grace of God, to bring my life somewhat into harmony with the teachings of Jesus, I see someone who has not come so far, and I find myself judging him automatically because he is not as patient or moral or generous or tolerant as I. In so doing I sin — just as he has sinned. He may be guilty of hostility or immorality; I become guilty of judging and spiritual pride. I am not at all sure who is the greater sinner, he or I, but it is quite possible that considering my opportunity and advantages, I may be a greater sinner than he. My self-righteousness may be a greater sin in the sight of God than his momentary sin of the flesh, which I tend to judge so hastily.

The Bible, then, is not necessarily a Book of moral standards, adhering to which will make us "good" persons meriting heaven; it is rather the wonderful story of God's almost unbelievable grace, His loving forgiveness, extended unconditionally to all who will receive it. It is the good news that God does not condemn us even when we fail, that He loves us, gave His Son for us, and accepts us, although we do not feel acceptable to ourselves.

But even as we speak of the unconditional love of God, we begin to feel vaguely uneasy: is not repentance a condition of our being forgiven? Must we not repent before God can forgive us? In answer, let me suggest that there is a difference between the idea of a God who "holds out" on us (somewhat in the manner of a union boss) until His demands are met, and a God who has created the universe in such a way that certain causes have certain effects. God's moral laws are much like His natural laws — the law of gravity, for example. They are not external "rules" with arbitrary penalties attached to them; they describe how things work. God's love and forgiveness are unchanging factors — just as unchanging as gravity or atmospheric pressure. Our "goodness" or "badness" do not affect these divine laws in the slightest. They operate as fixed laws of the universe, which is simply to say that they are unchanging aspects of the nature of God.

Our repentance is not a "condition" in our human, legalistic conception of the term. God is not waiting to extend forgiveness and love until we repent; it is rather that we are incapable of accepting the grace He eternally extends until we repent. "I change not," said God through the prophet. He has done everything necessary to forgive us. The cross stands forever as a symbol of this. He has taken the initiative; the rest is up to us. Our repentance is simply the way by which we bring ourselves into harmony with the pre-existent love and forgiveness of God. Even our response is, in a sense, the result of His divine initiative, but our wills make it operative when we open our lives to Him in glad response.

If we are not to gain Heaven by being good, by obeying the ethical teachings of Jesus, are there then no moral standards? Of course there are. But the supreme law is that of love, not morals. When asked what He considered the supreme law, Jesus said, " 'You shall love the Lord your God with all your heart, and with all your soul, and with all your mind and with all your strength.' The second is this, 'You shall love your neighbor as yourself.' " He indicated that one who has fulfilled this supreme law of love has, in so doing, fulfilled all the other laws as well.

If you desire to help people, whether friends or members of your family or acquaintances, do not judge them or criticize them. We are not the discerners of ultimate good in all matters. To judge or condemn or criticize may well be one of the worst of all sins. If you want to help people, let some of God's non-judgmental love be channeled through you. It is not our advice which the world needs, and however well one may cloak it in biblical phraseology, it is still egocentric advice-giving, and implies a virtue not possessed by the other. Love is the key, not advice.

Years ago I received an interesting letter. It consisted of eleven pages from a woman who said that God had commanded her to rise in the middle of the night to write me. In her letter she endeavored to straighten out my theology, personal life, attitudes, and preaching. It did contain some truth. It would have been difficult to write eleven pages without stumbling onto some truth. But being very human, I refused to accept the Olympian assumption that she had been authorized by God to sort out my private and public life.

She was right in much that she said, wrong in her assumption that such advice-giving was the way to help people. Human beings do not need our advice so much as our love. Of course there are times when they both need and want guidance; when they have lost their bearings, are confused, are about to wreck their lives; when they need the fixed point of an emotionally uninvolved person to help them see their way out. However, much of our well-meaning advice is born not of the Holy Spirit but of an egocentric need to run the lives of other people. Jesus said, ". . . first take the log out of your own eye, and then you will see clearly to take the speck out of your brother's eye."⁵ He was saying, "When your own personal life and relationships and motives are all properly straightened out, then you may see clearly how to help another."

Jesus did not call us to judge but to confess — and we go on judging. He urges us to confess, and we refuse. The Bible commands, "Confess your sins to one another, and pray for one another, that you may be healed"⁶ — a text on which few sermons have ever been preached, I cannot imagine a more unpopular text.

Confessing to another need not imply buttonholing a person on the street and saying, "I have some guilty secrets I want to share with you," or pouring out some sordid aspect of our lives to a random acquaintance; it does imply that in the environment of a small, loving group, or to an appropriate friend who is wise and filled with love and understanding, we are to share our spiritual deficiencies and failures. Does that bother you? Then it may be that you are troubled and need to share with another some of your problems.

In sharing with and praying for one another within a close-knit group, we have obeyed this command. What is more, we secure release from pent-up guilt; for impared emotions and attitudes (not necessarily the symptomatic acts) need to be shared so that we can experience the healing that comes from acceptance by others. Guilt long borne often assumes a neurotic value out of all proportion to its importance. When we share our difficulty, we find that others, too, suffer from the same or similar problems. God's love is mediated through them. Sensing their understanding and acceptance, we can begin to accept the forgiveness of God, which had been available all along.

I wish it were possible to change the image of the Church. Many people not closely identified with the Church think of us as respectable, ethical, sober, rather dull religionists, trying hard to be moral; and they suspect quite rightly that we aren't as good as all that. Perhaps some imagine that the primary business of the Church is to produce just such people. In this they are wrong. The Gospel which we are committed to accept, live, and proclaim, is the good news of God's redemptive love; of a divine love which is available to every human. Often those outside the Church, with a confused picture of what Christianity is all about, do not feel welcome in the Church because they don't feel like "good" people. If only we could make it clear that the Church's primary business, like Christ's, is to be concerned not with the righteous but with the unrighteous, not with the well but with the sick. It is our responsibility to make it known that the Church is not for "good" people, but for sinners, which is what all of us are.

In the church where I minister I have said, "I want alcoholics to know that they are welcome here. I would like for prostitutes to know that here they will find non-judgmental love and acceptance, along with those who have been equally guilty in other areas. Jesus said to the most moral people of His day that the traitorous tax collectors in the pay of Rome, and the prostitutes, would enter the kingdom of heaven before they did.

"One could wish that all of the lonely and the friendless, the people who feel guilty and inferior and confused, might discover that they would find a welcome in the

Church of Jesus Christ, along with the prosperous, cultured, confused people equally in need of God's grace. Before the world can sense this, however, we will have to change our own thinking and feeling, give up our judgmental attitudes, and know at a deep emotional level that some of the worst sins are not sins of the flesh but of the spirit."

Jesus sought to show the people of His day that they had a false concept of sin, and a large segment of the Church today still needs convincing on this point. Jesus stressed that sin was not simply the act but the motive and emotion prompting the act. The Bible tells us that the man who hates is already a murderer, though he has not killed; that one who lusts has already committed adultery and thus is guilty before God and the inner tribunal of his own heart.[7] Pride, covetousness, lust, jealousy, materialism — all these are stressed in the Bible as the corrosive sins of the spirit, and one who finds these emotions in his heart is, to the degree that he is in their control, in the grip of sin, though his outer life may appear blameless.

Projection is one of the most practiced of "oblique" sins and one of the least understood, because it is a totally unconscious device. It consists in preventing oneself from becoming aware of undesirable traits or feelings by attributing them to others. The trait which we find most objectionable in others is often one of our own problems, or latent problems.

Obviously, it is not always so; but when we discover an offensive personality trait in someone else which causes us to over-react to it, the chances are that we have not dealt fully with that tendency in our own lives. We cannot see it in ourselves, of course, for we find the trait so offensive that we blind ourselves to it or push it into the unconscious mind.

For instance I discovered after many years that one trait which I find objectionable in other people is one I possess. I dislike interruptions, whether by the telephone or an impatient listener. I am unreasonably bothered when anyone is interrupted. My rationalization has been that when a person is speaking I want to hear him out. I feel it is in bad taste to interrupt a dinner guest in the middle of a story with an invitation to have some more potatoes.

Though I like to think that I do not interrupt others unduly, I found by careful check that I have no hesitation whatever in interrupting a conversation or in stopping a secretary a dozen times in the midst of her work to give her some instructions or to ask a question. By observing myself over a period of months I saw that what I disliked intensely in others was something which I disliked in myself, and had not bothered to face fully.

To interrupt a person needlessly in the middle of a conversation is another way of saying, "What you have to say is of such little importance that I want to take over. Now let me talk!" It is an egocentric attitude, and I heartily despise it in others. I had endured it unconsciously in myself, but the fact that I reacted with an undue amount of resentment to this trait in others told me that I was one of the chief sinners. Even if I did not interrupt others as often or as blatantly as some, I am sure I had the inner urge to do so.

The person who is quick to condemn and find fault is usually projecting. The inordinately suspicious individual is really telling us of his own inner struggle with the thing he suspects in others.

Mr. Pontus was such a man. His relatives said that they had never known him to admit any defects of his own, though he spent a large part of his time condemning virtually everyone in the small town where they lived. He was enormously suspicious of the motives of others. He refused to permit his daughters to attend dances, for, as he carefully pointed out, dancing had strong sexual overtones, and he didn't want his daughters to get involved sexually. There was no sex instruction in the home, only dire warnings.

His personal conduct was always above reproach, but one sensed that there was a great inner struggle going on within. By attacking those about him he revealed to perceptive observers his hatred of his own unacceptable emotions. His suspicious nature indicated that he was doubtful of his ability to handle his own personal drives. As an elderly man he refused to let his eighty-year old wife speak to the gardener, for he was certain that the gardener had lustful thoughts toward her. This is a glaring instance of lifelong projection. Confession in his case would have meant not the confessing of outward acts but of sins of the mind and spirit, the root of all sin.

It bears repeating that our capacity to deceive ourselves is enormous. Our blindness to defects within us, so obvious to others, is one of the most amazing evidences of our inability to see our total selves: we cannot see ourselves as we see others and we rationalize and justify ourselves while condemning others. It is a kind of psychological smoke screen which we employ unconsciously, as though to say, "It is too painful to examine my personal life. Let's look at his." By focusing attention on the guilt of another we divert attention from the unconscious guilt we feel but are unwilling to face.

A counselee once told me that he was almost certain his wife had been unfaithful to him. He had had her followed. After a few counseling sessions, during which he persisted in the belief that his wife was "running around" with other men, he suddenly put his finger on the real problem. He asked, "Do you suppose the fact that I had a few affairs before I was married could have anything to do with my belief that my wife has been unfaithful?" I said, "Why don't you give that some serious thought?" He discussed this possibility for a time, then I asked, "Could there be a combination of two things at work here — the actual affairs you had prior to marriage plus a present fear that you may succumb to a similar temptation now?" He looked blank for a moment, for the mind often blocks out painful possibilities. I asked, "Could you be interested in someone else at the moment?" He was very thoughtful for a few moments, then he said that although nothing overt had happened, there was a woman where he worked in whom he could become interested. He was insistent, however, that he had done nothing wrong.

He came to see that his own prior guilt was the backdrop against which the present drama was being played. His partially suppressed interest in another woman was arousing the old memories and the pain of guilt. By a curious inversion he then became suspicious of his wife.

When Socrates, the wisest of Athenians, declared, "The unexamined life is not worth living," he was referring not to a casual once-for-all examination but to the need for daily re-examination of our motives; the urgent, constant need to dig one layer deeper beneath the levels of pretense and pride and rationalization.

There are several kinds of guilt which demand forgiveness. There is, first of all, guilt before God — those violations of basic spiritual, ethical or moral laws which in most cultures would also be considered violations of human personality or relationships. These involve such basic principles as the strictures in the Ten Commandments against such things as murder, theft, adultery and covetousness. The thing which distinguishes this kind of guilt is that it was specified by God in the Bible.

A second category (the categories overlap to some extent) is guilt before man, involving violation of a social ethic or taboo in a particular culture. This would include the violation of laws established by one's society to make for better relationships between the people comprising that culture. This would include everything from laws regulating marriage and divorce to traffic laws, income tax regulations and thousands of similar city, state and federal laws. That which distinguishes this group of laws from the basic moral laws of God is that these are sociological in nature and may change from culture to culture. In America, one drives on the right side of the road. In England this would be a violation of the law.

There are many such "cultural" rules and regulations, the violation of which may arouse guilt. One may violate some cultural nicety and feel guilty before man but not necessarily before God. Friends invite us to their home, and the hour is set at seven. To arrive an hour late without an apology or explanation is a flagrant violation of the social code, and one who does this without any feeling of guilt is not only lacking in social sensitivity but is a boor besides. If in addition he fails to thank his host for his hospitality, he has violated another important rule of social conduct. He may remember during the night that he failed in this respect, and may feel remorse. This is not guilt before God but before man. It registers, however, simply as guilt, for our inner tribunal has no categories reserved for specific kinds of guilt.

Another category concerns false guilt. This refers to our feelings of guilt where there is no actual guilt, either of commission or omission. One may not have knowingly violated any law of God or man and yet experience a deep sense of guilt. This false guilt usually stems from such things as rejection in childhood, causing the child to feel unwanted, unloved, and therefore worthless. This may persist through life in some diffused, indefinable form. The individual is not sure whether to call it a sense of guilt, inferiority, inadequacy, shame, or alienation. He simply feels vaguely "worthless," "no good," a "reject." Each of these feelings registers on the unconscious mind as guilt.

A child whose parents set unrealistically high goals for him may thereafter feel that he can never quite measure up, and so he judges himself a failure. He feels vaguely guilty and unworthy. Since he was unacceptable to his parents, he becomes unacceptable to himself. The cause may have been continued parental displeasure over his report card or his failure to measure up to many adult demands and expectations. He may go through life with an ill-defined feeling of futility.

If he had perfectionist parents he may never be able to satisfy the inexorable demands of his super-ego (roughly; conscience, or sense of "oughtness"). We come into the world with a conscience which says simply, "Do right." It does not tell us what is right or wrong. This comes largely from parents and is augmented by teachers, brothers and sisters, and our culture in general. In most instances, however, conscience is the product of mother and father.

In one group a highly intelligent woman said, "I always feel guilty or inadequate, I can't tell which. No matter what I do or how well I do it, my first instinctive question is 'What would Daddy think?'" Her father, it turned out, had been dead for years, but she still felt that he was peering over her shoulder. She said, "If I brought home a C on my report card, he felt it should have been a B. When I got a B, he made it clear that any daughter of his should make straight A's. When I did finally succeed in making straight A's there were other deficiencies which he pointed out. My piano playing was not progressing well enough, or my hair looked bad, or my posture was poor. I never could please him, no matter what I did. I still can't and he's been dead for years!"

To the credit of the group, no one made the fatuous remark, "Since your father is dead and you are a responsible adult now, throw off these foolish standards and make your own." No one said it partly because all felt within themselves some of the same problem and partly because they knew it would take her a long time to overcome fully the sense of guilt and inadequacy created in her by a perfectionist parent.

In tracing guilt back to one's parents it is not implied that we are in any sense blaming them. They did their best. They were *their* parents' children. In living up to the light they had, they fulfilled their responsibility. We are to blame neither parents nor teachers, brothers nor sisters, nor ourselves. There is no blame to be assessed.

Yet responsibility persists. We feel it strongly, even after having said that there is no blame. The real responsibility lies in beginning at this point to distinguish between false guilt and real guilt and to confess the latter.

Within the understanding circle of a sharing group one learns to distinguish. We discover gradually the real self behind the mask of pretense and rationalizations, and we learn in time how to offer this newly discovered self to God. This is true confession.

Occasionally someone, hearing about our groups for the first time, expresses considerable anxiety over the prospect of being involved in "group confession." The fear is wholly unfounded.

Very often, it is true, life-long defenses are shattered by some insight in the group, and a member may share some attitude or feeling about which he feels guilty. Nothing is shared which could be considered a morsel of gossip. Far from being a problem, the converse is true. Our reluctance to expose ourselves is normally so great that there is no danger of such a group becoming a "gossip center." The danger is not that we shall share too deeply, but that we shall deal in superficialities.

What is shared is the faulty emotion, the impaired attitude, the less-than-Christian relationship. It is the sinful self rather than the sinful act which is confessed. Often as the result of new insights and growing spiritual sensitivity, a person feels the need to share more deeply. In such cases the individual does so in a counseling session with a minister or professional counselor.

9. THE WAR BETWEEN THE SEXES

> No one can give mature love until he has
> achieved a considerable degree of emotional
> maturity; and we cannot achieve this so long
> as we are reacting to unconscious drives orig-
> inating in childhood, which have not yet become
> adult in their expression.
> — *Lucy Freeman*[1]

HISTORY records the Hundreds Years' War, but there is
another conflict which has been waged far longer. It is the
war between the sexes. Alfred Adler points out the origin
of this conflict.

The fallacy of the inferiority of woman, and its corollary, the
superiority of man, constantly disturbs the harmony of the
sexes. As a result, an unusual tension is introduced into all
erotic relationships, thereby threatening, and often entirely
annihilating, every chance for happiness between the sexes.
Our whole love life is poisoned, distorted and corroded by this
tension. This explains why one so seldom finds a harmonious
marriage. ...[2]

Assigned an inferior status for countless centuries, wom-
en have only in recent times achieved anything resem-
bling equality. Long denied equal educational opportunities and numberless social advantages, women found a
champion in the person of Mary Wollstonecraft, the first
ardent feminist, who launched her crusade in 1792. Unfortunately, her commendable zeal was not matched by equal
insight.

Two outstanding students of feminism, Ferdinand Lundberg and Marynia F. Farnham, point out that:

Far from being a movement for the greater realization of

women, as it professed to be, feminism was the very negation of femaleness. Although hostile to men and hostile to children, it was at bottom hostile to women. It bade women commit suicide as women and attempt to live as men. . . . Psychologically, feminism had a single objective: the achievement of maleness by the female, or the nearest possible approach to it. In so far as it was attained, it spelled only vast individual suffering for men as well as women. . . .[3]

Mary Wollstonecraft contended in her book, *A Vindication of The Rights of Women*, that men and women were essentially identical in their fundamental characteristics. It followed, then, that women should not only be equal before the law and be governed by the same moral laws but should also do the same work as men. Children were to be handed over to competent nurses or public nurseries, and their mothers were to hasten to the market place and enter into open competition with men.

The lot of women was extremely difficult in the eighteenth and nineteenth centuries, and the battle for equal rights did much to improve their condition. Some of the goals of the feminists were worthy, while others were neurotic. Although society has benefited enormously from some of the gains made by the movement, the evils of the neurotic goals are still with us, and the end is not in sight.

Marie N. Robinson, a psychiatrist, has written a remarkable book, *The Power of Sexual Surrender*. It could have been titled more inclusively "The Power Available to a Woman Who Will Surrender to Her Own Feminine Nature." She writes:

In so far as the feminist movement pitted itself against the male, and at the same time advised woman to masculinize herself or divest herself of her feminine nature, it was dreadfully neurotic, and we have been reaping the whirlwind this movement started ever since. The rage of the feminist was directed against herself. She speaks of the long list of masculine goals which the feminists advocated, and an equally long list of goals which ignored or denied the existence of feminine characteristics in womankind.[4]

Dr. Robinson and other students of the feminist protest movement analyze the unconscious hostility women feel toward men.

The feminist-Victorian antagonism toward men has survived, too. It has been handed down from mother to daughter in an unbroken line for so many years now that, to millions of women, hostility toward the opposite sex seems almost a natural law. Though many a modern woman may pay lip service to the ideal of a passionate and productive marriage to a man, underneath she deeply resents her role, conceives of the male as fundamentally hostile to her, as an exploiter of her. She wishes in her deepest heart, and often without the slightest awareness of the fact, to supplant him, to exchange roles with him.[5]

Marie Beynon Ray says concerning this unconscious female wish to exchange roles: "All — well, almost all — in their inmost hearts, wish they were men."[6] The fact that this is buried far below the level of consciousness, and originates in childhood envy of the privileged position of boys and men, makes it almost impossible for a woman to acknowledge it, much less deal with it.

This masculine protest, which Alfred Adler describes as a woman's resentment against masculine assumption of authority, causing her to refuse to accept her sexual role as a female, has understandable origins. Formerly a husband "owned" his wife, and any property which she possessed was his by right of marriage. This came about through laws made exclusively by men. Today in America, this is somewhat changed. Women now own between 65% and 70% of all private wealth, but it is still controlled by men, as one woman has pointed out. Even in our enlightened nation we have only recently passed laws granting women equal pay for equal work. The battle goes on, with considerable promise that women will gain successive victories in their fight for equality of opportunity. An ardent and articulate advocate of this crusade, Marie Beynon Ray, says, however, "The more women gain, the more intractable they become. The home is a battlefield, where the woman, having married the most superior male she can lay hands on, must now establish her superiority to him, and he must at all costs maintain his."[7]

Ashley Montagu, anthropologist at Princeton University, presents some interesting concepts in his book *The Natural Superiority of Women*. He argues that men achieve significance in more realms than women do because "they are overcompensating for a natural inferiority, the inferiority of not being able to have babies." Men are not likely to be greatly impressed by this argument, but Montagu contends that women are biologically superior, not in physical strength but in their capacity to endure pain, exposure, fatigue, shock, and illness. In every age bracket, the death rate for men is higher than for women. Women succumb to fewer illnesses than men and tend to endure illness with more equanimity.[3]

Women are also somewhat more stable emotionally than men, despite male contentions to the contrary. The proportion of men in mental institutions is higher. There are more male alcoholics than women. Women respond to shock somewhat better than men. Just because women are more emotional does not mean that they are less stable emotionally. Nature, because of the importance of the preservation of the race, appears to have given women some significant qualities not possessed by men.

The struggle of women for equal rights has unfortunately had some serious side effects. One of these is the misconception that since men and women are now more or less equal before the law, women and men are therefore equal as sexes and as persons. But men and women are not "equal" in the sense that they have equal and identical emotional or mental qualities, any more than an apple and an orange are equal. They were never meant to be.

A woman may be, for instance, intellectually superior to some particular male, but her mind operates on an entirely different wave length. It is not a matter of superiority or inferiority but a difference of approach. Men and women are simply wired differently — emotionally and intellectually. Largely because of the long uphill struggle for equality, women tend to be insecure with their newly acquired freedom. Prompted by the largely buried need to compete with the male, they often tend to push and prod, in a totally unconscious effort to discover how much strength there is in him and if possible to conquer him. The intellectual woman unconsciously seeks to confront, confound, oppose, defeat, or control the male by direct or indirect means; but the feminine part of her nature feels defeated and frustrated when she achieves this goal! She is then angry and even more frustrated than before, because he was not strong enough to oppose her. She may have married him partly for his quality of gentleness, and now she despises him for this very quality. She wants victory, insists upon being defeated, and desires to have the last word!

Carl Gustav Jung writes of "that peculiarly protesting character such as is unfortunately often encountered in intellectual women."

Such an intellect [he says] is always trying to point out mistakes in others; it is pre-eminently critical, with a disagreeably personal undertone; yet it always wants to be considered objective. This invariably makes a man bad-tempered, particularly if, as so often happens, the criticism touches on some weak spot, which, in the interests of fruitful discussion, were better avoided. But far from wishing the discussion to be fruitful, it is the unfortunate peculiarity of this feminine intellect to seek out a man's weak spots, fasten on them, and exasperate him. This is not usually a conscious aim, but rather has the unconscious purpose of forcing a man into a superior position, thus making him an object of admiration. The man does not as a rule notice that he is having the role of hero thrust upon him; he merely finds her taunts so odious that in the future he will go a long way to avoid meeting the lady. In the end the only man who can stand her is the one who gives in at the start, and therefore has nothing wonderful about him.[9]

Women have important traits and qualities which men do not possess. Women are more insightful than men. Women are more personal, more intuitive, and sense things which men, with their greater reliance upon logic, are prone to overlook.

A sidelight on this is contained in the story of a man who looked up from his magazine and said to his wife, "It says here that the trouble with women is that they take everything personally." His wife said quickly, "*I* don't!" It is this very quality of taking things personally, or relating ideas and experiences to themselves, which tends to make women more intuitive. They have a greater tendency to run each experience, comment, and concept through the blender of their own emotions. If they are emotionally mature, the result often may be superior to the conclusion arrived at by the male process of pure logic. If they are emotionally immature, or if the matter touches some area of insecurity, the results can be invalid — even explosive.

Jung speaks of the intellectual woman's tendency toward "a critical disputatiousness . . . which, however, consists essentially in harping on some irrelevant weak point and nonsensically making it the main one. Or a perfectly lucid discussion gets tangled up in the most maddening way through the introduction of a quite different and if possible perverse point of view. Without knowing it, such women are solely intent upon exasperating the man...."[10]

Men and women approach problems from entirely dissimilar points of reference, and it is small wonder that they often find discussions either unfruitful or impossible. For the woman, who thinks and feels far more in the realm of the personal, the world consists of people — fathers and mothers, sisters and brothers and cousins, husbands and neighbors. She may have an avid and well-informed interest in national or international affairs, and her opinions on these matters may be equal or superior to those of her husband, but inwardly and at the feeling level, she is more concerned with people and families. She is interested in details which, while important to her, can be an excruciating bore to a male.

The man's realm is his business or job, the city, and the world as a whole. His interests are more general than specific. Details, however important, are of less significance to him than general concepts.

Mary Esther Harding, psychiatrist and author, writes of "the development of the masculine side of woman's nature which has been so marked a feature of recent years. This masculine development is definitely related to her life in the world of affairs." Dr. Harding stresses the fact that this "affects her whole personality and has caused profound changes in her relation to herself and others."[11]

Camilla M. Anderson, Director of the Oregon State Hospital Outpatient Clinic, looks forward to the time when women will return to the business of homemaking, to the bearing and rearing of children, and to the business of living out the patterns which nature obviously intended for them.

They will do this [she declares] because they are forced into it. It wouldn't surprise me if neurotic behavior would then begin to decrease because women would have greater love for their children. They would no longer be seen as an accident, or something that interferes with bridge, or fun, or a career, or money making, or the figure. To the degree that women begin to think well of motherhood as something over and above all else *for them*, they will automatically lessen the feeling of helplessness among babies and children. The implications are obvious: when women find themselves as women, mental illness will decrease.[12]

Another significant difference between the sexes is the fact that to the woman her home is an extension of her personality. Her home consists of the actual residence in which she lives, together with all of its furnishings, her children, her husband, and all of the interests and concerns related to each person in the home. Her security is wrapped up in this extension of her personality. Where and how she lives, and the relationships in the home, mean more to her than to her husband. However much he is interested in his home the extension of his personality is his daily work. His wife spends a greater proportion of her time and interest being concerned about the home, and even if she works eight hours a day, keeping house on the side and possibly disliking it, enjoying the — to her — more interesting world of business, ultimately the home remains for her the major concern, while the job is a means to an end. The male, on the other hand, is basically so constructed that he gives the greatest proportion of his interest and energy to his work. If he did not do so, he would tend to lose out in what has become a highly competitive society.

The preoccupation of the husband with his work can be a source of considerable anxiety to his wife. He may come home tired and inwardly frustrated with aspects of his work — and his wife wants some communication. His mind may still be engaged in the issues of the day, and he finds it difficult to shift gears; or he is just too tired to be interested in what she has to say.

With her concentration on maintaining the home, she may remind him of some household repair job which has long needed attention. The exasperations she has endured during the day may cause her to tell him with some asperity that he promised to take care of the task weeks or months ago. From every point of view she seems justified. The matter does need attention. From his point of view, he has heard enough about it. He may have been resisting the matter unconsciously, perhaps because his wife reminds him of his mother's insistence on household tasks when he was a boy. It makes him feel unconsciously like a little boy again; at the mercy of a woman, forced to comply. So he may find a dozen excuses.

A far greater source of conflict in the home derives from the fact that husband and wife differ in their emotional natures as man and woman and that they each have different needs. The needs of both are legitimate, but they may be in conflict.

After a group session at a retreat, a charming couple came to me for counseling. She sat stony-faced and adamant, and his tense manner evidenced some of the frustration which had marred their marriage. He described the impasse. He had reached middle age and had attained the goal of financial security which, he had thought, would make him happy. But he found that he was not happy and wanted to launch out into a different type of enterprise. This would have involved selling most of their property, including their beautiful home, and moving to another area. She interrupted to say that she had moved twenty-three times in twenty-two years and had no intention of moving again. She liked the home in which they lived, and her security was wrapped up in all that it represented. "I'm not moving," she declared.

In her desperation she had begun ... to drink too much, which made him uneasy and angry. His steadfast insistance upon starting life over in another community, essential to the fulfillment of his inner needs, created in her all manner of insecurity and hostility. They had consulted a psychiatrist and a minister in trying to decide who was right, but at this point neither was prepared to yield an inch. She stated frankly that she would seek a divorce if he insisted upon what she termed "a foolhardy course — his effort to escape from life."

After listening to the details of their problem for some time I said, "I cannot see that either of you is wrong. Both of you have legitimate needs, but unfortunately each of you is being thwarted by the needs of the other."

I then explained to him that her needs sprang out of her feminine nature. She needed a home, a nest, a sense of security. Now that she at last had a home which was the fulfillment of all of her feminine dreams, the prospect of moving again was creating in her all manner of anxiety, with the resultant anger and frustration. He could not understand the deep attachment which she felt for that particular home, her friends, and social contacts. She had moved so often without being able to put down roots that now the possibility of another move was simply more than she could endure. These inner needs of hers, I explained to him, were God-implanted, not the neurotic demands of an unreasonable female.

To her I explained how her husband's sense of fulfillment was derived not so much from having his home and social contacts but from a sense of achievement. He was a man of considerable drive and ability. His earlier belief that financial security would give him a sense of peace was now dispelled. He was the sort of man who would always need the challenge of some new enterprise. At forty-five he was not so constituted that he could sit back and enjoy the fruits of his labor and maintain the status quo. He must have new fields to conquer, new challenges to meet. I explained to her that his need to achieve was as much God-given as her inner need for security.

"All right," he said, "where do we go from here? Granted that we cannot both have our way, what do we do about it?"

I said, "Neither I nor anyone else can give you a simple answer. You have been trying to discover which of you is right, and which one wrong. Both of you are right. Neither is wrong, yet your inner needs are in conflict. Therefore, unless or until you find these needs changing, there must be a compromise. If either of you wins out in this struggle, and the other gives in, there will always be a sense of frustration and anger on the part of the one who surrenders. You must not force the other to give in. One alternative is divorce, which you have both considered. I believe you can, of yourselves, find a happier solution.

"First of all, you can recognize the legitimacy of the needs of the other. Marriage and in fact all human relationships, involves a series of compromises. Where the inbuilt needs of one marriage partner conflict with equally valid needs of the other, some compromise must be effected. It is not my place to suggest how you work out the details of this compromise. I urge you to delay final action until you have considered every conceivable compromise. The final decision must not do too much violence to the desires and needs of either of you, though neither may be wholly satisfied with the final result. You tell me that you love each other, but now comes the test of whether your love is greater than your need to win a victory. You cannot each have all that you want. None of us can in this life."

They both accepted the principle, new to them, that each of us has inner needs which are incompatible with the needs of others. I saw them again at another retreat four months later. Both appeared happy and relaxed. I asked them how they had worked out their seemingly insoluble dilemma.

She said, "We seemed to get some relief from discovering that neither of us was necessarily wrong, and we gave up our struggle to resolve the problem immediately. Gradually I came to feel differently about the house. It didn't matter so much whether we sold it or stayed. He came to feel much the same way about moving and launching a new enterprise. Finally we both became relatively indifferent to what happened. I got to the place where I was quite willing to move, but he said he had lost a lot of interest in moving. Finally we put the house up for sale, because I came to see that it was really too big. When a sale fell through I was genuinely disappointed. Now neither of us cares very much about it one way or another. We are both free to move or not to move."

He smiled, and said, "That's about the way I feel too. It isn't too important either way."

More significant than the fact that their crisis had been resolved was the obvious change that had taken place in themselves. They solved the external problem when they resolved their inner feelings.

There are many basic ways in which men frustrate women and women frustrate men, and each marriage has its own catalog of variations. It would require a volume simply to list these innumerable frustrations, each born of the close personal relationship of marriage, compounded by the essential emotional differences between the sexes. However, some of the more basic frustrations which we encounter in groups can be catalogued. We shall deal first with ways in which men frustrate women.

Men frustrate women *by their refusal or inability to communicate*. Women may experience a similar difficulty in communicating, but it is more often the male who tends to retreat. In a typical situation, a discussion between husband and wife becomes an argument. Women are usually somewhat less afraid of their emotions than men, for in our culture boys are taught early in life to control their emotions. They may not cry, lest they be considered cry-babies. Hostilities expressed toward a parent is normally rebuked or sternly forbidden. A conditioned reflex is set up, with the result that the boy becomes a man who is afraid of his emotions. In particular, he fears his own hostility. He may become almost totally incapable of expressing a negative emotion without feeling that the roof is about to blow off. He is inwardly terrified at the apparent violence of his emotions. It is a reflex over which the conscious mind has no control. His standard procedure in such a case is to retreat. He may leave the room or simply retreat into an inner state of uncommunicative silence. This is extremely frustrating to his wife, who wants to talk things out.

Something else contributes to this impasse. Most men are less able to express themselves verbally than women, and they see themselves at a disadvantage. The male may begin with what he believes is a perfectly logical analysis of whatever the subject is. Before long he discovers to his consternation that somehow his relatives, his sundry failures as a husband and parent, and numerous other matters have been introduced. They seem relevant to his wife, but he feels himself utterly unable to discuss matters on this level. His anger is aroused, especially if he feels himself vulnerable on some of the counts, and from that point on he is unable to communicate; he and his wife are simply on different wave lengths. Or the discussion may get to a point where, at an unconscious level, he feels as he did when his mother accused him of something. He was defenseless then, as a child; and the inner child — always resident within the adult — responds as it did when he was accused by an irate or dominant mother. Feeling the threat of his own hostility and fearing accusations which, true or false, arouse still more anger, he withdraws from the discussion altogether. Consciously or unconsciously he feels hostility toward dominant women. His wife may or may not be dominant. The relevant factor is that he interprets her manner as dominant.

In many of our groups husbands and wives, usually in the same group, often learn to communicate for the first time. There is safety in the larger fellowship, which tends to maintain more creative and less emotionally charged communication. Fewer extraneous matters are dragged in. Accusations are toned down sufficiently so that the husband does not feel as threatened by his own emotions and the wife experiences less frustration, since her husband is not going to withdraw, physically or verbally.

When a woman is given to an excess of small talk, which the man feels is trivial and boring, it often means that she is bothered by some much more important problem of which she may be partially or wholly unconscious. She may have a deep sense of anxiety originating from some unresolved conflict within herself, or in the marriage. She may "feel" anxious about the minor issues of the day, but her tension is often the result of a mild "floating anxiety" which may attach itself to any issue and make a crisis out of it.

A sensation of inferiority or inadequacy, however diffuse, may manifest itself in overtalkativeness. It may result from a sense of rejection for which her husband is responsible or a generalized frustration which may be based upon many things, conscious and unconscious.

Some couples are able to communicate on such a thoroughly satisfactory level concerning their feelings that these things can be worked out between them. Unfortunately, the number of these couples is very limited. Usually it is necessary for them to be involved in a competently led group, where the basic feelings can be worked through. Sometimes a few sessions with a marriage counselor or skillful clinical psychologist will suffice. But in the minds of many husbands and wives the unfortunate idea persists that no one ever need see a counselor or join a group until a crisis of major proportions arises. And men, because of a false sense of pride and self-sufficiency, may reject the idea. Women, usually somewhat more realistic in this area, are often the first to suggest such a step.

The process seldom if ever involves the washing of dirty linen in public. There is simply an atmosphere in which neither husband nor wife feels threatened, and a profitable discussion can take place. For instance, in the first session of one group I asked husbands and wives to list just one thing they would like to change about their mates. The discussion proceeded with considerable humor, yet with an undertone of seriousness. It is probable that nothing basic came up at this first session, but one husband mentioned something he would like changed about his wife, and she said in genuine surpirse, "Why honey, we've been married fourteen years and I never knew you felt like that!" She was glad to know. He had never felt before that he could or should mention the matter, but surrounded by the good-natured, creative atmosphere of the group, his emotions became free of restrictions.

One of our demonstration groups consisted of three couples, surrounded by about forty others who were discovering for the first time how the groups function. The couples in the center were strangers to each other, and the setting was semi-public, hardly conducive to deep probing. There was the usual lightly humorous approach to the subject, to put the six at ease, and then I asked each of them to name just one thing they would like to change about their partners.

One thoughtful wife said, "Well, I'd like it better if he weren't so hostile. I never know what to say that won't provoke his hostility, so I just talk about what happened during the day at the office." I looked at him. He said, "One reason I'm so hostile is because I have what I consider a routine job. My wife has an administrative position and travels a great deal. When I come home from my humdrum, routine job, all I hear about is the perfectly fascinating people she has met, the places she has been, and the trips she is planning. I am hostile because she makes me feel inferior!"

Here was communication at a deeper level than they had been able to achieve at home, and in the presence of friends and strangers, yet without any trace of embarrassment. After all, every married person in the room had problems as great as, or considerably greater than, this one. They discussed their difficulty in the group for perhaps ten minutes. Later they told me that despite the fact that they had been to counselors, this was the first time that they had ever gotten down to the root of one of their problems. Communication had begun, not in the privacy of the home, but in a semi-public setting with others listening in. This is the magic of the group. It is simply less threatening and more productive for many persons than to undertake it initially at home.

Men frustrate their wives *by refusing to listen to them.* A husband may expect his wife to listen with rapt attention to business details in which she may be only vaguely interested, or not interested at all; but the same husband may answer with grunts from behind a paper or magazine when she wants to share with him some details of her day.

He feels they are trivial, yet they are the material of which her life is made. If she is a mother with small children, she wants some adult communication for a change. If she receives only casual attention, she is made to feel that her task as wife and mother is unimportant to her husband.

If she is so unwise as to begin talking the moment he enters the house, at a time when he wants only to mend the tattered edges of his soul, she may get anything from silence to pained and bored attention. The husband's responsibility to the marriage at this point is to learn to listen with interest. What she says may not be earthshaking from his point of view. Her conversation may reveal chiefly a need to talk to someone on an adult level, to communicate, to feel that her husband cares enough about her to listen.

Husbands frustrate wives *by their preoccupation with interests outside the home;* their work, sports, or any of the activities in which men engage. When most or virtually all of the husband's time is spent on non-domestic interests, and he fails to maintain an equal interest in what goes on in the home, his wife may feel frustrated. She may interpret his attitude as a lack of concern for her, since the home is an extension of her personality. Her exclusion from his outside life can threaten her sense of security.

Husbands frustrate wives *by failing to understand that "little things," as he sees them, are often big things to her.* The husband who is unsentimental may not remember birthdays, anniversaries, and special occasions. They may seem to be trivial to him, but to her they are important. Nations have special holidays commemorating important events. Christmas and Easter are commemorative occasions. Individuals and families, too, need to commemorate special days, to relive some of the significant events of the past. Men who think of anniversaries as unimportant simply refuse to recognize the valid emotional needs of others. A simple sense of doing the appropriate thing, of bringing happiness to each other, is a requisite for any happy marriage.

There are other areas where the sense of values differs between men and women. A husband not given to tinkering and puttering about the house may feel utterly frustrated by his wife's insistence upon some simple household repair job. To him it seems insignificant. To her it is important. This is a large part of her world. Furthermore, whether she is aware of it or not, she needs to know that he cares about the home and her. His willingness to undertake the task gives her a sense of security.

I was present when a husband and wife were arguing good-naturedly about the yard work. She wanted him to mow the lawn, and he insisted that it would have to be done by a gardener. He said, "I am willing to pay to have it done, but I will not do it myself." She said, "But I want *you* to do it!" Intrigued, I asked her, "Are you aware of your reason for wanting him to mow the lawn, rather than having the gardener do it?" She said, "Sure. It gives me a sense of security to see him working around the house!" He smiled. "I'll give you a sense of security in other ways, but I will not mow the lawn." The significance of their conversation lies not in the question of who mows the lawn, but in her awareness that she derives a sense of security from his being involved personally in the home. He did manifest a strong concern in other ways, perhaps far more than the average husband.

Men frustrate women *by their incapacity to understand the somewhat more volatile emotions of their wives*. Women often have strong mood swings, and may be depressed or made happy by events which would not affect a man. He may interpret these variations as evidence of emotional instability. Husbands are often incapable of understanding the therapy involved in a good cry. In our groups men sometimes come to realize for the first time that women are geared on an entirely different emotional basis, and they learn how to cope with the ups and downs of their wives' moods.

There are countless other variations. Any wife could supply a far longer list, depending upon her particular emotional needs and the type of man she married. Women do not understand themselves, and there is no point in the male's attempting this impossible task. But husbands can learn to understand and accept women's *needs* without needing to understand women.

The more basic ways women frustrate men appear to be the following:

Women frustrate their husbands *by being, or appearing to be dominant*. Few if any women ever see themselves as dominant personalities, yet the psychological tests used by many of our groups reveal a growing tendency on the part of women to dominate. During a three-year period, when nearly ten thousand persons took the personality inventories, the following facts were discovered:

50.2% of the women were significantly more dominant than their husbands.

41.1% of the women scored higher on aggression than their husbands.

10.3% of the women scored higher on *both* dominance and aggression than their husbands.

In essence, dominance is the inner urge to control people or circumstances, and aggression is the inner urge to change them. Neither of these personality traits is "good" or "bad" for either a man or woman, but in general it can be said that a too-passive husband tends to frustrate his wife by lacking in "drive," and a too-dominant or aggressive wife frustrates her husband by trying to control or change him. This tendency in a wife usually reminds the man, at an unconscious level, of his mother, making him feel like a little boy again. He may react against this feeling of helplessness with hostility or by retreating, both of which frustrate his wife.

This rather remarkable phenomenon, contributing in large measure to marital distress, is becoming more pronounced. In an effort to achieve equality, many women appear to have driven past their destination. They often end up competing with men, quite unconsciously of course. Men do not want to compete with women. They do not, as a general rule, reject intellectual women, as many women believe. They resent *the manner* in which many intellectual women argue, defend their position, and otherwise seek to outwit the male. Intellectual women *who accept their role fully* do not have this tendency to compete.

When a woman does not fully accept her feminine role at an unconscious level, there is an almost invariable tendency to compete with the male, and to try to outwit him. Men do not enjoy fighting or competing with women.

As women in our culture become more and more dominant they rear sons who tend to be passive. The passive son usually marries a dominant woman. In general, the sons in such a home will tend to be passive, the daughters dominant.

Knowingly or unknowingly, the average young woman

wants to marry a man who is strong and gentle. She may mistake his quietness for strength, and find later that she has married a passive male. In her efforts to force him to assert himself, she may succeed in doing nothing more than frustrating him. He feels dominated. His own passivity is as great a barrier to a happy marriage as her dominance, although many couples do have a successful marriage where there is a dominant wife and a passive male.

Women tend to think of dominance in terms of being domineering. On the contrary, some of the most dominant women are gentle and anything but authoritative, at least to all outward appearances. Many women dominate with gentle persistence. Some do it with an excess of oversolicitude, which the male interprets as dominance. Dominance is simply the tendency to control; and whether this is effected with a high hand and a loud voice or with quiet determination, the net results are very much the same.

A man related an experience bearing on this theme. He had saved for a long time to buy his wife a mink stole for their wedding anniversary, and he wanted to be sure to get her the kind she wanted. One evening as they were driving somewhere together he brought up the subject by asking her how much a good mink stole would cost. Just then he passed a turn he should have taken, and she said with considerable asperity, "What's the matter with you? Didn't you see that road sign back there?" He was frozen, emotionally immobilized. He suddenly became aware of all the times when she had used the same tone of voice, implying he was something less than bright, and his interest in the mink stole vanished.

He said later, "An emotionally mature person would have shrugged it off and would have gone on with the discussion. I was no more emotionally mature than she was. I simply lost all interest in the mink stole. It was not an effort to punish her. I just didn't feel like buying a mink stole for a wife who made a big issue over whether I had missed a turn in the road. I never did get it for her."

What he was reacting to, of course, was not the isolated incident, but the accumulated pressure of her dominant attitude through the years. It could be argued with some validity that both were wrong — the wife for adopting a hostile and dominant attitude, and the husband for reacting in an immature fashion. There remains the stubborn and ineradicable fact that women do frustrate men with a tendency toward dominance.

Women frustrate their husbands *by a tendency to become emotional in a discussion*. The husband who has some, or considerable, fear of his emotions dreads any discussion which could end in an argument involving strong feelings. If he wants a calm discussion and it erupts into an emotion-laden argument, he may retreat, not with the feeling of having been defeated, but with a distaste for the whole business of marriage. There is no question of "rightness" or "wrongness" involved here. The wife may be no more able to keep her emotions under control than he is to handle his fear of his emotions.

Women frustrate men when they *refuse to abandon the romantic dreams of girlhood*. A woman who has been married for some eighteen years had discovered from her evaluation slips that she was considerably more dominant and aggressive than her husband. In one group session she said, smiling a little as she did so, "I would like to have married a man who is very strong, and yet very gentle. He would be strong enough to put me in my place when I get out of line, but understanding and sensitive enough to know when I need to have my own way in certain areas. He would be tolerant of my occasional outbursts and emotional tantrums, and wise enough to see that I need a good cry. He would just pat me and console me without bothering to argue with me."

She went on at considerable length describing this paragon of virtue, strength and understanding, while her husband sat listening intently. When she had finished he said with a trace of bitterness, "There *was* someone like that once, but they crucified Him between two thieves!" He was not being irreverent, just perceptive. The group laughed, and even the wife, who sensed intellectually at least that her girlish dreams were unrealistic, laughed with them.

Then she had a sudden flash of insight: "If I had ever found such a man as that, what in the world would he see in me!" She had found her own answer to the adolescent dream of marrying a combination father-figure, lover, saint, and handyman. She had lived with a man for nearly twenty years whom she had, she said, picked out for herself; yet she still had her girlish dreams of the knight on a white horse.

Women frustrate their husbands with *a tendency to attack, often on issues which men feel are unimportant.* Karl Menninger writes about this characteristic:

> More painful to the man are those innumerable attacks upon his masculinity which the frustrated wife inflicts in the course of the daily routine of life — neglecting, reproaching . . . criticizing, ridiculing, interfering with pet hobbies and habits, playing the martyr, and giving the impression of being the victim of the husband's suspicion or cruelty. It seems invidious to make such a list, which must necessarily be not only incomplete, but equally applicable to husbands. . . . All the techniques available to a woman who is unconsciously hostile toward her husband she will use against him. He will react to them; they will evoke in him still more pronounced evidences of his own semi-controlled hates, and he will modify his infantile pattern of hostility in such a way as most comfortably to meet and defend himself against his wife's attacks. Because he is bound to her by law, by convention, or by his own passivity, he may remain within the bonds of matrimony, but he will find satisfactions for his frustrated love elsewhere. If he does not, his own self-destructiveness will overcome him. . . .[13]

One aspect of the problem was highlighted admirably in a letter written by a frustrated wife to Abigail Van Buren, who conducts a syndicated advice column. The woman wrote:

> "Dear Abby: My problem is getting my husband to be a man! I don't mean for him to be cruel, but if he would just show me that he is the boss I would be so much happier. I constantly try to get the better of him, but deep down I don't really want to win the battle. Why are men too dumb to know this? I am tired of making all the decisions and being the strong one. . . . Every time we disagree I secretly pray for his victory.
> Sign me, The Strong One."

Karen Horney describes girls who "cannot love a 'weak' man because of their contempt for any weakness; but neither can they cope with a 'strong' man because they expect their partner always to give in. Hence what they secretly look for is the hero, the superstrong man, who at the same time is so weak that he will bend to all their wishes without hesitation."[14]

A variation of this inner conflict experienced by such women is illustrated by the unconscious tactics of a certain type of woman who, as Karen Horney describes her, "marries a man because his existing or potential success appeals to her."

Since in our culture a wife participates to some degree in her husband's success, this may give her some satisfaction, as long as the success lasts. But she is in a conflict situation: she loves her husband for his success, and at the same time she hates him for it; she wants to destroy it but is inhibited because ... she wants to enjoy it vicariously by participating in it. Such a wife may betray her wish to destroy her husband's success ... by destroying his equanimity through enervating quarrels, by undermining his self-confidence through an insidious disparaging attitude. . . . All these destructive activities go on under the camouflage of love and admiration.[15]

A problem faced by both husbands and wives was illustrated by a young groom-to-be, waiting in my study for the wedding ceremony to begin. He appeared relaxed and leaned over to pick out a book to read. First he selected one titled *Man Against Himself*. He glanced through it briefly and put it down. Then he picked up *The Art of Loving*, looked at it for a moment, and finally settled back with *How to Live With a Neurotic*. In a sense all of us have neurotic tendencies which mar the marriage relationship. A neurotic can be loosely defined as "a person who is unreasonably bothered," or "one who consistently over-reacts."

The solution can be found in a serious attempt to apply the principles given us by the Apostle Paul in the thirteenth chapter of First Corinthians. In part he says, "Love is patient and kind ... Love does not insist on its own way; it is not irritable or resentful ... Love ... endures all things." Where love is seen not simply as a romantic attachment but as a lifelong effort to be "very patient and kind," the marriage can succeed.

10. FIGHTING BATTLES YOU'VE ALREADY WON

> Nearly all neuroses and psychoses manifest themselves as faults in human relationships. Only a group-to-person relationship can heal such faults. —*Howard E. Collier*

THE story is told of a deep sea diver who was walking around in his heavy diving suit investigating a wreck on the ocean floor. Above him was the mother ship to which he was connected by an air-hose. After he had been on the bottom for some time he heard over his intercom the anguished cry, "Come up at once! The ship is sinking!"

Robert, a dynamic minister who holds an important position in his denomination, was once faced with something of the same situation. As a boy he had grown up in a home where the father refused to support the family, and finally deserted them. His father had never offered him any encouragement. On the contrary he derided all of Robert's childhood accomplishments. Thrown more or less on his own at an early age, Robert left home and later joined a nearby church, partly because he needed social contact and acceptance, and partly because he responded naturally to religion. He had an unusual talent for leadership, but the very conservative minister disapproved strongly of some of the ideas the young man was putting into operation in the youth program. In the ensuing controversy Robert was told that he could no longer be a member of the church, that he was a disturbing force, and that he could never be accepted by any other church of that denomination. The boy had no way of knowing that this was not true, and at that point felt himself to be

149

thoroughly and completely rejected by both family and church.

At the age of sixteen he got a job in San Diego, California. Because he was under-age he could not secure a hotel room; and knowing of no other place to stay, he spent his nights in the park, sleeping on a bench. Quite often he was discovered by police, was awakened and was told that he was violating the law. He would then go to some other area of the park and try to get some sleep. Nearby in the park there was a zoo, and from time to time he could hear the animals snarling. His dreams were filled with nightmares in which escaped animals were attacking him.

Here, then, was a boy who had felt utterly unloved at home, rejected by his church, and now he was not even allowed to sleep peacefully in a public park. Human beings react differently to adversity, and fortunately Robert had sufficient creative aggression to face his difficulties. He did well at his job, and finally went back to school. Eventually he began, rather tentatively, to attend a church, and discovered one day, to his intense surprise, that what he had been told by his former pastor was completely untrue. He was made welcome, he united with the church, and became active in the youth program.

Eventually he decided to enter the ministry. He enrolled in a seminary, and upon graduation received a call to a large church. This was a rather remarkable thing to happen to a fresh young graduate, and gave evidence of the tremendous ability which he possessed. After a relatively short pastorate he was asked to assume the highest administrative office of his denomination, where he is providing excellent leadership.

In the case of both the diver and Robert, it was really the problems of those in authority over them, not their own problems, that caused them to be pulled off the job.

But rejection always leaves scars. Robert has had regular nightmares in which animals chase him. He has had recurring dreams of walking down the main street unclothed — a not uncommon dream, incidentally. He has dreamed of showing up to speak to large assemblies of people, only to find that he had forgotten his sermon notes and had no notion of what he was to talk about. Then he would discover that the congregation had all walked out. Often in his dreams he would shout aloud in terror.

There must have been other outward manifestations of his inner anxiety, because one day his wife insisted firmly that he was going to see a psychiatrist. He shared with the psychiatrist the story of his life, and the gist of the psychiatrist's comment was, "You're still fighting battles you've already won. You are trying to prove to your father that you *can* succeed in spite of all his dire predictions that you'd come to no good. You are trying to prove to that authoritarian pastor who rejected you that you do amount to something. Your frenzied activity and ceaseless drive to accomplish something worthwhile is due in part to your need to prove to them, and to yourself, that you can succeed. You've won that battle. Why not stop fighting?"

Robert reported that this was a great revelation to him. As a compulsive worker with enormous drive, he had rationalized his excessive busy-ness. There was much to be done, his responsibilities were tremendous, and there were innumerable calls on his time. Now he came to see that that there would always be more work than he could accomplish, more calls on his time than he could handle. Mere knowledge of this did not solve his problem, but it gave him a starting point for growth. The sharing with others of his true feelings of inferiority provided some release from the tension and started him on the road to a new sense of inner peace.

There is often a fine line between "being driven" and "driving." If one is driven by an inner compulsion originating in early feelings of inferiority, he is never in full command. Instead of driving, he is driven. If his goal is to make a fortune, having made it will give him no real satisfaction. He will need more, and more, and more.

One of the world's richest men was told by his father, "You'll never even be able to make a living!" Driven by an intense need to prove his father wrong, he was a millionaire by the time he was thirty. At fifty he had many millions. In his sixties he was one of the wealthiest men on earth; but, driven by an insatiable lust for more, he was unable to stop and enjoy his wealth. He said to a friend one day, "I wish I had taken time to learn how to get along better with people. I feel very inadequate socially." It would be safe to say that he is not likely to find any sense of peace or inner security, no matter how many millions he accumulates, unless he seeks the source of his compulsion, and instead of "being driven," discovers that he is fighting battles he has already won.

Jud, a delightful and highly competent man of about 35, shared with his group the inner compulsion which caused him to try to dominate every conversation and to top every story. He said, "I get home and I think, 'I did it again. I dominated the entire group,' and I hang my head in shame. Then I do the same thing the next time I am with people." In the group he was asked to share some of his earliest memories, and over a period of time he dredged up many partially buried incidents of his early childhood. They had lived on the wrong side of the tracks, as he put it. He did not always feel accepted in school by his associates.

As he came to see the source of his feelings of inadequacy, he ceased to blame himself. He did not blame his parents, his schoolmates, or anyone else. There was no one to blame. He saw that his responsibility was to accept himself as he was, and move on from there toward spiritual and emotional growth. We observed how, gradually, he tended less and less to dominate the group discussion. Since he was learning a greater degree of self-acceptance, he did not have the same deep need to win temporary acceptance and approval. It was as if he was carrying his own self-approval about with him, and did not need to pluck the sleeves of his associates with the unspoken plea, "Look fellows, I'm here too. Notice me. Accept me." He had stopped fighting battles he had already won.

Louise grew up in a home where the mother quietly ran the family; but the father appeared to do so. He was a rather ineffectual person who had a great deal to say, always in dogmatic tones; but it was mother who usually made the decisions. Louise felt a strong need to identify with her father and please him. But no matter what she did, she should have done it better, according to him. No household task she performed was ever done quite to his satisfaction. He criticized her, browbeat her, and ran her down; yet she kept on trying to please him, never sure that he loved her.

At thirty-five, still unmarried, Louise fell in love — "I guess it was love" — successively with three different alcoholics. Each was a pleasant, affectionate, delightful person. Each romance ended for one reason or another —

she was never quite sure just why. In one case she balked at the last minute; in another, the man kept postponing the wedding; and Louise finally came to a group for help. In her efforts to win the approval of each man, she had done everything she could to please them, to adapt, to secure the love her father had denied her.

In time she came to see that she was trying unconsciously to win, not a battle she had already won but a battle that could never be won. Her father was no longer living. Even had he lived, she could never have won his approval, for he had none to give anyone. But in each man she met, she was seeing her father and trying to win his approval. She saw in time how she had unconsciously chosen men who were dependent, and who sought a strong, mother-type figure to whom they could relate. Their dependent need for her evoked a sense of accomplishment in her. "Now at last someone needs me, someone approves of me," was her unconscious response, and she interpreted it as love. Louise finally discovered what her real problem was and came to terms with her deep need for love, learning self-acceptance through group acceptance.

Wendell's first experience with a group was at a retreat with fifty other people, among them half a dozen ministers, some group leaders, and members of a dozen or more churches. An Episcopal minister, Wendell introduced himself to the others by saying, "I am Father McCloud." During the sessions he sat in the farthest corner of the room, and from time to time shared some of his true feelings. At one point he said to one of the women, "For some reason you bother me. I suppose it's your very dominant manner. I just can't take dominant women." His smile only partially concealed the extent of his hostility. The group leader asked Wendell to share his feelings toward his mother. Reluctantly at first, and gradually with much more freedom, he told of the broken home from which he came, the ambivalent feelings he had toward his parents, and the deep resentment he felt toward his mother.

On subsequent days he spoke quite frankly of his rejection of certain women in the group. In each case it was someone who reminded him of his mother. He was aware intellectually of his reason for disliking these particular women, but feelings which have been a part of one for thirty or forty years do not yield instantly to intellectual arguments.

By the end of the retreat, Wendell was well liked by everyone. He was basically friendly, and when he got over being Father McCloud and became Wendell, a human being with problems like everyone else, he proved to be a delightful person. When he returned to his church he organized a group, then a second one, and from time to time attended a group for ministers where he proved to be a discerning and highly perceptive person.

A year later when Wendell arrived for the annual retreat, he was much more relaxed. He introduced himself to newcomers as "Wendell McCloud," dressed informally and, instead of sitting in the farthest corner as before, he chose a seat nearer the center. He participated easily, and no longer launched verbal attacks on women in the group.

In the short space of a year he had begun to come to terms with his long-buried hostility toward his mother and to women in general. He had begun to see that he had many different feelings toward women: he loved, feared, hated, and needed them. His marriage, which had ended in divorce, had not helped resolve his difficulties in this direction. Now that he could pin-point the origin of his mixed emotions toward women, and no longer blamed his mother for her mistakes, or himself for his anger, he was free to relate to women on an entirely different basis. Gone were the barbs cloaked in pleasantries. He had ceased to fight battles he had already won. The group had helped him see more clearly the source of his problem. No one had rebuked him for his hostile remarks to women in the group. He had been accepted just as he was, hostility and all, and he had become a different person.

It was at the same retreat that Ben, a quiet young man, expressed a desire to go for a walk with me on the beach. I waited for him to open up, but he was finding it difficult. Finally I said, "Did you feel that the group was a little hard on your wife yesterday?" His wife was an exceedingly dominant and aggressive young woman, and had unwittingly demonstrated a number of very masculine traits, as well as a tendency toward arrogance.

In response to my question Ben blurted out, "I can't tell you how much I hate my wife! And I feel so terribly guilty about feeling this way about her." This was an honest expression of his true feelings. I said, "I understand how you feel — and why you would feel guilty over harboring such feelings. Let's see if we can get to the root of it. Tell me about your mother."

His mother had been a dominant person, and unconsciously he had sought out a wife very much like her. He needed a strong woman in his life, but not this strong! As we talked about his feelings and his early life, he saw that it was not really his wife he hated so much as his own weakness and passivity. He saw too, as the group sessions continued, that there would be no quick, easy solution. He was the end product of his environment, as was she. Attitudes and reactions were firmly embedded. It would take time for him to give up his dependency and become a stronger person. It would take time for her to surrender some of her extreme aggressiveness and feel comfortable playing a less dominant role in their marriage.

As in most homes, theirs was not so much a vague marriage problem as a "person problem" — the problem of two persons trying to live together in harmony. Knowing that one *should* love, *should* forgive, *should* always be tender and understanding, is little help if there is a basic personality clash. In fact, our *shoulds* and *oughts* can become tyrants, producing guilt feelings without providing solutions.

As we parted after our walk on the beach my friend said, "I feel better already. In fact I don't feel as hostile as I did. Just sharing it, admitting it to someone, has robbed it of its intensity. I think that with the help of my group I can begin to grow toward a more mature reaction to life and show more tolerance and understanding to my wife, while she is growing toward the same goal of spiritual maturity."

Ben was not fighting a battle he had already won, but he was doing something similar: he was fighting with his mother, who was no longer on the scene. The buried hostility he had felt toward his dominant mother was now coming into consciousness. He was at last aware of his deep resentment and could admit it to himself, to God, and to a fellow-minister.

I was walking down the street with a young man of about thirty-five whom I had come to know only a short time before, when he said suddenly, "Wait a minute. Let's go in here." It was a jewelry store, and I waited while he looked at a dozen or more different rings. At one point I thought he had found just what he wanted, but finally he decided against the purchase and we left.

A few blocks farther along we paused to look at the display in another jeweler's window and went in. We spent about ten minutes there while he looked at rings and tried them on. Again he left without making a purchase.

Four times that day he stopped at jewelers to look at rings. Finally, I said, "Just what kind of a ring is it you're looking for? I noticed you already have a beautiful one on your left hand." He said, "Oh, I just like rings. They have always fascinated me."

Out of curiosity I asked, "Do you spend a lot of time looking at rings?"

"Yes, I go into every jewelry shop I can. I love rings. Anything wrong with that?"

"No," I said smiling, "it's a reasonably normal hobby. But there is a motive behind all of our actions. Would you like to try to find out why you are so fascinated by rings?"

"Sure, but I don't see anything neurotic about liking beautiful things."

I said, "Tell me about your earliest recollection of a ring, or rings."

He thought for a moment, and then said: "I had almost forgotten about it, but now that I think of it, my first experience with a ring was tragic. My father bought himself a beautiful ring. When I saw it I wanted one like it, but a kid my age had no reason to have such an expensive ring. I asked my dad if I could wear it to school just once. He agreed but said, 'You'll probably lose it.' And I did. I never found it, and my dad gave me a bad time about losing the one valuable piece of jewelry he had ever owned."

"So," I said, "you've been looking for the ring ever since!"

My friend was astounded. "And all these years I didn't know I was driven by a neurotic urge to find a lost ring. I just thought I liked rings. I did, really, but I didn't know why."

My friend was beset by a fairly harmless compulsion, from which he is now freed. At least he is free to collect rings or not to collect them. He is no longer driven by an unconscious urge to appease his father by finding the lost ring. His minor compulsion, expensive and time-consuming as it was, did not interfere seriously with his life. It illustrates, however, ways in which we can continue to fight battles already won or to continue a hopeless search for which there is no longer any need.

Norine, a member of one of our groups, made enormous spiritual growth during the first six months or so. She shared freely during the sessions and maintained a daily discipline of reading and prayer. The growth was evident and dramatic. Her mask began to disappear, and in its place there came to light a very lovely person. One evening she told the group that she had never had a satisfactory relationship with her father. She had wanted very much to feel loved by him, but had never achieved anything beyond a casual, rather distant relationship. This seemed to be a source of great concern to her.

One day she came to see me to share some things she did not care to discuss in the group. She told me that as long as she could remember she had been falling in love with different men. Even as a happily married woman, she found herself feeling physically attracted to other men — dozens of them, scores of them. She was unable to say whether it was love or mere physical attraction. Whatever it was, it was a powerful force, vastly more than a casual, flirting relationship.

I asked her to elaborate on her relationship with her father. It appeared that as a little girl she had done everything in her power to win her father's love but never felt that she had succeeded. "He just sort of ignored me," she concluded.

I asked her if she could see any relationship between her frustrated attempts to win her father's love, and her compulsive need to conquer men, or at least to win their affection. She saw it, of course.

"Now that you see the connection," I said, "you will not necessarily be free of the drive to attract, win and conquer men. But it need no longer be a compulsion over which you have no control. You will be able to control it — if you want to. You can be free now. At a subconscious level you were deeply disappointed by your relationship with your father, though at a conscious level you thought you were seeking something entirely different. You were driven. Now you can drive — if you wish. You are free to choose your course of action, whereas before you were in the power of a compulsion you could not understand, and which led only to a succession of unhappy incidents."

She made remarkable progress in the following year, and became forever freed of her compulsive need to "conquer" men.

It is difficult for many people to accept the fact that at least eighty per cent of our actions are motivated by unconscious inner needs. We like to feel that we are rational, intelligent beings in full control of our actions; but it has been demonstrated many times that most of our decisions are the result of totally unconscious drives. Having made the decision, we feel an immediate need to rationalize it, so that we can maintain our feeling that we always act on the basis of rational logical choice.

Robert had no way of knowing that his tremendous drive for achievement, which made him a compulsive worker, stemmed from a buried need to prove his worth to his father and to the minister who had humiliated him. Jud did not know until he sorted out his feelings in a group that his compulsive need to dominate a group sprang from his early childhood poverty. Louise did not know that in seeking a certain type of man, and balking at marriage, she was responding to impulses set in motion when she sought her father's approval. Wendell had little awareness that his hostility toward women sprang from an impaired relationship with his mother. Ben did not know that the hostility he felt for his wife was a carry-over from the time when he had identical feelings toward his mother.

My friend with the compulsion to buy rings had no way of knowing that his neurotic urge sprang from a buried need to appease his irate father. Norine, the young wife with a penchant for affairs, discovered that her need to conquer men was based upon a frustrating relationship with her father.

Are we responsible then? And if so, to what degree? This question is dealt with in detail in another chapter, but at this point we can emphasize the attitude of Jesus, who Himself did not condemn the sinner and commanded that we should not judge. He, whose purity of mind and purpose enabled Him to perceive the inner drives and motives of men, felt no need to judge. He dealt with the repentant sinner with infinite compassion. He prayed for those who took His life, "Father, forgive them; for they know not what they do."[1]

Only God could know how the countless cross-currents of environment, heredity, human will and human frailty, pride and inferiority, anxiety and stress have formed our lives and decisions. Only God can judge. We cannot.

We can, however, come to know ourselves at a much deeper level by developing ruthless honesty with ourselves, with others, and with God. Out of such honesty in a loving group can come insights which can make us more than we are, more like Christ, who accepts us as we are but longs for us to be more.

11. YOUR SELF-IMAGE

> In the world to come I will not be asked,
> "Why were you not Moses?" I shall be asked,
> "Why were you not Zusya?"   —*Rabbi Zusya*

THE conscious and unconscious feelings you have about yourself constitute your self-image. This self-image you will act out in life. You will always tend to act in harmony with it.

The Bible recognizes this. The author of Proverbs writes, "For as he thinketh in his heart, so is he."[1] When the Bible uses the term "heart" it refers to the emotions, among other things, "the center of our being." Modern psychology confirms the insight of Proverbs: Whatever you feel yourself to be at the center of your emotional nature, that is what you really are, existentially, and your actions will be in harmony with your self-concept.

In Proverbs 4:23 we read, "Keep thy heart with all diligence; for out of it are the issues of life";[2] or, as we might paraphrase it, "Watch very carefully what you put into your unconscious mind, for it will determine your very destiny."

The ideas of ourselves which our parents and other early authority figures gave us have a great deal to do with our self-image. One group member with a very weak self-image reported that he could not recall any praise which either parent had ever given him. He did recall, however, that his father — a very austere and demanding figure — told him over and over. "You'll never amount to anything. You're just no good. That's all there is to it;

161

you'll never succeed." As a small child he had no alternative but to accept this verdict. It required many years of struggle to establish a valid concept of himself.

The young child has no clear picture of himself. He sees himself only in the mirror of his parents' evaluation of himself. "Have I been a good boy, Mommy?" is partly the desire for reassurance and love, and partly to check with the ultimate authority to gain some concept of "goodness" or "badness." A child who is told repeatedly that he is a bad boy, or is lazy, or no good, or stupid, or shy, or clumsy, will tend to act out this picture which the parent or some other authority figure has given him. He tends to believe and act out what he has been told. The emotional structure of the child is formed by the time he is six years of age, probably much earlier, in the opinion of many psychologists. Some insist that what happens in the first six months of life plays an enormous part in the developing emotional structure of the child. Subsequent events affect, alter, redirect earlier impressions, but cannot completely erase them.

For instance the inordinately shy child, made so by some subtle mixture of hereditary factors upon which environment has impinged with still greater force, may in later life become a seemingly extroverted personality. Associates may term such a person gay, witty, outgoing and anything but shy. But at the center of his being he can still feel the shyness, the tendency to retire from close contact with others. He has "reconditioned a conditioned reflex" by acting contrary to traits he dislikes in himself. But in some degree he is inwardly the same shy, retiring person he was as a child. He is acting differently, and may feel reasonable comfortable with people, but the ancient fear is there, buried deep within. The conflict is sufficiently resolved to enable him to live a creative, rather than a defeated life.

Fortunately for us, we need not be forever the victims of all our earlier conditioning. We can change. People do overcome handicaps. We are not the blind victims of either heredity or environment, with no power to alter our destinies. There is a divine inner capacity which enables us to be more than we are. It is important, however, that we do not deceive ourselves, and that we recognize the deep inner feelings planted there long ago, and which still reside within. Why bother? Simply because self-honesty is essential to honesty with God. We cannot know God any better than we are willing to know ourselves. If we are afraid of our own deep inner feelings, we will to the same degree fear God, though even this fear may be repudiated and buried deeply with the other emotions.

Paul shared with a group his irrational feeling that he might be fired any day. His employer had never offered any serious criticism of his work, and he was, he felt, turning in a relatively satisfactory performance. "I know it's irrational, but I simply feel inwardly that I could be fired at any time. I won't even take a vacation, partly because I don't feel I've earned one."

Paul had not participated in group dicussions for the first few weeks. He seemed to fear the possibility of rejection. When he was finally able to share some of his feelings about himself he began to discover emotions he had never dared admit before, even to himself. He dug around among half-buried memories and eventually discovered intensely hostile feelings toward both his authoritarian father, and his mother, whose religious convictions seemed to be a mixture of fear and rigid moralism. He recalled a deep sense of failure, of fear of punishment, of displeasing his parents and of failing to perform satisfactorily. The sum total of his earliest environment had given him a picture of himself as physically weak, mentally below average, and a person destined to experience almost certain failure.

Far from being incompetent, he was a very able person; but his own self-image, given him by overly strict parents and a very outgoing older brother, was that of an inadequate person. He was now in his thirties, acting in perfect harmony with his own self-image — frightened of his employer, and constantly passive, fearful of impending disaster.

By dredging up his early feelings about his environment, Paul learned that there was no reason to blame his parents, who had done the best they could. He came to see that it was not simply what they did, but how he reacted to them that determined his self-image. Within a year he had made such progress in self-understanding that he was leading his group, and revealing rare insight into the problems of others. His self-image was changing. He began to see himself as a different kind of person. He no longer felt overwhelmed by the early childhood picture of himself. To some degree the earlier feelings will always be there, but he is *now acting in harmony with an entirely new self-image.*

The childhood self-image need not be permanent, a kind of albatross hung about our necks to blight the rest of life. On the contrary we can, with the help of a group, discover our highest potential and act in harmony with an entirely different self-image. The reason this is best achieved in a group is that the loving acceptance of the group members, coupled with utter honesty, helps us to see ourselves as we are, and as we can be. If we have been crippled by having a weak self-image which bears no real relationship to the true inner capabilities which others see in us, the group can give us a true picture of what we can become.

"Where two or three are gathered in my name," Jesus said, "there am I in the midst of them."[3] This is often quoted by people who have not the slightest idea what it means, who believe that Jesus said it but who have never experienced it. Jesus was God in the flesh, when He walked the earth. When He left the earth He said, "I am with you always."[4] God in Christ is willing to be present in power wherever two or three or a dozen of His followers are gathered in genuine Christian love.

His manifest presence seems to be conditional. Simply that two or more Christians are talking about a baseball game, or meet in a committee session, does not necessarily mean that Christ is there in power. But when a few of His followers are willing to relax their tensions, prejudices, and barriers, and turn their attention to Jesus Christ, He is there. The reality and intensity of their love for one another seems to be one of the conditions for His presence to be felt. In such a setting honesty can flourish. The group can learn the value of "speaking the truth in love."

It was in just such a group that Jesus gave Simon a new self-image. Jesus was alone with the twelve, and suddenly asked them, "Who do you say that I am?" Simon replied, "You are the Christ, the Son of the Living God!" Where-upon Jesus answered, "Blessed are you, Simon Bar-Jona! . . . And I tell you, you are Peter, and on this rock I will build my church . . ."[5] In this dramatic way Jesus changed Simon's name to Simon Peter, which means Simon the Rock.

This was said to a man who had been, and continued to

be for a time, notoriously weak and vacillating, a man of passionate affirmations and vehement denials. In giving him a new name Jesus was not implying that unstable Peter had already become a towering rock of strength. Rather He was giving him a new self-image which would become reality in the course of time. He was saying, as it were, "Men may see in you evidences of great emotional instability. You are only too well aware of this, and you hate it in yourself. But I see the true Simon within. This is what you *can* be, what you *will* be — a Rock. Instability will give way to stability, weakness to strength." And Peter began to mature into the new self that Jesus pictured for him.

There are untapped resources in all of us. We can love more, be more, achieve more, and acquire more quiet inner strength. When we learn to cooperate with the divine laws of God, and become willing to have His best for us, when we no longer fear His will but seek it as the supreme good for our lives, we can believe what God already believes about us — that we can be vastly more than we are. We can come to have a new self-image and act in harmony with that new concept.

For forty years Dave lived in complete harmony with the self-image which his father had given him. He told his group: "My father told me hundred of times, 'You're no good.' And I wasn't. I cheated and stole. I was caught by the cops, and my father always bailed me out. He had plenty of money, and I learned two things about him very early in life — that he thought I was no good, and that no matter what I did, he would bail me out of any difficulty. I got to feeling that I was not only no good but that I was immune to punishment of any sort.

"Now at the age of forty I am a no-good gambler and a liar. But I am beginning to get a new picture of myself. I see that I need not act the rest of my life in harmony with that false picture my father gave me of myself. I am still driven by a compulsive need to gamble; but I no longer lie as an accepted way of life. I can tell the truth to my wife and to myself and my customers. I am beginning to feel a sense of guilt over things I always accepted as normal."

The power of God was beginning to stir in Dave, and through loving acceptance of the group he came to have a much better concept of himself. He is still growing. One seldom discards the habits, attitudes and self-image of forty years in a matter of days or weeks. Dave learned the meaning of honesty with himself and with God and became able to open up in the group without fear of rejection. As his fear of rejection lessened, his own capacity for self-acceptance improved. He is on the way.

Earl is a minister with the barest suggestion of a stutter. He is a good speaker, and the slight pause he makes in order to search for a synonym or to take a quick breath actually enhances his style of speaking. It was not always so. He shared with me the fact that his parents had been rigid and demanding. They were determined that none of their children would ever become puffed up or conceited from being praised, and consequently they never commended their children for anything. There was an abundance of criticism but no counter-balancing with warm praise and acceptance.

Inevitably Earl grew up with a weak self-image. Fortunately he had enough aggression to react rather strongly to his environment. When freed of parental control he began to develop a feeling that he could succeed, despite the oft-repeated statement that he would come to no good. Gradually he revised his self-image, and in time he became a highly effective personality. A less determined person might have become resigned to being timid and passive.

There are many factors at work in any family. There is the matter of the place in the family constellation — whether one is an only child, a second, third, or fifth. There may be unspoken love mingled with seeming rejection. The family atmosphere may be accepting, despite a lack of demonstrativeness. In the case of Earl, there was also the degree to which he identified with his father and the kind of person his father was. All of these variables make it impossible ever to judge or evaluate fully a family relationship. Thus there can be no blame, either of family or of self, but only the question: where am I at the moment, and how can I permit the grace of God to flow into my life to a greater degree so that I shall become more than I am?

Roger, a young minister on the staff of a local church, could not carry a tune and never took part in congregational singing. It was a source of great embarrassment to him to be the only person in the group unable to sing. He told the senior minister one day the origin of his difficulty.

"It must have been in the third or fourth grade," he

said. "The teacher was preparing the class for participation in some school function and wanted us to show up well. We were to sing, and she drilled us diligently. She finally heard a few discordant notes from one side of the room. There were three of us who were not singing to her satisfaction. She separated us from the others, and put us in the rear of the room, saying, 'Those in the back are the sparrows. You children here in front are my song birds'."

It seems incredible that a teacher could be so insensitive; yet it happened. Roger never tried to sing again. He had been told by an authority figure that he could not sing, and he accepted that verdict. Now at twenty-five he was certain that he couldn't carry a tune. But in his work with young people he felt a great need to be able to lead the singing, so he consulted the choir director, who assured him that it would be quite possible for him to learn to sing. In a few sessions with the director he discovered that he was not tone deaf as he had always supposed. He began to participate in congregational singing, and eventually he led the singing for large groups of adults and did excellently. He told me, however, that after each such experience he was emotionally exhausted. This of course diminished with time.

Roger had been the victim of a conditioned reflex. The word "music" and "singing" had always left him with deep feelings of inferiority. As an adult he simply reconditioned the conditioned reflex by the laborious process of doing the thing he feared. The James-Lange theory gives us the clue to this. In essence it is this: If we check or change the expression of an emotion, we thereby change the emotion itself. Put another way, if we "act as if" we feel a given way, in time our feelings catch up with our actions. Roger began to "act as if" — to pretend to himself that he did not fear music or the sound of his own voice, and in time he began to shed the old fear. Gradually he gained a feeling of confidence in himself. The trepidation which he felt at first when leading the singing was a holdover from the past, which gradually diminished as time went on. He had changed his self-image.

Many people protest that to act contrary to their feelings makes them feel hypocritical. As a young minister in my first pastorate I felt some of this when I first tried to apply the James-Lange theory. When calling in a home I found myself wanting to talk about the church. I was quite uninterested in the seemingly trivial details of the lives of the people whom I visited. I was a poor conversationalist, with a strong dislike for small talk. This was a distinct handicap, for when calling on members, I found that *they* wanted to talk about things that interested them — their children, a new piece of furniture, the little incidents of the day. I had read about William James' "act as if" principle, and I decided to see if it actually worked.

Upon entering a home I began deliberately to pay attention to the children, to notice details, such as the pictures on the mantel, antiques — everything which seemed of importance to the family, and to comment on these things. I even tried to enjoy the cats which shed hair on my dark suit. At first I felt uncomfortable and hypocritical: after all, I wasn't genuinely interested in these details. I wanted to get down to the really "important" subjects, such as their relationship to God and the church, their problems, and the responsibilities I hoped they would accept in the church. But in time I began to enjoy my experiment and felt less hypocritical and insincere. Before long I was discovering a genuine interest in the details of their lives — the picture of the young sailor on the mantel, the small child who wanted attention, the cat that wanted to jump up on the chair — because they were important to the people on whom I was calling.

Ultimately it became second nature. I ceased to think of myself solely as a budding young prophet possessed of transcendent truth which must be proclaimed to an expectant world. I came to be genuinely interested in people and in anything which mattered to them. It was not simply a new technique but a new self-image. I began to "see" myself as a different kind of person and to act in harmony with my new image.

There is a "goal-seeking mechanism," as it were, within each of us, very much like an automatic pilot. God has given us this impulse; it needs only to be understood and directed. It operates something like this:

With the conscious mind one may settle on some desirable goal. It may be the securing of an education, the ability to make friends, a personality change, or even a material possession. This is determined by the conscious mind and is the result of our ambitions, desires, and sense of values. One may desire with all of his heart a worthy or unworthy goal. What he seeks may be destructive or creative.

However, the universe is so geared as to aid us in reaching worthy and creative goals. "The stars in their courses" are on the side of one who dares to dream great dreams if they are consistent with God's will.

It is only as we spend time in honest soul-searching in the presence of God that we dare to dream these great dreams and ask Him to help us attain them. For one it may be to have a happier home; for another, to secure a life mate. One may long to serve God and man in some significant way. He may want to be rid of obvious personality handicaps. Whatever the goal, once we *know* that it is within the will of God, the next thing to do is to visualize it. See it clearly on a mental screen and hold it there day after day, month after month. It must be more than wishful thinking. It must become a kind of quiet obsession. Not in doubt and fearfulness, but in humility one offers this goal to God with the understanding that if this is an unworthy or inadequate goal it will be discarded. One who honestly wants the will of God, and who sees His will as involving the supreme good, can dare to set goals beyond anything he has ever dreamed of before. "In everything God works for good with those who love him. . . ."[6] "God is at work within you, both to will and to work for his good pleasure."[7] This tells us that God is at work, not just in outer space, but in our inmost being, helping us to will the highest and best, and adding His power to our human capacities.

Another promise tells us that God "is able to do far more abundantly than all that we ask or think."[8] The danger is not that we shall ask too much but that our dreams will be too small. "Without faith it is impossible to please him."[9] He is pleased when His children dare to set worthy goals.

When through prayer and meditation, we come to the inner assurance that we are working together with God toward a worthy goal, the goal-seeking mechanism goes into operation. Let us say that you desire to become a far more effective person, rid of your fears or feelings of inadequacy; that you want to learn how to give and receive love; that you wish to become capable of being happy, and effective. Your old self-image may tell you that you are inadequate, fearful, and basically an unhappy and ineffective person. If you visualize that vividly and constantly, your goal-seeking impulse will see to it that you continue to remain just that! On the other hand, if you can "see" yourself as potentially a highly effective personality, able to give and receive love, and to achieve far more than you have up to this time — if you set this goal-seeking mechanism to work, all of your inner forces, and the power of God working in you, are available to bring it into reality.

When Jesus gave Simon a new self-concept symbolized by the name Peter — a rock — He set in motion this divine inner mechanism. God was now at work in Simon, helping him to become Simon Peter, Simon the Rock of towering strength.

Several conditions must be met to make this effective. There must be strong motivation. There must be nothing wish-washy about the desire. It can become a reality only as one makes this a supreme concern. Second, one must work at it. There is no cheap grace, no easy path to spiritual maturity, no celestial Santa Claus to grant our childish petitions. It is work. The work one does is simply that of keeping the new self-image vividly on the mental screen, and holding it there consistently for weeks and months. The work involves screening our desire through the fine mesh of God's will, and visualizing the change as already accomplished. One must keep the visualized dream vividly on the screen. God does the rest, through this remarkable goal-striving mechanism which He has built into us.

This is no cheap and easy way to "get things." You will need to spend half an hour a day in quiet meditation, "seeing" vividly the person you want to become. In this quiet time with God you will not beg Him to change you or others. Rather you will affirm that your desired self-image can become a reality because God has promised it. It must be a self-image that is in harmony with the teachings of Jesus.

This inner mechanism works for us, striving toward the goal we have set. Brother Lawrence has said that those in harmony with the will of God "go forward even in sleep." God is pleased when we dare to dream, to aspire, to long to be more, to do more, to love more. When you dare to see yourself as more than you are, with far more capacity than you ever dreamed of, you can become that person.

A group member wrote, concerning her struggle to acquire a new self-image:

My biggest problem was a lack of self-acceptance and a proper self-love. I am coming to believe that I am as worthy of receiving love and joy in life as others, and that I don't have to be perfect in order to be acceptable.... Also, I have come to see that I can be myself without any apologies. I don't have to fit a certain pattern of behavior in order to please people; all I have to do is to be myself while I use God's guidance for directing my activities.

I wonder how I could have managed without the marvelous help and new insight into religion which I have received from this group. It has given me a completely new life. As I look back I feel that my emotional upset really caused my cancer. I now understand that Jesus' healing of the sick was not just a "fairy tale" or imaginative exaggeration, but the natural consequence of inner peace and power — a peace which I, too, am coming to have.

12. WHAT TAKES PLACE IN A GROUP?

The unexamined life is not worth living.
—*Socrates*

THERE are many kinds of groups and group discussions, each with its place and purpose. Some of the different types follow:

1. *The Committee.* This is normally a group of several persons who have a function to perform on behalf of a larger organization to which they belong. The committee may be assigned, for instance, the duty of planning a social event or some special program. They deal not so much with general principles as with specific details. There may be differences of opinion, the sharing of information, and finally, if all goes well, the committee will decide on a course of action.

Committees do not always work rapidly. They can be frustrating. There is the story of a minister who stood in the Smithsonian Institution looking at Lindbergh's plane, *The Spirit of St. Louis.* A little old lady in the group said admiringly, "And just think, he did it all alone." The minister, apparently the victim of many a church committee, said wryly, "He would never have made it if he had done it with a committee!" This is probably quite true, for committees tend to adopt the conservative and traditional method, which in many situations is precisely what is needed. For a unique project, requiring a creative and dynamic spirit, one person can often achieve vastly more. But there is a specific place for committees.

2. *The Discussion Group* is usually drawn together by a common area of interest to be studied, such as racial intolerance, plans for community betterment, or Bible study.

The sharing of ideas and concepts in such a group can prove stimulating and helpful. There is give and take and the airing of opinions; and often a kind of corporate opinion evolves.

There is a common tendency to believe that a discussion group engaged in talking about the Bible, commitment, or involvement in important movements, will somehow produce spiritual growth. There is, however, no assurance that such discussions automatically produce spiritual maturity. Such groups often share mere opinions. An intellectual debate about the Bible or Christian principles has little to do with spiritual growth. In fact, members of such groups often safely sidestep basic problems, such as their own barriers to emotional and spiritual maturity. A group of this nature can become a modified debating forum, tacitly agreeing to avoid sharing true feelings. It is much less threatening to deal with opinions than with basic feelings.

3. *The Bible Study Group.* Traditionally minded persons assume more or less automatically that if we can get people into Bible study groups, their spiritual growth would be assured. Important as Bible study is, the truth remains that the mere acquisition of Bible facts does not guarantee spiritual growth. One may be able to recite all the books of the Bible, recount the journeys of the Apostle Paul, and quote many Bible verses without effecting the slightest change in his spiritual nature. The Pharisees did not lack knowledge of the Law, yet they were evidently the chief group Jesus condemned! Nor did they lack moral uprightness. They were ethical, decent, religious, knowledgeable social and religious leaders. But their attitudes were all wrong. They never seemed to have taken a good look at themselves. They were completely satisfied with outward morality and a thorough knowledge of the Old Testament.

This need not disparage Bible study, for the Bible is the basic source of our spiritual knowledge. However, if the minister of your church announces a series of Bible studies, the chances are the place will not be crowded. As one minister put it, "People say to me frequently, 'I wish I knew more about the Bible' but when I announce a Bible study course they stay away in droves!"

4. *Prayer Groups.* A generation or two ago church members came together in small groups for prayer. These sessions were often highly effective, and startling things were frequently achieved. There are many groups of this kind in operation today, ranging from the traditional Wednesday night affairs — often a mixture of Bible study and highly unedifying prayers by people who are committed to this type of traditionalism — to dynamic groups of Christians who gather for effective prayer. Where these sessions are vital it is always because the traditional approach has been abandoned; and genuine spiritual growth has taken place in the lives of the persons involved.

One difficulty with most prayer groups is that many Christians have little idea of what prayer is. They assume that prayer consists of telling God about the problems here on our little planet, informing Him of the needs of this person and that cause, and asking Him to do something about it. When little or nothing happens as a result, they assume that either they lacked faith or that God does not answer prayer.

Christians as a whole believe in prayer, and even non-Christians will often pray in a crisis. But if announcement is made in the average Christian church that a prayer group is being formed, the attendance is disheartening. Still more discouraging is the fact that if an outstanding authority in the field of prayer is brought in to conduct a course of study in how to pray, only a handful will be present in most churches. We have then the anomaly of Christians believing in prayer, being unable to pray effectively, and being unwilling to study the principles of communion with God.

5. *Sharing Groups.* Such groups are not strictly discussion groups, Bible study groups, or prayer groups; yet they involve elements of all three. They differ primarily in the way the group is formed — which is on the basis of need — and how they function.

Jesus dealt with people on the basis of their needs. Whether it was blindness, spiritual need, physical illness, bereavement, or a need for forgiveness, He met them where they were. He was not interested solely in solving a personal crisis, but He used the crisis as a starting point.

Someone has said that Jesus envisioned a man as an island, and He sailed around it until He found a point of need, and He landed at that point.

Rollo May says,

A human being will not change his personality pattern when all is said and done, unless he is forced to do so by his own suffering. Advice, persuasion, requests from the outside will effect only temporary change in the cloak of the personality. . . . The human ego is a recalcitrant and stubborn affair; it fights off disturbance, for it very much fears the profound insecurity that comes when its style of life is shaken. . . . Fortunately the wheels of life do grind relentlessly on and bring a just portion of suffering as a penalty for every neurotic attitude. When this misery becomes so great that the individual is willing to give up his wrong attitude, in fact to give up everything, he has arrived at the state of desperation which Kunkel says is prerequisite for any cure at all.[1]

The inner need which prompts the seeking of an answer may be the sharp stab of a crisis or the dull throb of frustration long endured. It may be the crisis of marital disharmony, of personal illness, or the diffused pain that comes when one finds life slipping away without his having experienced anything significant.

We are reluctant to admit inadequacy. It is painful for many to confess that they have problems which they are unable to resolve alone. Such an admission is somehow taken to suggest a confession of weakness. I have known literally hundreds of husbands who, when a marriage seemed on the verge of breaking up, would resist their wives' suggestion that they see a minister or marriage counselor. "We're adults, and we'll handle this like adults," is the common attitude, which really cloaks a deep feeling of inadequacy and an unwillingness to face the need for change.

Sharing groups are distinguished from other types by the very fact that the group members are humble enough to confess a need for help. The need may be simply a desire for greater spiritual growth. The individual is vaguely aware that life holds vastly more for those who will seek it. Some are prompted by the growing awareness that their religion has not provided them with some of the love, joy and peace which Christ promised His followers.

Others are motivated to join a group by the need for

greater marital happiness. At least four-fifths of all marriages could be improved significantly if the partners learned to communicate more effectively. In a sharing group they learn the art of communicating their true feelings.

The dull throb of frustration can provide motivation for some. Life is frustrating. The moments of true, unalloyed happiness are relatively rare. The difficulty is not that life does not *offer* more joy and happiness, but that most people have not learned how to be open to it.

Sharing groups function in different ways, depending upon the needs of the persons in them. Some groups begin at the point of seeking a deeper commitment to Christ. They may see this as their greatest need. In the process of seeking this commitment, they will usually discover that they do not really know how to pray effectively. In studying Jesus' teachings about prayer, and by reading some of the great classics on the subject, they begin to discover that there are often inner barriers to effective prayer and to ask themselves, "What is my personal barrier to knowing God at a deeper level?"

One husband confessed that he had joined the group initially only at his wife's insistence, since he was unaware of any needs. He smiled ruefully as he said, "I now see that I had needs as great as those of my wife. I thought she was the one who needed changing. It has gradually dawned on me that every living person needs changing if we are to discover God's full will for our lives."

Another member said, "I didn't know what to expect when I joined the group. I had no problems I could put my finger on, but in these past six months I have found dozens of them. Before, they were a kind of spiritual blur, dulling my capacity to experience all the blessings God has made available to us. I have found that I was afraid of God, and I feared what His will might involve if I yielded to it. I have discovered that I hated my parents, and that this unconscious hatred I wouldn't admit to myself had dulled my capacity for joy and happiness. I have come to see that I am filled with fear. I couldn't admit this to myself before, for it would have been an admission of weakness; but we can't handle an emotion we won't face. I am learning to face my buried fears."

What actually goes on in a sharing group? So many different things happen in so many varied ways that there is no "typical" session; but here is a highly condensed version of a part of one session.

The group of twelve consisted of four married couples, two single persons, and two wives whose husbands were not members. They ranged in age from thirty to forty-two. The meeting was held in the church parlor. The announced starting time was 7:30 p.m. and upon arriving, each person got a cup of coffee from the table in the corner of the room and took his seat in a close circle. For fifteen minutes they chatted, and since it was their first session and they did not all know one another, the atmosphere was restrained.

At 7:45, when all were present, the leader said, "Here are some copies of the book which we will be reading. Pay for your copy any time in the next month. Al, here, can take your money. If you will turn to page forty-three you will find a tremendously stimulating passage which we may want to discuss tonight. In the next five minutes or so we will have a period of silence, during which you may read, meditate or pray. Read this passage if you wish, and try to be open and receptive in the period of silence, so that God can speak to you."

There followed a period of silence during which some read, while others closed their eyes in silent prayer and meditation. The atmosphere was one of quiet, "structured permissiveness."

Then the leader said, "In the passage to which I called your attention, the author suggests that the reason many of our prayers are not answered is not because God is unwilling but that we each have certain barriers which limit our faith and capacity to receive. He also suggests that in our spiritual blindness we often pray for the wrong thing, such as the removal of a symptom, when we should be praying about the real problem, which is usually a faulty attitude.

"For instance, he mentions four basic barriers: fear, hate, inferiority, and guilt. You might underline those, and we can talk about them. The only rules in the group are that we will be personal rather than abstract. Tell what you feel, not what you think."

One of the men interrupted, "What's the matter with thinking? Has it gone out of style?"

The leader smiled: "No, but the 'think' group met last night. This is a 'feeling' group. We want to discover our feelings and offer these to God. For instance, these four barriers to spiritual growth are all feelings. Let me share mine. As I look at the four feelings, or barriers, I discover that I am troubled more by one than any of the others. Resentment is one which has troubled me as long as I can remember. I don't resent mildly. I resent with my whole nature. I do not often express it, because if I did I would have no friends and probably no family. For instance, I frequently resent my children. I love them and resent them. At least I resent the noise they make, their quarreling, and their disobedience."

"You shouldn't feel that way," said one of the women. "After all they're only children."

The leader said, "In the group we don't tell how we should feel. We feel whatever we feel. We do not pretend that our feelings are good or right or noble or Christian. We just admit them freely and honestly."

"Well, I don't care much for digging up all this stuff," one of the men said. "I always say 'let sleeping dogs lie.' I just put these unworthy thoughts out of my mind and try to think nice things about people. Jesus taught that, you know. But I'll tell you what my real problem is. It's none of these four. I am not troubled by those things, but I am bothered a great deal by unanswered prayer. I have arthritis and I've prayed about it for years, and it just gets worse. I wonder if maybe this is just one of the ways God has of keeping us humble. Or maybe I don't know how to pray. I wish I knew."

The leader looked around the group. There was a moment of silence, and one of the women asked, "Didn't I read somewhere that arthritis is supposed to have something to do with our emotions?"

One of the men said, "Maybe you're referring to a book written by Dr. Loring T. Swain. I think it's called *Arthritis and Spiritual Laws*. My mother had arthritis, and someone sent her the book. I read it. He's a Harvard Medical School specialist in arthritis. He claims that rheumatoid arthritis results from negative emotions such as hate and fear and resentment."

The member with arthritis smiled gently and said, "Why, that may be so for some people but I am not aware that I have ever hated anyone. My mother always taught me that love and forgiveness were the great Christian virtues. I remember her saying that you couldn't be a

Christian and hate. She felt very strongly about it. I recall having a big argument with my older brother once, and I shouted, 'Jim, I hate you!' Mother came into the room just in time to hear me, and she punished me."

Someone asked, "How did she punish you?"

The arthritic smiled his gentle smile. "Well, she was usually pretty firm about these matters. She had strong Christian convictions; and she was right too."

Another group member said, "I think you avoided the question. You didn't tell how your mother punished you."

"Oh, didn't I? Well, she took a stick to me. Quite a licking. I hadn't thought about that for years. Come to think of it she left a lot of welts on my back, and they were sore for a week or more. But Mother was right, and I knew it. I bore no resentment."

Someone said, "Tell us about your father."

"Well, he was one of the kindest people I ever knew, quiet and gentle. I never knew him to say a hard word about anybody. He had arthritis too, and was pretty badly crippled up when he died. He died of a heart attack in his forties. But look, I'm taking up all the time, and I don't want to monopolize the discussion. Let's move on to someone else."

The leader hadn't said much, but at this point he said, "Actually we are all participating through your sharing. Perhaps others in the group can sort out some of their own feelings while listening to you. Tell us more about your mother and your feelings about her. Maybe when we find out exactly how you feel about your parents we will know how you feel about God."

The arthritic, a mild and unassuming man, went on: "You asked how I felt about my mother. I never felt anything but the deepest love for her. I had asthma as a child, and her devotion to me was beyond belief. I guess I did think a time or two that my older brother — he's a highly successful lawyer — was the favored one, but of course all children think their brothers and sisters are the favored ones. Mother sacrificed to send my brother through law school, and I peddled papers during those difficult years. But we got Jerry through law school, and I'm proud of his success as a lawyer."

Someone asked, "What do you do, Ted?"

"I'm a grocery clerk, and I live with my mother. I never married for one reason or another, and Mother needs me.

She has high blood pressure and is a partial invalid. But look, we've spent far too much time on me. I have no serious problems. I just joined the group to learn some of the techniques of effective prayer, and I'm sure in time I'll get some of the answers. Let's talk about someone else."

In subsequent sessions, as Ted became more and more honest with his emotions, he was able to admit to himself for the first time that he did have some deeply buried resentment toward his mother and older brother. He discovered that he could share these resentments with the group and that they accepted him and his hostility.

In a later session he told them, "The fact that the group could accept me and my great load of buried hostility enabled me to accept it more fully myself. I have come to see that one cannot surrender to God what he will not admit to himself, that I could not be rid of my arthritis until I admitted my true feelings to God and to the group. For the first time I could accept myself. I saw that it was partly a sense of dependency which kept me tied to my mother. It was true that she did need me, but her need had kept me dependent. I am now becoming free to be my true self."

At the first session, when the discussion veered away from Ted, someone else brought up the matter of one's feelings toward parents. It was Marjorie who said, "I guess I joined the group partly because I have never known how to pray effectively, and I thought maybe we'd be discussing principles of prayer. This business of digging into our emotions bothers me a little. I don't see what this has to do with religion. In fact, I think it may be dangerous to be tinkering with our deep feelings. Maybe we ought not to be so self-centered. I think perhaps we should just focus on God and learn how to be more committed Christians. The past is gone, and so far as I'm concerned it's a waste of time to be digging it up and bothering with all these morbid things."

The leader said, "Marjorie, you said you had difficulty in praying, in feeling that you were 'getting through' to God. Will you tell us how you envision God?"

"Well, God to me is the greatest thing, or power or force, there is. God is love. But sometimes I feel so unworthy and guilty — and even fearful — when I pray that I just don't pray as often as I should. I know it's all in me, because I do believe God answers prayer. I just don't have faith."

A group member said, "I read somewhere that no matter what lofty thoughts we have about God, we tend to feel toward Him as we did toward our fathers or some other authority figure. Marjorie, tell us about your father."

Marjorie said, "I loved my father, but he was pretty stern. I was afraid of him when I was very little. I used to try to climb up into his lap when I was four or five years old, and usually I got the feeling that he was too busy to pay much attention to me. I remember sitting on his lap only once. I hadn't thought about it for many years, but I remember taking him something I had made in school. He was reading the paper, and I said, 'Look Daddy, what I made for you in school today.' He just sort of grunted, looked at me for a minute and said, 'Yes, that's nice. Now go and play,' or something like that. I think I felt rejected. If I ever wanted anything I asked my mother, rather than my father."

Someone said, "I suppose if we learned as children that father was too busy to pay any attention to us, we tend to project this same feeling onto God, as though He couldn't possibly be interested in our little needs and problems."

"What's that got to do with it?" asked one of the men. "We're big boys and girls now and know that God is never too busy to be interested in our smallest needs. Jesus taught that God noticed the fall of even a sparrow, so surely He would be interested in anything which concerned His children. I don't see that what happened when we were kids has anything to do with the way we feel or act today. We have learned the truth from Christ, and He said, 'The truth shall make you free.'"

There was a pause, and one of the members asked, "John, do you feel that your prayers are effective? Does God answer your smallest needs as well as your crises?" John hedged slightly. "Well, not always, of course. I'm not the Christian I ought to be, but I am convinced that if I really believed, God would answer my legitimate need."

"Was that an intellectual concept, or a deep feeling?" someone asked.

"Intellectual, I guess," John said. "But I'm not so sold on this splitting the intellect off from the feelings. Feelings may be important, but what happened when I was a kid isn't going to affect my life today. I am an adult now and intend acting on what I know."

The leader said, "It is pretty well agreed by students of the human mind that our emotional structures are formed at least by the time we are six years old, probably much earlier. Some think the first few months are tremendously important. Let's go back to Marjorie, who knows that God answers prayer but feels that God probably isn't interested in the smallest details of her life. Do we see any connection between this feeling and her feelings toward her father?"

"Sure," someone said, "if she felt rejected by her father when she came to him with some childish need, or even wanting to express love, perhaps she'd feel now that God is some kind of a distant deity who runs the universe and is too busy to be concerned with mundane details of ordinary living. Maybe we have to re-educate our feelings as well as the tops of our heads. I've known for years, intellectually, that God is not too busy to be concerned with me, but for some reason I don't pray until I am confronted with a crisis. I don't know whether this is because I am egocentric and hate to admit I need help, or because I feel toward God as I did toward my father. He was a busy, harrassed contractor who was always bushed when he came home at night. I can remember Mother always cautioning us to be quiet because Dad needed to rest before dinner. And after dinner he usually went to his den and worked on his papers. Now that I am an adult with my own family responsibilities I know what he was doing — just trying to keep enough money coming in to feed a large family; but at the time I think I felt that Dad was a pretty remote figure. Maybe I still feel that same way toward God — remote, and someone whom I shouldn't disturb with my little problems."

"All well and good," another member interrupted. "So some of us grew up feeling our fathers were remote figures, and maybe some of us have buried hostility toward our mothers which we can't accept because we felt then, and still do, that somehow it isn't right to admit these feelings. So what! Here I am thirty-eight years old, just beginning to discard some of my immature childhood feelings about God. How does it help me to know all this stuff about my childhood? What if I do dredge up all these forbidden feelings? How does it help me? What I think we all ought to do is to get over being kids and become committed Christians. The world is in a mess, with people hating each other and nations ready to go to war, and here we sit in the midst of a world threatened with atomic extinction tinkering with our emotions, wondering if we really did hate our parents. Let's get on the ball and be Christians for a change, and try to lend a hand to a threatened civilization."

There was a pause, while they thought it over. Then someone said, "Joe, I agree with you in part. I think we ought to be committed Christians. The minister challenged us to a deeper commitment last Sunday. You were there. Why didn't you respond and decide to be a more committed Christian?"

Joe said, "For one thing he didn't tell me specifically where to begin, how to get hold of it. I wish I knew."

One of the women, a fairly close friend of Joe's wife, asked, "Joe, since you seem to want a starting point, and since we can't solve the world's problems in one fell swoop, what about starting in our own homes?"

"What do you mean?"

"Well, maybe I've no right to ask this, but I understand we can be as frank as we want to in this group, so I'll ask it. How do you and Francine get along at home?"

"Oh, about as good as the rest of you," Joe said a little defensively. "Every married couple has their differences. We have ours. Part of the time I'm wrong, and part of the time Francine is. When I'm overworked I get testy, and when she's out of sorts she is short-tempered with the kids, and then I blow my cork, and we really go at it."

Francine who had not said anything as yet, spoke up. "I guess our home life is about normal, with our ups and downs; but I'm not satisfied with it. I was thinking when the minister was talking about a deeper commitment last Sunday that I don't feel much like trying to solve the race problem, or get involved in discussions about world peace and all the rest, when I am so filled with resentment at home. I don't even know who I am. How can I commit a 'self' I don't understand? How could I possibly help to solve the world's ills when I can't even solve my own personal problems? I think all this talk about commitment 'out there' is for the birds. I want to work on my inner nature, the part of me that's 'in here,' and when I can get some of my personal and domestic problems solved I may be some good in helping to solve the problems of others.

"Right now I'd like to know why Joe and I argue about inconsequential trifles, why I get so upset over the kids, why I am filled with anxiety about nothing in particular, why I'm so touchy, and why I say things I regret later and am then too proud to say, I'm sorry. To tell you the truth, I doubt if anyone in this group, or in our church for that matter, has their own lives sufficiently in order so that we can do much good sorting out the problems of the world."

Francine was normally a rather quiet person, but she was really wound up — and expressing her true feelings. Her husband said, "Francine, I didn't know you felt that way." She said, "Of course not. We never talk at home, at least not about anything important. We don't really communicate. We talk about how the kids are out of hand, or about the overdraft at the bank, or yell at each other. That isn't communication. If we do try to communicate a little about anything that matters the kids are there demanding attention and we never get down to anything really important."

The leader said, "That is one purpose of the group, to provide a place where we can really communicate with each other. Here we can say whatever we feel like saying. We can be our true selves, even if that self is not always the nice self we show to the world at large. And the surprising thing is that we will always feel more acceptance and love when we express our honest feelings. People can't love a mask, or communicate with a mask; and most of us wear them much of the time."

Joe said, "Look, I didn't join a group to wash my dirty linen in public. If I have sins I'll confess them to God and not to this or any other group. Jesus said that when you pray you should go into your closet and shut the door, and pray to your Father who is in secret. I don't go for any of this public confessional kind of thing." He was feeling a little threatened, apparently, lest Francine bring their family disagreements out into the group.

Francine said, "Joe, I think the only two passages of Scripture you know are the ones about praying in secret, and the one about not letting your left hand know what your right hand does. There's another passage somewhere — I don't remember just where — that says, 'Confess your faults one to another, and pray for one another, that you may be healed.' I don't think this means we have to blurt out all our sins in some group, but it must mean that the guilty feelings we have about ourselves can be — ought to be — shared with others. Maybe when we get them out and find that no one rejects us, we can begin to like ourselves better; and if the group accepts us, maybe we can get it into our heads, or our feelings, that God accepts us, sins and all. I guess I've said too much already, and Joe, maybe you're mad at me for telling about our arguments at home, but for some reason I feel more like being honest here than I do at home. If I say what's on my mind at home you get mad and walk out, and when you're real honest with me I burst into tears, and you get mad when I cry. Right now I feel like I have communicated more in these few minutes than I have at home in the ten years we've been married. And I feel good about it!"

One of the women said, "Francine, I've known you for years. You've always said the proper thing, at the right time, and have always been your sweet, demure self. I really never got to know you, and I wanted to. Now that you have let your hair down I feel I really know you. You *do* have feelings, and I like your real feelings better than the pretty, proper mask you always wear."

Francine smiled her gratitude and said, "I think I feel more like a real person now that I have found a place where I can let go and be myself without that awful fear of rejection that I have always had, the fear that if I let people really see what a mess I am inside they'd reject me."

Bert spoke up. "I'm glad to hear someone else talk about this matter of communication. I feel a little better, too, knowing that there are other homes where there is some hostility and an absence of real communication. I hadn't intended to let this out, but since the rules permit it, I may as well admit that Helen and I have our arguments, too. We have some real dillies. About once a week things build up to a crisis and the roof blows off. I never know what is going to trigger it, but, right or wrong, I get the idea that she digs and digs at me until I let go with some strong language, she bursts into tears, and we make up, and things are all right for maybe another week."

Helen came to life. "I just had an amazing insight. I never saw it before. Bert said I seem to dig at him until he blows his top. I just realized that my mother did that to my father. My dad was a kind of easygoing person, like Bert. Mom had to make most of the decisions, and I think she wanted Dad to take more of an active hand in family affairs. I expect her nagging, if that's what it was, was an unconscious effort to push him into assuming more of a masculine role. It took a lot of nagging to get my dad to blow up, but when he did it was awful. I just now realized that Mother would cry when he blew up, but she always seemed to feel better afterwards. I thought it was the good cry that helped her. I suppose it was simply that she felt better when Dad would tell her off. Good grief! Is that what I've been doing all my married life?"

Bert grinned, "Look kid, if that's what you need, you'll get plenty of it."

Then in a more serious vein, "I realize I am rather passive, and I hate it in a way, but it's the only way I know to be. I'd like to be more dominant. I think part of Helen's dominance she got from her mother, and maybe part of it is just insecurity, or anxiety. Maybe she's just needling me to assume a more masculine or authoritarian role. I think most dominant women are mixed up. They want to run things and be the boss because they're human, but being female they want someone else to take the dominant role. They just can't decide which they want most. I think they want to have their cake and eat it too. Helen married me, I suppose, because she was dominant like her mother, and I was passive and easygoing like her dad. She wants to be bossy like her mother, but the female in her wants me to be stronger. Personally I feel a lot of hostility about this whole thing — the more dominant role women are taking, while wanting me to be more aggressive and dominant. I think women ought to decide what they want."

One of the women asked, "Bert, are you hostile toward women in general for this reason, are you hostile toward your somewhat dominant mother, or are you really mad at yourself because you are so passive?"

Bert looked startled. You could almost see the wheels going around. Finally he said, "Well, I hate to admit it, but I just now saw that my answer is 'Yes' to all three of your questions. I think I did feel, and still feel, a lot of hostility toward my mother's quiet dominance, and for that reason resent all dominant women; but deeper than that, I feel self-contempt for the fact that I cannot be more sure of myself. I think of myself as amiable, easygoing, and easily pushed around. I'd really like to be a strong, self-confident male, but that isn't the way I'm wired up, at least not at the moment."

The leader asked, "Do you suppose, Bert, that as Helen lets up little by little on her dominant role, that you can gradually assume more of the role you seek for yourself?"

"It rings a bell," Bert said. "I think maybe that may happen, especially if we can come here once a week and thrash things out. The Lord knows we can't, or won't do it at home."

Toward the close of the meeting, which had lasted close to two hours, someone said, "We started out by talking about our domestic and personal problems. I'm just beginning to see, or rather to feel, something I can hardly put into words. Maybe it's something like this: that prayer is not just a bunch of words and requests, but an attitude of mind, plus some deep feelings about God and others and ourselves.

"Maybe," she said as if thinking out loud about her feelings, "it's like Jesus said, that we must learn to love, to love Him and others, and in the process learn to love ourselves properly. I have been feeling something during this session. I have felt, with each one in the group, a mixture of feelings — compassion, and concern, and I think the stirring of genuine love for each of you. I've known some of you fairly well, but in these two hours I know you far better than I had ever dreamed possible. In knowing you at a deeper level I have come to love you. Maybe it's that when we develop the capacity to love people unselfishly, we can then love God also at a deeper level. And maybe seeing that others can know all about us, or more about us at least, and still love us, enables us to love ourselves.

"It's certain that I need some self-love. I have felt self-rejection as long as I can remember. I've always felt inferior and inadequate, and I've been reasonably sure no one could ever love me if they really knew what I was like inside. But I feel that this group can love me even when you know all about me. Maybe the early Christians had a group like this. . . . I didn't intend to say all that, but it just came out. . . ."

The leader picked it up. "What a beautiful summary of what we expect to accomplish in this group! To carry her thought just a bit farther, perhaps all of us sense that we feel less like praying when we are loaded with feelings of guilt and inferiority. As we learn to accept our emotions, and can accept God's acceptance of us, we will feel more like praying because we will feel — at a deep level — that He truly loves us.

"Now let's close with silent prayer, thanking God for His love and offering to Him in perfect surrender whatever we have discovered about ourselves. He accepts us and our guilt even more readily than we have accepted each other here tonight."

After the period of silent prayer each took a sheet of paper, and at the direction of the leader wrote down the name of each group member. Opposite the name they wrote some prayer request. During the week they were to spend some time — thirty minutes a day if possible — in a quiet time of meditation, reading, and prayer. During this period they were to pray for each one in the group by name, remembering the prayer request.

The leader explained that it was not the verbal request which constituted the real prayer but holding the other person in loving attention before God, asking for God's perfect will for that individual, and remembering the expressed need of each one in the group.

As the group broke up at 10 p.m. it was as if they had all been intimate friends for years. There was a warmth in their parting such as one seldom sees in a standard church group. They were beginning to know each other at a deep level and had begun to sense some of the power inherent in love. They had experienced in one session that it is possible both to share at a deeper level than they had ever imagined and to be accepted and loved and understood.

This is basically what each of us desires deep within — to know and be known, to love and be loved. The group had begun their search for love and understanding and for the meaning of life.

13. HEALING IN THE GROUPS

> This is the great error of our day in the
> treatment of the human body, that physicians
> separate the soul from the body. —*Plato*

THERE is a remarkable resurgence of interest in spiritual
healing today. Interest in the subject had waned considerably through the years, owing in part to the activities
of charlatans, and to the fact that certain religious groups
had brought it into disrepute by extravagant and unsup-
ported claims. But today healing services are being held in
churches of many denominations.

God is not limited to any one method of healing. He
heals a cut finger by a set of unimaginably intricate
processes, so complex that if it happened only once we
would call it a miracle. The fact that it happens every day
tends to rob it of its wonder and mystery. God heals
through competent medical skill, through proper rest and
diet, through operations, and in many other ways. Alexis
Carrel, Nobel prize winner, reports observing at Lourdes
the almost instantaneous healing of a patient whose numerous illnesses had been diagnosed by several competent
physicians as incurable. His conclusion was that the normal healing processes had simply been speeded up by
spiritual forces not understood today.

Jesus healed people instantly, and we call the healings
miracles; but many people believe that such events were
not outside "natural law;" that He was able to heal
because He lived on a spiritual plane where energies of
tremendous power were at His disposal; that He did not

violate natural law but rather invoked higher laws not commonly available to men whose spiritual forces are dissipated by inner conflict. In this sense His acts of instantaneous healing would not be "miracles" in the ordinary sense of the word. The important thing is that the same powers used by Jesus to heal the sick are available to us. This is clearly indicated in His command, "Heal the sick, cleanse the lepers." The Apostle Paul, writing to the Christians at Ephesus, said, ". . . how tremendous is the power available to us who believe in God. That power *is* the same divine energy which was demonstrated in Christ when he raised him from the dead. . . ."[1]

On one occasion Jesus censured His disciples for lacking faith to effect a cure.[2] There is ample biblical warrant for our expecting physical healing through the exercise of spiritual power. What is required is that we meet certain conditions.

The borderline between emotionally induced illness and organic illness is almost impossible to define, since emotional conflict can, in time, produce an organic disease. Medical men agree in general that body, mind, and spirit are a unit. What affects any part of our nature tends to affect the whole person.

In one group of which I was the leader I witnessed the complete healing of a case of what had been diagnosed by numerous physicians as severe neurodermatitis. The woman had suffered from it for nine years and had been hospitalized on numerous occasions. At no time in the group did she pray for physical healing, but as she grew in love and self-awareness, and brought her emotions under the control of the healing Christ, she was healed.

In the same group a partially arrested alcoholic was "cured," in the sense that she found a new relationship with God, with others in the group and acquired a wonderful new sense of self-acceptance and forgiveness. Another member of the group, an expert in his field, had been out of work for over a year, completely unable to function normally. He spent much time at home weeping. The thought of going out to seek employment was sufficient to produce a splitting headache and other physical symptoms. A little over a year from the time he entered the group he sat down one day to outline the ideal job, in terms of working conditions, geographical location, salary and other factors. One day soon thereafter he applied, more or less at random, at a firm within walking distance of his home. He was employed on a temporary basis, and a few months later was hired permanently. Virtually all of the physical and emotional symptoms which had immobolized him have disappeared.

His wife, who had joined the group only to encourage her husband, said later, "I have discovered that my problems were as great as his. My spiritual and emotional growth have been phenomenal. Our relationships in the home have improved to an amazing degree."

Another member suffered from "fear of speaking," as he described it. A lifelong distrust of people originating in childhood had made him extremely timid and limited his effectiveness. He wrote later: "My fear of speaking was lifelong. When the reason for it showed up, in the group discussions, and as I shared my feelings, I felt the change. I may falter a bit on occasion when I try to speak, but the old fear will never be the same. My faith has been strengthened, and I have come to experience fondness, good-will, and sympathetic understanding for the group members, and for everyone else whom I meet."

Annabelle had been a very dependent child. She was about eighteen when her father died. Soon thereafter she began to exhibit serious signs of emotional illness. She was committed briefly to a mental institution, but nothing specific was done for her. She was released under heavy sedation, and she later saw a psychiatrist a few times. She continued to be dazed, uncommunicative, and incapable of continuing her schoolwork. She suffered occasionally from hallucinations. In one rather lucid interval she tried to attend college, but she failed to keep up with her class.

Annabelle and her mother participated in a group led by a layman in a local church. Here she began to experience something which she had never encountered before — complete openness and unconditional love. She found that no matter what she shared, it was kept in complete confidence; and, far from rejecting her, the group members expressed great love. She could feel it! In a sense the group became her family, providing the nonjudgmental acceptance she had always needed, and she began to respond.

Invisibly, gradually, the mother began to experience some of the same growth as her daughter. She became aware of some of the ways in which she had made

Annabelle overly dependent. She saw, too, that she was simply repeating what her own mother had done to her.

As mother and daughter grew toward wholeness of mind and spirit, a new quality entered their relationships. Annabelle saw her mother in a new light as she heard her confess her own shortcomings. Her anxieties lessened as she learned that Christianity is not a creed to be believed, nor a set of morals to be obeyed, but a quality of life to be received from Christ, the source of all spiritual and mental health.

Eventually Annabelle shared her fear of boys and her failures in school, and she sensed the complete, unconditional acceptance and love of the group — her family, the family of God. She continued to see the psychiatrist occasionally, but both she and her mother agreed that her healing came chiefly from the insight, love and security provided by the group. Subsequently she returned to school, graduated, and secured a position where her work proved quite satisfactory. A bit later she fell in love with a fine young man whom she married.

The mother's growth paralleled that of her daughter. She began to discover, as she explored her feelings, that she was emotionally dependent upon her own mother, a ninety-year-old woman who dominated every aspect of her life. She was eventually able to resist.

"At long last," she said, "I simply gained courage to stop fearing and obeying my mother. Gently but firmly I put her in her place, and to my surprise the roof didn't fall in." Soon thereafter she decided to go on a diet, being greatly overweight, and within the next few months she lost forty-five pounds. Freed at last of domination by her mother, no longer dependent upon her emotionally, she had no difficulty in losing weight. She said, "I feel like a whole new person, inside and out. And Annabelle is, too!"

It is a painful but inescapable fact that many of our physical and emotional disabilities are self-inflicted.

In *Faith for Personal Crises* Carl Michalson writes: "According to ... Freud much of our suffering is self-inflicted."

[This] is our way of escaping the burden of life. As children, when the going got difficult, we could run home to mother. As men, we have the same desires to run, but we express them in socially acceptable forms, such as illness. A crippling allergy is much easier to explain to your friends than a failure in business. . . . One learns to trade major pains for minor. . . .⁸

The mind and spirit hand their pain over to the body. Even when we are unaware of any emotional distress, some physical disability will often point to the fact that it is there just the same. A highly effective man of fifty-one wrote as follows:

The most unexpected incident was triggered by the evaluation slip I got relating to health. Before I was married I was refused life insurance because of high blood pressure and abnormal heart action. In more recent years I have been able to pass the insurance examination, but have been troubled by excessive heart pounding upon exertion, and extreme fatigue from long and irregular hours. On top of this I was subject to frequent and prolonged nosebleeds. My slip on excessive concern over my health was a bitter pill to take, because I have always ridiculed people who appeared to have a lot of psychosomatic ailments. . . .

Having faced this thing squarely, and painfully, all the symptoms were suddenly gone — instantly. No more labored pounding of my heart, no nosebleeds, and even with the exertion of long hours, I am convinced that my heart works as well as the next fellow's of my age. The Bible, and church, have taken on an altogether different tone for me. Now the casual contacts with people that don't get beyond the weather, sports, and TV programs, are pretty flat. . . . People have become so much more interesting!

As many authorities in the field of psychosomatic medicine have pointed out, the appearance of some disease often goes hand in hand with reduction in anxiety. The mind has simply handed its anxiety over to the body. The anxiety is now temporarily relieved. It is being borne by the body in the form of a symptom. If and when the physical symptom disappears, the anxiety has a way of reappearing unless one has come to grips with the source of his anxiety. None of this is conscious, of course. It all takes place in the unconscious mind, and the sufferer is understandably indignant if anyone suggests that he may have developed a physical symptom as an unconscious escape from mental or emotional conflict.

This is not to say that all pain and suffering are self-inflicted. Much of our suffering comes to us from the corporate evils of society, as in the case of communicable diseases.

The Apostle Paul speaks of his inexplicable adversity, the "thorn in the flesh," which he prayed three times might be removed. He says, "A thorn was given me in the flesh, a messenger of Satan to harass me." He saw that his disability was not sent by God but by Satan. Jesus speaks of a woman "whom Satan has bound" with illness. "The knowledge that God does not intend our suffering minimizes the agony of this present age . . .", as Carl Michalson has pointed out. "Our affliction will not last forever, and you can stand almost anything if you know that it is not going to last forever."

Despite the knowledge that not all suffering originates in our emotions, it is well to ask ourselves, "Am I an 'injustice collector?' Is there some attitude on my part, wholly unconscious, which predisposes me to adversity? Is this physical or mental pain which I endure the result of some inner need to punish myself for unresolved guilt or conflict?"

In a group led by a layman the members decided to take the spiritual growth inventory. One group member who had served in the second world war had all manner of physical symptoms. In the book being studied along with the weekly evaluation slips he came across the statement that many physical symptoms originate in unresolved guilt feelings. At one session he felt led to share with the other members an experience of twenty years before. He had been responsible for making a decision which resulted in a plane crash. Bodies of the victims were scattered over a hillside. He now became aware of the almost totally buried sense of guilt which had haunted him ever since. The feeling of guilt over his decision had never been fully resolved, and the inner pain which he felt had been handed over to his body in the form of various ailments.

The evaluation slip which he received triggered the release of the partially buried memory, and he sought the spiritual healing which comes from sharing with an under-standing group. What relief he experienced from discovering the acceptance within the group! A number of other interesting things followed. The group "opened up" as the result of his sharing, and dynamic things began to happen. He no longer felt any need to punish himself for his long-held guilt. He was free to give up his physical symptoms; for the inner pain of guilt and self-accusation was no longer there. He became a liberated and "well" man for the first time in twenty years.

I believe it to be a valid inference that Jesus did not heal men's bodies without doing something of great importance to them spiritually. It was not so much that Jesus set out solely to heal people's bodies as that His dynamic wholeness, undergirded by loving compassion, overflowed into the lives of those He met. If the need was physical, He met that need. If it was another need, He met that one; but in each case it appears that Jesus dealt with the whole person, not simply with an individual's physical illness.

Mark records the case of a father whose son Jesus healed. The father said, "If you can do anything, have pity on us and help us." Jesus said, "If you can! All things are possible to him who believes." The father then cried out, "I believe; help my unbelief!"* As I see it, the father was not simply believing in the fact of Jesus' power to heal; he was believing in a Person. Something significant must have taken place when the distraught father looked into the face of the Son of God.

In the presence of Jesus people either recoiled in unrepentant guilt and unbelief or knelt in surrender to One whom they sensed was more than man. Something of a transforming nature went on in the minds and hearts of those whom Jesus healed.

When He went back to His home town of Nazareth, "He could do no mighty work there . . . because of their unbelief." Mark records that He laid his hands on a few and healed them, but His power was greatly limited by their unwillingness to believe in Him.* Because He could not reach them spiritually, He could not heal them physically.

Virtually all instances of healing seem to be accompanied by a new spiritual awareness. Man is a unit. We cannot separate mind, body and spirit, for they are one. The *British Medical Journal* once stated that "no tissue of the human body is wholly removed from the influence of spirit." Many people believe, erroneously, that there are just two main types of illness: organic disease and psychosomatic illness. They operate on the assumption that organic disease is "real" and that psychosomatic illness is largely imaginary.

On the contrary, it is now known that psychosomatic illnesses can become organic. There is no doubt in the minds of authorities in the field of psychosomatic medicine that such emotions as fear, hatred, jealousy, and anxiety produce stress in the body. This stress creates a chemical imbalance resulting in malfunction of glands and other organs. The body then becomes unable to provide resistance to germs which are otherwise held in check. When Jesus commanded love instead of hate and urged us to avoid anxiety, He was not concerned with some arbitrary decree of God dealing with these emotions. It is simply that the mind, spirit, and body of man operate far more effectively in an atmosphere of love and good will.

Since the mind tends to hand its pain, guilt, and grief over to the body by an unconscious process, we find it easier to endure physical illness than mental anguish. For one thing, we receive sympathy, which is a form of love, when we are physically ill; but the person suffering from mental anguish or depression is likely to be told to "snap out of it" or to "pull yourself together."

We have recorded scores of instances of physical and emotional healing which took place in groups. Healing came when the sick persons dealt with the underlying causes: guilt, fear, hostility, inferiority resulting in self-rejection, jealousy, envy, or whatever they were. These and other negative emotions seem to register on the unconscious mind (the spiritual nature) as guilt or unworthiness, which are really the same thing. Guilt demands punishment or forgiveness. It is not God who demands it but an inner mechanism. Until we resolve the guilt through the securing of divine forgiveness, the guilt persists as a kind of warning bell. If we delay in securing forgiveness and a change of attitudes, the guilt takes its toll in the form of self-punishment.

Guilt feelings, like pain, were meant to serve as a warning. The inner self is shouting, "Guilty!" As children, when we were guilty of wrong-doing we were usually punished, and we came to expect it. The punishment may have been physical or simply the withdrawal of parental love. The unconscious mind came to relate the two: "wrong-doing is followed by punishment." A conditioned reflex was set up, and in the adult the "inner child of the past" still operates on the old basis: guilt demands punishment. We may be able to quote chapter and verse on the forgiveness of God, but if at a deep level we equate wrongdoing with punishment, if our parents were punitive in word or gesture, we will automatically and unconsciously seek a form of self-punishment for our real or imagined guilt.

Hegel said, "The sinful soul has a right to its punishment." The findings of modern psychology confirm the existence of an inner judicial mechanism which demands that we secure forgiveness or endure suffering as punishment.

As we said previously this self-punishment may take the form of being trouble-prone, accident-prone, sickness prone, or it may take some other form; for the inner self is often punitive and accusatory beyond belief. Freud affirms that some of his patients seemed deliberately to resort to wrongdoing because of the punishment sure to follow. The punishment eases the sense of guilt which has its origin elsewhere, usually in the unconscious.

One suffering pain or discomfort is likely to say, "It's all very well for you to talk of this originating in my emotions, but I feel a specific and almost unbearable pain. Don't tell me it's my emotions. It's real pain!" Of course it is. A woman who had come in for counseling told me that she had an appointment with a surgeon because of great pain. Her physician had hinted at the possibility of an operation. She had previously secured some relief from sharing with me certain traumatic events of her early life, but I was confident that she did not yet feel forgiven at a deep level. Her need for forgiveness, I assured her, was probably no greater than mine, but for some reason she had not been able to secure a sufficient sense of forgiveness so that she could forgive herself. I felt reasonably sure that there was a correlation between her excruciating pain and her spiritual dis-ease. This was evident more from her manner than from anything she had told me.

I said to her, "I know nothing about your physical difficulty, but I do know something of your spiritual struggle. I would hazard a guess that your surgeon will tell you that your pain originates in anxiety, which is one of the by-products of both conscious and unconscious guilt." A few days later she reported that the surgeon, after exhaustive tests, had stated flatly that her condition was caused by anxiety and tension.

A sense of unresolved guilt, a diffused sense of inferiority, shame, or rejection in childhood, all register on the unconscious mind as guilt and unworthiness. This is the cause of many physical and emotional symptoms. If only we could learn to accept and *feel* the forgiveness which we know, intellectually, God has offered! When one can feel at the center of his being that he is acceptable to God, to man, and to himself, he can usually be healed. Many have experienced this sense of acceptance for the first time in a sharing group. We tend to bear our guilt in secret, feeling somehow unacceptable and unworthy.

It is a healing experience to discover that virtually everyone else in the group feels very much the same way. When we become able to share in the group, little by little, some of our feelings of inadequacy and guilt, we discover that instead of being rejected we are loved all the more; and the healing effect of love and acceptance begin to be felt.

People ask frequently, "Why must I share the sordid aspects of my life with others? I confess my sins to God. Surely that is enough!" The answer is that these are not "confessional groups" in which members are required to bare the past. In general it is the destructive emotions which are shared rather than the symptomatic acts. However, on occasion, an individual will feel the need to unburden himself further, usually to a counselor; though I have been in numerous groups where the atmosphere of loving acceptance was so great that it was perfectly natural for a member to share at a still deeper level. *Invariably* I have observed — not rejection or surprise but understanding and love. Some persons are unable to experience the forgiveness of God except as it is mediated through such a group.

A Methodist minister wrote describing four instances of physical and emotional healing experienced in a group. He related one case at some length. The wife came to see him first. She was certain that it was all her husband's fault, and she was planning to secure a divorce. Her manner was highly nervous and compulsive and she had numerous physical symptoms. She and her husband joined a group, and when their spiritual growth slips began to arrive the wife learned that not only did the husband have some problems but she had some serious ones herself. Through their spiritual growth slips they discovered, week by week, the areas of their lives which needed attention.

They found, too, that both of them had far more positive qualities than negative and that they could complement each other. Formerly the husband had alternated between feelings of dependence and a determination to dominate. As he began to understand himself and to understand why he reacted as he did, and as she began to see the connection between her spiritual needs and her numerous physical difficulties, the symptoms began to disappear. The minister wrote in conclusion "The spiritual growth slips were a means of reconciliation. They are now living together happily."

Lee provides a graphic illustration of the way guilt takes its toll. "To hell and back" was the way Lee described his experience. "If hell is any worse than what I have been through, then one should avoid hell at all costs!" His return from mental illness through his group experience is dramatic because of the intensity of his need.

He was thirty-eight when he entered the group. A professional man, he had not been able to work for over two years because of a crippling and terrifying phobia. "About six years ago," he told them, "I went to a party, where I had too much to drink. I drove a young woman home and attempted sexual relations with her. She was quite willing, but for some reason — perhaps because of my strict religious background — I was unable to go through with it. But the intent was there just the same, and later I felt terribly guilty and ashamed, because I had disgraced myself and my family.

"In the succeeding weeks and months I tried to bury the memory as much as possible. To think about it made me uncomfortable, so I just tried to put it out of my mind. As a child I had come to believe in a punishing God, one who will grant your prayers if you are good, but if you are bad He is almost certain to punish you in some way. It was a very childish and immature concept of God.

"I had been a 'good boy.' Neighbors often complimented my mother on how good I was. I never disobeyed or talked back to her. As I see it now, she was over-protective, and I became a passive, obedient person, repressing all of my resentment toward her. I have come to see that it is normal for a child to feel a mixture of resentment and love toward parents. Resentment, however, was partially repressed. I could not express myself to my mother about her over-concern, as I did not want to hurt her feelings.

"The summer after my experience with the young woman I was terribly depressed, but did not know why. I saw no connection between my depression and the fact that I felt disgraced, and feared exposure in some way.

"At work I began to check on things unduly. Then I would recheck. Sometimes I would go back to see if I had dropped any papers, or had locked a door. The checking continued to increase, but I did not associate it, of course, with my sense of unresolved guilt. I did not realize that this was the beginning of a compulsion that was going, in time, to threaten my very sanity. The compulsion to check gradually spread to every aspect of my life. In driving, if I hit a slight bump I would go around the block and inspect the place where I had hit the bump. Eventually I was checking and double-checking on everything I did, often as many as ten times.

"About a year after the onset of my guilty experience I took a routine physical examination. The Wasserman test was incomplete, I was told. The physician said that this often occurred. They took another test, and it too was incomplete. I was certain by now that I had syphilis and that the incomplete tests were simply evidence of it. The third test proved negative, and the doctor assured me that I was physically in fine shape, in every way. But the idea persisted. Maybe I *did* have syphilis! Maybe the test was inaccurate.

Now began a routine of handwashing, showering and cleaning that grew steadily worse. I checked things eighteen hours a day. I stood in the shower daily from half an hour to forty-five minutes soaping myself. I washed my hands until the skin was white from the soaping. I was spending so much time checking every detail of my life, bathing and worrying, that I was incapable of going to work. I went home to my parents and lived with them. Little by little I withdrew from all social contact. Walking downtown was an ordeal, as I spent every minute of the time checking, checking, checking. Finally I was totally paralyzed with fear, completely incapacitated.

"My family was worried, and of course urged me to 'snap out of it'; but when they saw that this did no good, they took me to a psychiatrist. I went to him for a year. He was a splendid man, and I liked him, but I grew consistently worse. Eventually he assured me that the only hope of a cure was shock therapy, and recommended that I be hospitalized. I was in a mental institution for ten days, but members of my family could not bring themselves to agree to the shock therapy. Finally I went home, worse than when I had begun the psychotherapy a year before.

"A brother-in-law learned through a client of his that significant results were being achieved by people with all sorts of problems, through some type of group, and in my desperation I signed up to join a new group.

"I liked the group from the outset. Even in my half-paralyzed mental state I responded to them. There was a man who had lost his job as an engineer because of a severe emotional problem; his wife, who had joined mainly for her husband's sake, and then found any number of areas where she could make spiritual and emotional growth; there were two 'dried out' alcoholics seeking spiritual growth; a woman of great personal charm and culture who finally revealed a great sense of inferiority. It was just a cross section of society. All of them shared their needs little by little, but I couldn't bring myself to do so. It was too personal. Dr. Osborne knew about it, for I had revealed it to him before entering the group. He had said, 'You don't need to share anything in the group unless you wish to. You may participate as much or as little as you like.'

"In this permissive atmosphere I began to enjoy these people. The meetings often lasted from 7:30 to 10:30 P.M., and then we stood around visiting, and loving each other. The love that grew up in the group was similar to the love one experiences in a family. It *was* a family, too, and I think I resented it whenever anyone was absent. I also resented it when Dr. Osborne brought a new couple into the group. After all, what right did he have to introduce other people into the 'family' without our permission? But in a few weeks I learned to accept them, too, as members of the family. I came to realize that these people also had problems and needed help.

"In the discussions, and in the assigned reading, I began to discover a different kind of God than the God of my childhood. I came to see that He is not a vengeful, punishing deity, but that He wants to forgive us more than we want to forgive ourselves. I had some conferences with

Dr. Osborne about the nature of God, and His forgiveness, which reinforced my growing feeling about a God who forgives us and accepts us just as we are.

"I came to believe intellectually in this kind of God, but there remained the problem — how to forgive myself? It had been six years since the event which had precipitated my guilt and fear, and unconsciously during all of this time I had been waiting for God to punish me. When He didn't, I began to punish myself. I came to see in the group how I was punishing myself by checking and re-checking, by fear and depression, and by refusing to permit myself to live like a normal human. If God would not punish me, then I would punish myself, is about the way my unconscious mind worked, I suppose.

"I still had not shared the details of my problem with the group. All I had told them was that I had a compulsion, and was immobilized by fear. I did share with them a fear of speaking. I had begun to stutter when I was five, and though this gradually diminished through the years, I still had a great reluctance to speak, through fear that I might stutter. I began to notice that in the group I was less and less reluctant to speak. I shared more, talked more than I had in a long while. I began to become less passive and more dominant.

"At first, when I tried out this less passive personality at home, my mother was startled. I found I had no difficulty in telling her when she was being too bossy, or too protective. My seventy-four-year-old father watched and listened with great interest when I was able to tell my mother exactly how I felt about her. At first I spoke with some force and irritation, then as I got used to my less passive nature, with more tact and understanding. Finally, I noticed, my passive father began to stick up for himself. At last, after fifty years of marriage, he began to be able to defend himself, just from observing my new-found freedom of expression.

"Mother was flustered at first, but finally I could see that she was enjoying her new role. I observed, too, that my brother-in-law, married to one of my sisters, listened with amazed interest as a formerly passive son and father defended themselves. Visiting in his home some time later I saw that he had started to learn the art, too. My sister is quite dominant, and he, passive. But now he was attempting to defend himself, to express himself, and to stop retreating.

"These were important dividends but there still remained the checking, the fear, the phobia, the ceaseless hand-washing. True, the symptoms were lessening, but I still could not go out and apply for a position. I had been in the group about nine months when I began to see the cumulative effect of all that had transpired. Dr. Osborne explained that it was the 'rock in the swamp' principle. You dump a load of rocks in a swamp to make a road, and they disappear. A second and third, and maybe a tenth load disappears, but the eleventh shows up and you begin to have a road. By the end of the tenth month I was looking forward to going out to interview prospective employers, but had not yet brought myself to it. But gradually I was opening up my horizon. I was making trips, engaging in sports, talking freely to people, checking less; and finally, about a year after I entered the group I knew I was ready to go back to work. I experienced no difficulty in applying for a position. Talking to prospective employers was much less effort than it had ever been, because I was no longer afraid to speak.

"I have secured a position now, and I am a far better integrated personality than I was, even before I became emotionally ill. In a sense, I am glad I had this trip 'to hell and back,' painful as it was, because I have grown spiritually and emotionally. I have a new concept of God, and of His love and acceptance. I am less selfish. I have gained a vast new insight into myself which has changed my personality. I have become interested in other people, and their needs. I no longer feel I have to be perfect to merit God's love. The paralyzing effect of trying to be a morally and spiritually 'good boy' in order to avoid God's wrath has given way to a new maturity in which I want to be my highest and best under God, not to avoid punishment, but because this is the only creative way to live.

"I have seen everyone else in the group grow, too. Their fabulous maturity, in every instance, has made me feel that they are and will always be a part of a very special family. Maybe this is the 'family of God' you hear about but seldom see."

A nurse in an Eastern city writes of her healing, in which a spiritual growth group played a significant part:

"After an automobile accident in which I received a

severe head injury which kept me from working for six months, I had a complete emotional breakdown, and tried to commit suicide. Then followed almost a year in a state hospital. While in the hospital I was visited almost every week by the minister of a church I had attended from time to time.

"I left the hospital on a bitterly cold February day; but the problems of ex-mental patients are staggering — no real home, relatives who considered me a disgrace to their name, no job, no money and no friends. This last, no friends, was so bad that I pretended to be an alcoholic and went to AA meetings for a year just to be around some people who would accept me. I went to church every Sunday, probably out of gratitude to the minister who was willing to give me so much of his time.

"About a year ago I joined a group at the church. I still had my fear of people, and sat through many sessions without saying a word. I kept a totally blank expression which revealed nothing; but as time went on I began to like these people, and stopped fearing them. I felt that they loved me, and cared what happened to me. Shortly thereafter I got my first job in nursing.

"I now attend a Sunday school class where I am not afraid to take part in the discussion. I sing in the choir, and serve on a number of committees. The greatest thing that has come out of this is that I have learned about love. First, I learned in counseling sessions that 'God is love, and loves you.' You see, I had been so hurt by parents who cut me to ribbons that I never learned to give or receive love. They said they would love me if I got the best marks in school. They would slap me and then say, 'But we love you.' Love based on an 'if' or a 'but' is never love. It was a glorious thing to realize that the God of the whole universe loved me, and that His love was not based on anything I did. I didn't have to earn it.

"To sum it up, what I got from the group was the first genuine love I had ever known, and because of this I gained the ability to love these people, and ultimately many others. Long ago a psychiatrist asked me, 'Do you think you can ever accept or give love?' At the time I had to answer, 'I don't know.' Today I know. The answer is 'Yes!' to both."

Numerous factors were at work in helping her to discover the healing power of love. A compassionate and understanding minister played a vital part: in visiting her and in private counseling. She had psychiatric care over a fairly long period of time, but she feels that it was in the group that she first came to understand the meaning of love. And it is love which heals, for love is of God, and it is through love that He performs His miracles of healing.

A woman whose hatred of her daughter was so strong that it resulted in a complete physical and emotional collapse has written at some length about the healing which she experienced in her group:

"We had a daughter who had left home, married, and become a nurse. She finally left her husband and returned home with her baby. Eventually she remarried, and left home with her child. The second marriage broke up, and this time we tried to help, but were told to stay away and let her work out her problem. Finally, she found she could not hold down her job as a nurse and care for the three children, so she gave two of them to her husband, and we took the oldest one, now a teen-ager, to raise."

The breach between mother and daughter widened. Each felt rejected by the other. The mother described her growing hostility toward her daughter: "Hate grew in my heart, and I told people my daughter was dead. I destroyed most of the things she had given me through the years, sentimental things from her youth. I hated her and fought her father who tried to help me think clearly. He was heartsick, too, but still loved her and wanted to help her. We had not seen her since the last time she had told us to go away and leave her alone. This went on for two more years, and I became ill, sick in heart, mind and body. I attended church services, but could not sing. I fought back tears every time I tried to sing, yet kept on going to church, in order to maintain some semblance of a religious atmosphere for my grandson.

"When we were invited to join the Yokefellow group we responded. I knew we had to have something. I had suffered a 'nervous breakdown,' had ulcers, and had been hospitalized. With resentment seething within me I began studying, and attending the group meetings. I wondered what God could do for me now, with all my hate.

"We joined in September. In October I was called into court to testify against my daughter, who sought custody of her children. She had remarried an older man, and was happy now, and able to care for them. I prayed about it, and in the group I talked out my resentment. I struggled with resentment and pride as I stood before the judge. It was like entering Heaven and being judged. I realized suddenly that I could not forsake the daughter I had borne. I said, 'Judge, I cannot be a Christian, profess to love God and not give my daughter another chance. I do believe she will make good if given another chance. I will give up the child I have cared for.'

"My load was lightened, my heart washed clean. I had thrown out all resentment. My daughter and I became friends again. For Christmas, she and her new husband bought me a lovely poinsettia. I watched it grow, blossom, and die down. I could not throw it away, so I kept it, and it continued to grow, and somehow became a symbol for me. I nourished it, and it came out anew, strong and beautiful. The next year it blossomed again, and I rejoiced in this symbol of the new life I had given my daughter. Now she and I have a happy relationship, and understanding through suffering. We both realize how far apart we had gotten, and try harder to keep the relationship growing.

"It was through my time of prayer and study, and the strength of the group, that God worked the change in me. How can I ever let Him down? I have found happiness again. What a blessing the group has been to me! Thank you so much for bringing the Light into my life. May God bless you in your wonderful work!"

14. LOVE

> Love is such a power that it unites all things.
> Therefore love Jesus, and then everything that
> He has will be yours.
> — *The Cloud of Unknowing*

A BRILLIANT and very attractive young woman had come
several thousand miles to attend the annual Prayer Therapy Workshop conducted at Santa Barbara, California, by
Dr. William Parker. I was the leader of the group to which
she was assigned.

She did not participate in the discussion during the first
session. At our second group meeting I turned to her and
asked if she had anything she cared to share with us. She
said, "No, I think not. I will just listen." There was a
pause. Groups like this are not afraid of silence. Finally
she said, tentatively, "Well, there is this one thing that has
been on my mind." Then she told about it, for forty-five
minutes. No one interrupted or felt that she was monopo-
lizing the time. She shared her loneliness, the pain over
her broken marriage, and her frustration over an impaired
relationship with her mother. The group members listened
with deep understanding, and occasionally someone would
ask a gentle, probing question.

There were five group sessions during the Workshop,
and in three of them she shared her needs. At the last
session she told of a dream she had had the night before.
"I was in a warm, comfortable house," she said. "I went to
the door and looked out. It was night, and the moon shone
on a dark, bitterly cold landscape. It was dreadfully bleak.
Finally I closed the door and went back into the warm

house. That was all." I asked her what the dream meant to her. She said, "I think it means that here in this group I have found warm, loving acceptance, and I suppose I dread going back home, which, in my dream I pictured as a bleak, cold world."

I assured her that I would endeavor to help establish a group in her home city, where she could continue the spiritual growth begun in the workshop. The significant thing is that in a few short group sessions she had discovered a relationship in which there was more love and acceptance and understanding than she had ever experienced in either the home in which she grew up or in the relationship with her husband and children.

We often tend to exaggerate our own guilt and inadequacy; and when we discover, in a warm group relationship, that others can know all about us and still accept us, it enables us to accept ourselves. This had happened in the case of the young woman. A proper self-love often begins in just such an experience; when we find that others love and accept us, despite our failures.

In a group session in which I was participating, attention was focused for some time upon a woman whose score on "depressive" was extremely high. She shared some of the painful rejection which she had experienced as a child. She had felt unloved and now could feel no love for parents, brothers, or sisters. She felt loved by no one in all the world. There was a silence, and finally someone, in an effort to be helpful, said, "*God* loves you." She had no doubt, she said, that God loved her, but she wanted to be loved by *persons*, too. She recognized that she was virtually incapable of receiving such love, even when it was offered. The pain of rejection in childhood was so great that, like many others, she had erected a protective barrier which effectively prevented her from feeling love. In fact, she could feel little besides depression.

It is probable that no one has ever developed into a well-rounded personality, or has lived an effective life, unless he has experienced the love of another person. Normally this begins in infancy. The infant learns about love from parents, brothers, and sisters, and other human beings around him. We can never love others or experience a proper self-love unless we have had the experience of being loved. We develop the capacity to love by being loved.

"Whether it be a soft whisper or a loud scream, the essence of the cry is the same: 'I am alone, unloved, unwanted. What am I to do? How can I get love . . .?' "¹

In his splendid book, *The Art of Loving*, Erich Fromm describes how the infant reacts to the experience of being loved in the earliest months and years of life:

" 'I am loved. I am loved because I am mother's child. I am loved because I am beautiful, admirable. I am loved because mother needs me . . . *I am loved for what I am*, or perhaps more accurately, *I am loved because I am*. This experience of being loved by mother is a passive one. There is nothing I have to do in order to be loved . . . mother's love is unconditional. All I have to do is *to be* — to be her child'."²

What transpires in those earliest years, especially from birth to six years of age, is all-important in the development of the child's personality. Many factors are involved — the relationship between the parents and between parents and child, brothers and sisters; the emotional maturity of the parents; or an older child with whom one must compete. A thousand and one factors invariably affect the growing child. The degree to which he will be able to give and receive love later in life is determined almost exclusively by what transpires in these earliest years.

Two University of Wisconsin psychologists, Dr. Harry F. Harlow and his wife, Margaret K. Harlow, have studied several hundred monkeys at the Primate Laboratory in an effort to discover clinically the place which love plays among monkeys. The Harlows discovered ample evidence pointing to the conclusion that one must learn how to love before he can learn to live.

They also discovered that it was just as important for monkeys to form healthy relationships with other monkeys their own age as to have good relationships with their parents. Learning to love, like learning to walk or talk, cannot be put off too long without having damaging effects upon the child's personality, Dr. Harlow believes.

An individual whose capacity to give and receive love is seriously impaired invariably had a childhood in which he did not feel loved. He may well have been adored by one or both parents, but must have been unable to receive love in the form in which it was offered.

Can one who lacks the ability to give and receive love

ever learn this art, or are we forever handicapped by early environmental factors? The answer is that we can learn to love and to receive love, though at considerable effort. An illustration is found in those children who are reared in an environment where two languages are spoken. They grow up bilingual, able to speak two languages with more or less equal fluency. In the Holy Land, where the children of missionaries are reared among the Arabic-speaking children, they speak English at home and Arabic with their playmates; and their Arabic is without a trace of an accent. However, missionaries and others who study the difficult Arabic tongue later in life find it an exceedingly complex task, and they will always speak it with an accent.

In much the same way, those who learned the art of loving as children usually experience no difficulty in giving or receiving love. If for some reason our love relationships as children were impaired, and we felt rejection, we must learn the art of loving as one learns a language later in life — the hard way. We will not be as proficient in the art as if we had learned it in infancy and early childhood, but *it can be learned*.

A child who feels rejected for any of a number of reasons learns that it is painful to love, and subsequently he may automatically retreat from any close relationship. Without reasoning it out, he simply reacts negatively to love. He has, as it were, become the victim of a conditioned reflex: "Love equals pain." The reflex action is to avoid any relationship in which love or warmth may prove a threat. This is all below the level of consciousness.

All persons have "islands of immaturity" within, saints as well as sinners. If one of these islands has to do with one's inability to love, it does not necessarily follow that such a person must be labeled "immature." He may be in every other way a very capable, mature personality. But in some degree the effectiveness of one's entire life hinges upon the ability to love. Therefore, it behooves us to learn this difficult but rewarding art. "The final goal in all therapy is to release within the individual a greater capacity to love."* In this sense religion, group therapy, spiritual growth groups, and psychotherapy all have the same ultimate goal.

A good place to begin is in the small group. Unfortunately, those who resist this approach are usually the very ones who need it most. Their reluctance to establish any sort of a close relationship, even with eight to twelve persons, is evidence of their underlying fear of people; and fear of people is fear of love. Paradoxically, men are less realistic in this area than women. Husbands more often resist the idea of going to a marriage counselor than their wives; and they sometimes resist participating in a group for the same reason.

Men are usually more afraid of their feelings than women. They were taught in childhood not to cry, which is the expression of an emotion. In our culture, they are taught that it is "manly" to suppress emotions. Consequently, men tend to fear any experience in which feelings are involved. They may rationalize this by saying "No, we are adults. We'll work this out ourselves." They are really saying, "I want to avoid any situation in which feelings are exposed. I feel safer when I am dealing with them." As in certain other areas, women are more realistic, and more often seek help from a counselor or in a group. The fact that this male reaction is unrealistic is evident when we observe the fact that a man has no hesitation in surrendering his car to a mechanic who knows more about an engine than he does; or in going to a dentist when he has a toothache, or in calling a television mechanic when the TV needs to be repaired. It is only in the realm of relationships that men display their intense fear of emotions.

We derive our self-image, our sense of identity, early in life. If the child does not grow up with a strong sense of self-worth, he may be limited in his capacity to relate creatively to others. His limitation may take the form of timidity, or he may cover this innate shyness with a brusque or aggressive exterior, a way of saying, "I am not really shy at all." He may even deceive himself in this manner. He may compensate for inability to love by achieving something significant, such as the amassing of money or status symbols ("I *do* amount to something, after all! If I cannot have love, I will have your admiration, or your envy, or power over people or things.")

Women have fewer means of compensating for a sense of inferiority and for feelings of being unloved. A man may compensate to some extent through achievement in business, sports, or the acquiring of some distinctions or honors. The range of their opportunities is wider. Women, on the other hand, are more seriously thwarted if they are unable to love or be loved. Their opportunities are limited, usually, to the realm of the home and domestic achievement. Though they may be employed, they do not usually compete very readily in business, which is dominated by men. The loss of love or inability to love thus plays a much more important part in the woman's life than in the man's.

The Greeks had three words by which to designate different aspects of love. We say, "I love God," "I love my family," and "I love ice cream." We have only the one word with which to describe the loving relationship with God, physical love, the affectionate regard in which we hold parents, children, husband and wife, and the degree to which we find objects pleasing.

This semantic difficulty often confuses people who read the New Testament admonition to "love one another," and to "love your neighbor as yourself." The difficulty arises over the fact that many people confuse love with affection. The love which Jesus urged us to manifest may have nothing to do with affection. It is rather the attitude implied in the Greek term *agape*, an unselfish, active concern for the well-being of another.

Erich Fromm has pointed out that the final test of love is whether we can love the "stranger," who may not share our values, or our culture or who, for that matter, may not be particularly admirable himself. Loving him does not in the slightest imply the adoption of his values or approval of any of his traits which we may dislike.

Paul Tornier has written:

Love is not just some great abstract idea or feeling. There are some people with such a lofty conception of love that they never succeed in expressing it in the simple kindness of ordinary life. They dream of heroic devotion and self-sacrificing service. But waiting for the opportunity which never comes, they make themselves very unlikeable to those near them, and never sense their neighbor's need.

To love is to will good for another. Love may mean writing with enough care so that our correspondent can read without spending time deciphering; that is, it may mean taking the time to save his time. To love is to pay one's bills; it is to keep things in order so that the wife's work will be made easier. It means arriving somewhere on time; it means giving your full attention to the one who is talking to you. . . .[4]

In the family relationship, we move into another aspect

of love. In addition to *agape*, Christian love, we normally
expect a degree of affection to be expressed. In a group
session a woman told of her husband's seeming inability to
express affection. He had been reared in an undemonstra-
tive family, and felt uncomfortable in attempting to show
affection. She, on the other hand, was a warm, outgoing
person who longed for physical demonstration of affection,
such as had been expressed in the home in which she was
reared. To her, there was something wrong with him. To
him she seemed overly effusive — "sticky," as he expressed it. Each was demanding that the other react on
the basis of their individual childhood memories. He
expressed his love with generous gifts and was, she admitted, extremely thoughtful of her in every way. "But," she
said, "I want him to *show* his love." She had never been
able to express her need for greater affection until the group
provided the proper climate.

Fromm comments:

In any number of articles on happy marriages, the ideal
described is that of the smoothly functioning team. . . . The
husband should "understand" his wife, and be helpful. He
should comment favorably on her new dress, and on a tasty
dish. She, in turn, should understand when he comes home
tired and disgruntled, she should listen attentively when he
talks about his business troubles, and should not be angry
when he forgets her birthday. All this kind of relationship
amounts to is the well-oiled relationship between two persons
who remain strangers all their lives, who never arrive at a
"central relationship," but who treat each other with courtesy
and who attempt to make each other "feel better."[8]

Let no one disparage the "well-oiled relationship," as
Fromm describes it, for as compared to a bickering,
hate-filled home, one would much prefer the atmosphere
of mutual respect and tact. However, what the author is
pointing out, I believe, is that the smooth relationship
achieved by tact is an inadequate goal in marriage. Many
a couple might well improve the atmosphere by expressing
as much tact in the home as they normally use with
strangers whom they will never see again. But they should
do this with the understanding that it is only a first step
toward a deeper relationship, in which they seek to
achieve a growing sense of oneness, of understanding, and
of love based upon unconditional acceptance.

If a husband and wife can learn to communicate, the details will take care of themselves. Communication is everything. If communication can be established on the feeling level they can discover that it is not fatal to share negative emotions. Hostility, or irritation, which is normal in any human relationship, can be expressed in such a way that neither need feel threatened by it.

In our groups hundreds of couples have acquired the art of communication for the first time. They have been surrounded by the friendly warmth of others who have similar or identical problems. Spiritual and emotional growth need not be a solemn affair. Humor and hilarity often relieve the tension. In such an atmosphere many who have found it difficult to communicate discover that they can be themselves, express themselves, and communicate true feelings more readily than ever before.

There is never any fear in such a group that "things will get out" and be discovered outside the group, for one cardinal rule is that nothing which transpires in the session is to be shared elsewhere. Members come to feel toward each other much as members of a family do; and an affectionate loyalty is generated, which effectively prevents the sharing of confidences outside the group.

It bears repeating that a proper self-love is the starting point for loving another person. If we do not love ourselves properly we can never truly love someone else; for we tend to project upon others our own disguised self-contempt. Self-love does not imply narcissism, egocentricity, selfishness, or a warped self-interest. It does imply: I, too, am a person, loved of God. I have as much right to love myself as to love another person. In fact, I am required to love myself. There is no virtue in despising or depreciating oneself. We are commanded to love our neighbor *as we love ourselves*. In fact, we will always esteem our neighbors about as much as we esteem ourselves. We are assuming here, of course, a mature, non-egocentric self-love, the loving of oneself simply as a person who is loved by God, who has needs, goals, and rights.

What is implied in loving ourselves properly? It means, first of all, to learn self-acceptance. We tend to reject ourselves if we did not feel unconditional acceptance as small children. Such unconditional acceptance is relatively rare, and to some degree all of us experience self-rejection. We can work toward mature, adult self-acceptance by learning to accept divine forgiveness and then by forgiving ourselves. The only reason we reject ourselves is because we do not feel "acceptable." Yet God accepts us, and if the infinite God can accept us, we can learn to accept and love ourselves. Jesus manifested this unconditional acceptance when He fraternized with those who were called "sinners." Though He set the ultimate as a goal — "You, therefore, must be perfect as your heavenly Father is perfect" — He accepted unhesitatingly and without question those who had utterly failed! He is telling us by this that God extends unconditional acceptance; that while He lures us toward the ultimate in spiritual maturity, He takes us where He finds us without condemnation.

We can take the first step toward self-acceptance by saying to our souls, "I have difficulty in accepting myself but God accepts me, and I will accept myself." We may need to make this prayer of affirmation numberless times before we succeed in counteracting the effect of years of self-rejection. The process can be speeded up immeasurably in a group experience, where we discover that others are suffering from the same problems; that, surprisingly, the more they know about us the easier it is to accept and love us; that the things we often despise in ourselves are present, too, in the lives of others. One cannot love a mask. One can love only persons; and as we gradually remove the mask of pretense behind which we have hidden the real self, it is gratifying to discover, instead of the rejection we had half-expected, a growing affection and acceptance by others.

Soren Kierkegaard made the wise observation that:

"When the commandment [to love one's neighbor] is rightly understood, it also says the converse, 'Thou shalt love thyself in the right way.' If anyone, therefore, will not learn from Christianity to love himself in the right way, then neither can he love his neighbor. He may perhaps ... cling to one of several other human beings, but this is by no means loving one's neighbor. To love oneself in the right way, and to love one's neighbor, are absolutely analogous concepts, and are at the bottom one and the same."[7]

Joshua Loth Liebman stresses the need for self-acceptance:

"He who hates himself, who does not have a proper regard

for his own capacities ... can have no respect for others. Deep within himself he will hate his brothers when he sees in them his own marred image. Love for oneself is the foundation of a brotherly society and personal peace of mind."[8]

This self-love is not a morbid preoccupation with ourselves and our own interests. It is not, to use Liebman's term, a "paralyzing egocentricity." Nor is the achieving of a proper self-love an easy task; it requires discipline and preoccupation with this goal as the supreme effort of life. But it is worth whatever it costs.

I recall a shiftless farmer of my boyhood days who was wont to say, when asked why he didn't mend his fences or repair his house, "You know, I have half a mind to do that." Having "half a mind" to do it, he never managed to achieve anything except a precarious existence just short of starvation. "You will seek me and find me, when you seek me with all your heart," said God through the prophet Jeremiah; and the God whom we must seek with the "whole heart" is the God of love. When we find love we shall find Him; and when we find Him, we have found love. As Rollo May has put it: "To love oneself, to love others, to love God — all these require almost a transcendent effort for most of us. The road is narrow, and 'few there be who find it.'"

In *Existence*, by Rollo May, Ernest Angel, and Henri F. Ellenberger, the statement is made:

"Knowing another human being, like loving him, involves a kind of union. One must have at least a readiness to love the other person, broadly speaking, if one is to be able to understand him."[9]

In the group experience, when it is person-centered rather than idea-centered, it becomes possible to establish this kind of union with others. The very act of participating in such a group indicates the "readiness to love the other person," and thus one begins the thrilling process of understanding other persons and being understood by them.

Thomas Kelly writes:

"In the Eternal Now, all men become seen in a new way. We enfold them in our love, and we and they are enfolded together within the great Love of God as we know it in Christ.

Once walk in the Now, and men are changed, in our sight, as we see them from the plateau heights. They aren't just masses of struggling beings, furthering or thwarting our ambitions ... or utterly alien to and isolated from us. We become identified with them, and suffer when they suffer, and rejoice when they rejoice."[10]

Dora had been through a divorce and was trying to pull her fragmented life together. She had been drinking heavily for quite a number of years, but had made no serious effort to attend AA or to resolve her drinking problem in any other way. She showed up for the first group session swaying slightly, as she did at every subsequent session. She persistently kept her sharing at the opinion level, quoting passages from the Bible, and sundry devotional books which, she assured us, she read daily. It was obvious to everyone in the group, especially to two or three who had been members of AA, that she was a confirmed alcoholic who was probably consuming large quantitites of alcohol daily, and was in a constant daze.

From time to time the group gently tried to get her to be personal rather than abstract, but the threat of removing her mask was too great. It was not so much that she feared rejection by the others as that she was unable to look at herself. She had engaged in self-deception so long that she had virtually come to believe her own lies. Carefully measuring her "ego strength," the group never pushed too hard; but they persisted in refusing to let her get away with all of her fantasies. After six or seven months, during which she appeared to have made little or no progress, the leader "opened the gate," as it were, and silently encouraged the group to work with her. This they did, ruthlessly, tenderly. One man said, "Dora, we love you, but we could love you so much more if you'd stop all this pretense about how much you drink. We don't reject you because you drink. If there is any rejection here at all it is because you won't let us know the real you. All we can see is your mask of pretense. Why don't you tell us the truth? There are three other alcoholics in the group. One of them showed up here one night loaded to the gills, and was received with the deepest love and affection. Why won't you take your mask down and let us know you?"

Dora persisted in assuring the group that she was not an alcoholic, nor even a problem drinker. "I do have a drink at night, before dinner, just to sort of relax me, you know. Doesn't everyone?" As someone said later, "If we had lit a match in the room there would have been an explosion," for her breath belied her insistence that she had only one drink a day. But under the relentless, loving pressure of the group, which was determined that she be honest with herself, she finally said, "All right folks, I'll tell the truth. I have a pint a day! There — now at least give me credit for telling the truth."

There had been laughter throughout the discussion, but underlying it all was a deep seriousness of purpose. Now there was an atmosphere of acceptance and relief. "Dora, we can relate to you, knowing that you've faced the truth," one person said. But Dora had a long way to go. She had lied to herself, to God, and to everyone else for so long that the road back was not easy. Her physician told her that her liver was "in terrible shape," and one morning she was found in a coma. At the hospital she was given treatment for a month, and when she returned to the group she did not weave when she entered the room. There was a new look of self-respect about her, more calm self-assurance, less defensiveness. The love expressed by the group was a healing experience for her.

She moved away later to be nearer relatives, but her letters to group members continue to reveal some of the same glowing assurance and self-honesty she had come to learn. Love was the healing factor, for in a loving group she had the courage finally to look at herself, to find herself, and to offer that self to God.

When asked what he considered the greatest law of all Jesus replied that the one supreme law was loving God with all of one's nature, loving one's neighbor, as oneself. Modern psychology has revealed the reason for Jesus' insistence upon love as the supreme virtue. Erich Fromm says that failure to observe the command to love one's neighbor is the basic cause of unhappiness and mental illness. "Whatever complaints the neurotic patient may have, whatever symptoms he may present, are rooted in his inability to love, if we mean by love a capacity for the experience of concern, responsibility, respect and understanding of another person, and the intense desire for that person's growth. . . . If this aim is not fulfilled nothing but surface changes can be accomplished."[11]

Fromm also points out that "love by its very nature

cannot be restricted to one person. Anyone who loves only one person and does not 'love his neighbor' demonstrates that his love for one person is an attachment of submission or domination, but not love."[12]

Ralph W. Sockman points out that Toyohiko Kagawa, the Japanese Christian leader, distinguished three levels of love. The first is physical love, which holds persons together in families. Kagawa would also classify as physical love the bonds which bind individuals to their nation or their labor union or any other group which benefits them materially.

"Above this level is a plane which he [Kagawa] calls psychic love. Every true marriage rises above physical attraction into an affinity of minds and interest. Psychic love also includes our association in friendships, in professional and social groups, and in all those relationships which rest on community of mental tastes."

Kagawa then designates a still higher level of love based upon conscience. "If one is walking along the road with an enemy on his right hand, and a sinner on his left, and if he can walk with them without accusing them, or if he can halt his progress to help them, then he has risen to the plane of conscientious love. Such was the love which Jesus manifested, and to which He summoned his followers, bidding them to do good to those who hated them. . . ."[13]

There are many misconceptions concerning love and many false methods by which we seek to express or gain love. Paul Tournier describes the misguided love which parents sometimes offer their children, using gifts to bribe them for some desired behavior. This procedure Tournier continues,

will undermine their whole affective relation with the child. "If you succeed better in Latin you will get a bicycle." There is no relationship between bicycles and Latin. The parents are happy to give one to their child, but they want to kill two birds with one stone; they want to taste the joy both of giving a bicycle and of the child's progress in school. The child, however, does not so understand it, and he resents the conditional gift because it means a conditional love: "I love you if you are good, if you work hard, and if you are obedient." Such a child does not really feel loved.[14]

Knowing only conditional love impairs the child's subsequent capacity to accept the unconditional love of God and, in some degree, limits his future capacity to accept the love of persons; for deeply ingrained within, at a feeling level, is the concept that one must "deserve" love, instead of being loved for oneself. Such a person may never feel fully forgiven, completely worthy of God's love, unless he measures up to some real or imaginary standard.

Another false concept — really a perversion of love, is found in the dependency relationship often observed between a parent and child. In one of our groups a woman described her relationship with her demanding and possessive mother. As the mother grew older, her demands increased until the daughter could no longer enjoy being near her mother and, in fact, resented the demands deeply. When the daughter secured a divorce, the mother began to make plans for them to live together. She owned considerable property, and through the years had made it clear that in order to inherit this her daughter must conform. The daughter said to us, "I don't want her money, and I won't live with her. I want to establish my own identity. I don't want to be dominated and controlled. I will now have to earn my own living, and I would much rather do this than to be dependent in any sense upon my mother. She has always tried to shower gifts upon me, but they were usually conditional. If I did not please her, she would ask for the return of the gift."

Here was a clear-cut case of a mother-daughter relationship based upon the mother's dependency; the mother seeking to dominate, but actually dependent upon, her daughter. The more she sought to dominate the life of her daughter, the more the daughter retreated from her, thus increasing the mother's anxiety and determination to "win my daughter's love." She confused love and dependency.

A similar situation is often observed when a mother is reluctant to have a son or daughter leave home to marry. On the conscious level the mother is anxious for the child to find happiness and establish a home; but unconsciously she feels a need to have the "child" dependent upon her. Thus she herself becomes the dependent person. This is a far cry from love.

Young couples often mistake physical attraction, which is the God-given sex drive in operation, for love. Each is attracted to the other for a variety of reasons: some valid and others simply a manifestation of their own needs, which the other seems to fulfill. To attempt to explain to young people all that is involved in love and marriage, as I often do when they come to me to discuss their wedding plans, seems at times almost fruitless; their eyes are filled with star dust. The possibility that their romantic dreams could ever turn to intense hostility seems to them incredible. They often look at me with undisguised amusement as I suggest some of the means by which they can avoid the more obvious pitfalls in marriage. Usually it is only later, when their frustration and pain becomes insupportable, that it is possible to offer any real assistance; and often it is too late when they return for help.

Frequently in our groups a couple learns the art of love by discovering first how to communicate true feelings. It is a deeply gratifying experience to observe the lowering of the barriers between a husband and wife as they begin to "know" each other for the first time.

"It is easier to love God than people," as Frank Laubach has pointed out. "The God we see in Jesus Christ is the most lovable Being in the universe — but *people* are often contemptible. We must school ourselves to love people because they need love and not because they are attractive. . . . The people who need us most are those whom others do not love at all. They are likely to be irritating. They are often bad-mannered and bad-tempered."[15]

Laubach also points out the difficulty which Christians experience in this area. He refers to the fact that "the closer they draw to God, the more clearly they see the sins and weakness of human nature. And the greatest temptation of one who is trying to be a Christian is to be critical of those who do not share his Christian ideals. So it is often said that the hardest man to live with is a saint! . . . How to hate wrong, yet feel love and tolerance for one who does wrong is a problem every Christian must face. The problem does not grow less; it grows greater as one's dedication to God increases."[16]

We must continually remind ourselves that a person does not truly love until he loves himself, until he loves God, and in the process acquires the capacity to love others unconditionally. With some, the ability to love begins with loving people; with others it appears to start with a loving relationship with God. Perhaps it is not too important where one enters the circle of love — whether with self, with God, or with others.

Wendell McCloud, Episcopal priest who attended one of our retreats at Asilomar in northern California, and whose experience was told in chapter 11, has written of his spiritual journey at my request.

"My forte is hostility. Since I am so full of hostility, I have a compulsive need to talk about love. The best way to talk about love is to tell a love story. The love story I can tell best is my own. My story began when a learned lawyer asked a competent Carpenter one question involving legal technicalities.

"Because his answer evidenced familiarity with legal jargon and understanding of legal priority the Carpenter amazed everyone, especially the lawyer. The first part of the Carpenter's response to the lawyer's entrapping question was, 'Thou shalt love the Lord thy God with all thy heart, and with all thy soul, and with all thy mind.'

"For forty-eight years I struggled with the Carpenter's answer, for forty-eight years I tried to love with all — with all my heart, soul, and mind. For forty-eight years I tried this love stuff and got nowhere. I got nowhere because I lacked even the faintest notion of what He had been talking about. I did not know what He was talking about because I had mis-learned the lesson of love. In its love relationships our family adhered to a system of barter. This seemed especially true of the exchange involving Mother and me. To barter is to exchange one commodity for another. Mother's commodity was 'love.' My commodity was 'good boy.' I bartered with Mother exchanging my 'good boy' for her 'love.' These sharply calculated interpersonal risks were poor preparation for loving with all my being. Inevitably my infantile attempts to love God with all my heart, soul, and mind failed, for in God's economy of love 'barter' means nothing and therefore produces nothing.

"The Carpenter continued his answer to the attorney by saying, 'Thou shalt love thy neighbor . . .' And I continued my answer to the Carpenter by failing to love my neighbor in the same manner I had failed to love God. Unfortunately I hid this second failure, and hid it so well that all the time I was hating I thought I was loving. In my seminary days the social gospel was the greatest and I was the greatest for the social gospel. I cared inordinately for the underdog, which in my case was a way of hating inordinately the top kick.

"For twenty years I deluded myself into believing that I was a gentle loving soul, but in reality I was a first rank hater. I hated one group by pretending to love another, opposite, 'enemy' group. Under the camouflage of loving one group I was hiding from myself that I hated much more than I loved.

"In 1956 when my wife precipitously left me, this pretense ended abruptly. She took flight and I took to falling apart. This collapse of my personal, most intimate world eventually convinced me that I had to take a long perceptive look at myself. With this conviction came awareness — awareness that I had heard only part of the Carpenter's answer to the lawyer. For forty-eight years I had perpetuated that peculiarly human trait. I had heard the words but not the meaning of the words. Somehow those last two, primely important words, 'as thyself,' had escaped me. I was trying to love everybody but myself. I had heard what the Carpenter had said but not what he hàd meant. Because it forced me to understand those words my world's collapse was a major blessing.

"I have been so intolerant of so much that fulfills life that I am appalled by my prodigious capacity to tolerate so much that frustrates life. But, God be praised, even a glutton for punishment eventually reaches his point of supersaturated frustration. In my forty-eighth year I had reached mine. Life terrifies me at this juncture, because it confronts me with choice when I am least competent to choose. It terrifies me, because on this pin-pointed fulcrum of choice, hate hangs balanced against love, death against life, and self against God. I panic because so little can tip the scales so finally. I panic because I'm certain that the scales will tip to my destruction, against love, against life, against God. At this juncture, I disbelieve that the scales will as easily tip to my redemption for love, for life, for God. Finally there was the question raised by an established pattern: I had chosen wrong so far, why should I make a right choice now — at this juncture?

"Although the logic of past performance guaranteed another wrong choice, that wrong choice was never made. Which shows you how illogical logic can be. That wrong choice was never made not because I suddenly 'got smart;' but because God cares for me, he moved me to attend my first therapy group. In a group God opened my mind and my heart to the meaning of His Son's words, 'Love thy neighbor as thyself.' Three years in a group has helped me in my search for meaning, enabling me: 1. To see me (self-understanding); 2. To free me (self-acceptance); 3. To be me (self-love). Relentless honesty with oneself and constantly increasing love of others accompanies this growth in life's meaningfulness.

"One year after my first group experience I was leading two Yokefellow groups. Last year I led three groups. Next year I'll lead four. This is my way of loving others as Christ has loved me. As a consequence of His love operative in these groups I have seen in the past and continue in the present to see human life awaken to the Godly life for which it was created. As a consequence of this awakening, I have seen the obdurant forgive, doubters become faith-filled, the despairing filled with hope, the sad filled with joy, the haters turned into lovers; in fact, I have seen chaotic marriage become holy matrimony.

"For myself I am certain that to whatever degree it is true of me [that:] I can see me, free me, be me; I can love God with all my heart, mind and soul; I can love my neighbor as myself; [it is] only because I believe in

> God the Father who created me for love,
> God the Son who redeemed me for love,
> God the Holy Spirit who empowers me for love,
> God the Holy Trinity who through groups establishes
>   His Kingdom on earth as it is in heaven."

Raynor C. Johnson, in *Watcher on the Hills,* gives a detailed account of many persons who have experienced the ultimate reality of God's love. Though the details of each experience differ, a common thread runs through all of them. The experience of Sir Francis Younghusband, reported by Johnson, is typical:

"I had a curious sense of being literally in love with the world. There *is* no other way in which I can express what I then felt. I felt as if I could hardly contain myself for the love which was bursting within me. It seemed as if the world itself were nothing but love ... At the back ... of things I was certain was love — and not merely placid benevolence, but active, fervent, devoted love, and nothing less. The whole world seemed in a blaze of love, and men's hearts were burning to be in touch with one another."

I have reason to accept the validity of this, for I once had a similar experience. I had been preparing a sermon on the love of God. For a week I had read and thought about the subject. On Sunday morning I went over my sermon notes; and then, for some reason, I decided to walk to church rather than drive, as I usually did.

Upon opening the front door of our house it happened: I walked out into a world I had never seen before. The familiar things were there as usual, but they were all different — clothed in a radiance and beauty beyond description. The grass was infinitely greener than I had ever seen it before. I glanced at the trees, silhouetted against the deep blue sky, and their beauty was thrilling beyond measure. I became a part of the whole, embracing it; and it embraced me. I almost feared to breathe lest the experience dissolve, but the apprehension was only in the back of my mind, for the rest of me was experiencing an ecstatic joy that came from something other than visual beauty. Suddenly I knew what it was. It was love! The whole world was a vast system of love! I felt it rather than thought it. Love, I sensed, was at the heart of everything, and God was in everything, and everything was in God, and God was inexpressible love.

A white house which I had previously thought of as rather ordinary in appearance now seemed amazingly beautiful. The trees lining the street were no longer simply trees but an integral part of this system of love permeating the entire universe. I recall feeling love for the trees. It was a warm, affectionate feeling, as if we belonged to each other. I glanced at the dark brown earth between the curb and the sidewalk. Eucalyptus seeds lay there in great profusion, and I felt, rather than thought, that they were the loveliest things I had ever seen. I loved them in their beauty, for they were a part of this universe of love. Two strangers approached me and I felt a sudden surge of affection for them. I greeted them warmly, and their obvious surprise did not matter in the slightest. The rest of the way to the church was filled with beauty and love, and when I greeted several people standing at the entrance to the church I felt something which can only be described as overwhelming love, and warmth, and affection. We were all one, and there was no barrier between us. They were just parts of God's glorious, wonderful, joyous, loving universe, and they were beautiful.

It was an awareness of the ultimate reality of love. I was seeing people and things the way they really are, not clouded by hate, and guilt and anxiety and fear. The experience lasted on a diminishing scale for the next hour, and I still felt a glowing warmth toward everyone at the close of the service. It did not matter that they and I had faults. We were all forgiven,, loved, united, and in love. It was not brotherhood; that is much too feeble a word. It was Oneness, in which we were "in" God, and God in us. I did not feel sadness as the feeling gradually diminished, because I sensed that I had been given a glimpse into reality beyond what we humans call "normal."

Love is at the heart of the universe. It pulsates in every atom and molecule. It throbs in every tree. It is alive in every human, in the dust of the earth, in the heart of God. God is love, Heaven is love, and we were all made to love, to live in love with God and man.

St. John of the Cross, who had many long glimpses into ultimate reality, has written: "When the evening of life comes, you will be judged on love." For love is everything.

ACKNOWLEDGMENTS

CHAPTER 1

[1]*The Meaning of Persons*, Paul Tournier, Harper & Row, 1960
[2]From *The Listener* by Taylor Caldwell. Copyright© 1960 by Reback and Reback. Reprinted by permission of Doubleday & Company, Inc.
[3]Exodus 3:5
[4]John 13:34; 16:24; 14:27; 13:17 (KJ); 10:10; 17:3
[5]*Call to Commitment* by Elizabeth O'Connor, Harper & Row, 1963
[6]*Emotional Maturity*, by Leon J. Saul, J. B. Lippincott Co., 1960
[7]*The Art of Counseling* by Rollo May, Abingdon Press, 1949

CHAPTER 2

[1]*Alternative to Futility* by Elton Trueblood, Harper & Row, 1948
[2]*The Art of Counseling* by Rollo May, Abingdon Press, 1949
[3]From *The Undiscovered Self* by C. G. Jung, copyright©, 1958 by C. G. Jung. Reprinted with permission of Atlantic-Little, Brown and Company Publishers.
[4]*Ibid.*
[5]Luke 24:49
[6]*Alternative to Futility* by Elton Trueblood, Harper & Row, 1948

CHAPTER 3

[1]Proverbs 14:30, An American Translation, University of Chicago Press
[2]Phil. 4:6, 7
[3]*Love Against Hate* by Karl Menninger, Harcourt, Brace & World, 1942
[4]John 16:33
[5]*The Dynamics of Personal Adjustment,* by George F. J. Lehner & Ella Kube, ©1955. Reprinted by permission of Prentice-Hall, Inc., Englewood Cliffs, New Jersey.
[6]*The Vital Balance* by Karl Menninger with Martin Mayman and Paul Pruyser, The Viking Press, 1963
[7]*The New Group Therapy* by O. Hobart Mowrer, D. Van Nostrand Co., Inc., Princeton, N. J., 1964

CHAPTER 4

[1]*The Neurotic Personality of Our Time* by Karen Horney, W. W. Norton & Co., New York, 1950
[2]*The New Group Therapy* by O. Hobart Mowrer, D. Van Nostrand Co., Inc., Princeton, N. J., 1964
[3]Matt. 18:20

CHAPTER 5

[1]Mark 9:23
[2]Matt. 6:33

CHAPTER 6

[1]*New Approaches to Dream Interpretation* by Nandor Fodor, Citadel Press, New York, 1962
[2]*Guilt and Grace* by Paul Tournier, Harper & Row, N. Y., 1962
[3]James 5:16
[4]Luke 16:19-31
[5]I John 4:8
[6]Luke 9:54, 55
[7]I John 1:9
[8]*In Search of Maturity* by Fritz Kunkel, Charles Scribner & Sons, 1943
[9]*Prayer and Personal Religion* by John B. Coburn. Copyright, 1957, by W. L. Jenkins, The Westminster Press. Used by permission.
[10]Matt. 23:33
[11]*Psychoanalysis and Religion* by Erich Fromm, Yale University Press, New Haven, 1950
[12]*Time and Eternity, A Jewish Reader,* N. N. Glatzer, Editor, Schocken Books, New York, 1961

CHAPTER 7

[1]*Neurosis and Human Growth* by Karen Horney, W. W. Norton & Co., 1950
[2]Matt. 6:14-15
[3]Job 42:8, 10
[4]*The Myth of Mental Illness* by Thomas Stephen Szasz, Hoeber-Harper, New York, 1961
[5]*The New Group Therapy* by O. Hobart Mowrer, D. Van Nostrand Co., Inc., Princeton, N. J., 1964
[6]*Ibid.*
[7]*The Transparent Self* by Sidney M. Jourard, D. Van Nostrand Co., Inc., Princeton, N. J., 1964
[8]Romans 3:23

CHAPTER 8

[1]John 8:11
[2]Luke 15:11-24
[3]John 4:25, 26, (KJ)
[4]Mark 12:30, 31
[5]Matt. 7:5
[6]James 5:16
[7]Matt. 5:21, 22, 27, 28

CHAPTER 9

[1]*Search for Love* by Lucy Freeman, World Publishers, Cleveland, 1957
[2]*Understanding Human Nature* by Alfred Adler, Premier Books, Fawcett Publications, New York, 1954
[3]*Modern Woman, the Lost Sex,* Ferdinand Lundberg and Marynia F. Farnham
[4]From *The Power of Sexual Surrender* by Marie N. Robinson. Copyright© 1959 by Marie N. Robinson. Reprinted by permission of Doubleday & Company, Inc.
[5]*Ibid.*
[6]*The Importance of Feeling Inferior* by Marie Beynon Ray, Harper & Row, New York, 1957
[7]*Ibid.*
[8]*The Natural Superiority of Women* by Ashley Montagu, Macmillan
[9]*The Undiscovered Self* by Carl G. Jung, copyright©, 1958 by C. G. Jung. Reprinted with permission of Atlantic-Little, Brown and Company, Publishers.
[10]*Ibid.*
[11]*Woman's Mysteries* by Mary Esther Harding, Random House, Inc., revised edition, 1955
[12]*Saints, Sinners and Psychiatry* by Camilla M. Anderson, The Durham Press, Portland, Oregon, 1962

[13]*Love Against Hate* by Karl Menninger, Harcourt, Brace & Co., New York, 1942
[14]*Neurosis and Human Growth* by Karen Horney, W. W. Norton & Co., 1950.
[15]*Ibid.*

CHAPTER 10

[1]Luke 23:34

CHAPTER 11

[1]Prov. 23:7 (KJ)
[2]Prov. 4:23 (KJ)
[3]Matt. 18:20
[4]Matt. 28:20
[5]Matt. 16:17, 18
[6]Romans 8:28
[7]Phil. 2:13
[8]Eph. 3:20
[9]Heb. 11:6

CHAPTER 12

[1]*The Art of Counseling* by Rollo May, Abingdon Press, Nashville, 1949

CHAPTER 13

[1]Eph. 1:19-20 (Phillips)
[2]Mark 9:19
[3]*Faith for Personal Crises* by Carl Michalson, Chas. Scribner's Sons, New York, 1958
[4]*Ibid.*
[5]Mark 9:24
[6]Matt. 13:58

CHAPTER 14

[1]*Search for Love* by Lucy Freeman, World Publishers, Cleveland, 1957
[2]*The Art of Loving* by Erich Fromm, Harper & Row, New York, 1956
[3]*Man, Animal and Divine* by Wm. R. Parker and Enid Aldwell, Scrivener & Co., Los Angeles, 1956
[4]From *The Strong and the Weak* by Paul Tournier, 1963, The Westminster Press. Used by permission.
[5]*The Art of Loving* by Erich Fromm, Harper & Row, New York, 1956

[6]Matt. 5:48

[7]*Works of Love*, Soren Kierkegaard, Trans. by David Swenson, Harper & Row, New York, 1962

[8]*Peace of Mind* by Joshua Loth Liebman, Simon & Schuster, New York, 1955

[9]*Existence, A New Dimension in Psychiatry and Psychology* by Rollo May, Ernest Angel, Henry F. Ellenberger, Basic Books, Inc., N. Y., 1958

[10]*A Testament of Devotion* by Thomas Kelly, Harper & Row, 1941

[11]*Psychoanalysis and Religion* by Erich Fromm, Yale University Press, New Haven, 1950

[12]*Ibid.*

[13]*Man's First Love* by Ralph Sockman. Copyright© 1958 by Ralph W. Sockman. Reprinted by permission of Doubleday & Company, Inc.

[14]*The Meaning of Gifts* by Paul Tournier, John Knox Press, Richmond, Va., 1963

[15]*Channels of Spiritual Power* by Frank Laubach, Fleming H. Revell Co., Westwood, N. J., 1954

[16]*Ibid.*

[17]*Watcher on the Hills* by Raynor C. Johnson, Harper & Row, N. Y., 1959

INDEX

235